PROFIT FROM INTELLECTUAL PROPERTY

Ron Idra

James L. Rogers
Attorneys at Law

SPHINX® PUBLISHING
AN IMPRINT OF SOURCEBOOKS, INC.®
NAPERVILLE, ILLINOIS
www.SphinxLegal.com

First Edition, 2003

Published by: **Sphinx® Publishing, An Imprint of Sourcebooks, Inc.**®

Naperville Office
P.O. Box 4410
Naperville, Illinois 60567-4410
630-961-3900
Fax: 630-961-2168
www.sourcebooks.com
www.SphinxLegal.com

This publication is designed to provide accurate and authoritative information in regard to the subject matter covered. It is sold with the understanding that the publisher is not engaged in rendering legal, accounting, or other professional service. If legal advice or other expert assistance is required, the services of a competent professional person should be sought.

*From a Declaration of Principles Jointly Adopted by a Committee of the
American Bar Association and a Committee of Publishers and Associations*

This product is not a substitute for legal advice.

Disclaimer required by Texas statutes.

Library of Congress Cataloging-in-Publication Data
Idra, Ron.
  Profit from intellectual property : the complete legal guide to
copyrights, trademarks, patents, permissions, and licensing agreements /
by Ron Idra and James L. Rogers.-- 1st ed.
     p. cm.
  Includes index.
  ISBN 1-57248-332-6 (pbk.)
  1. Intellectual property--United States. 2. License
agreements--United States. I. Rogers, James L., 1965- II. Title.

KF2980 .I37 2003
346.7304'8--dc21
                                    2003014607

Printed and bound in the United States of America.

VHG Paperback — 10 9 8 7 6 5 4 3 2 1

CONTENTS

USING SELF-HELP LAW BOOKS

Before using a self-help law book, you should realize the advantages and disadvantages of doing your own legal work and understand the challenges and diligence that this requires.

The Growing Trend

Rest assured that you won't be the first or only person handling your own legal matter. For example, in some states, more than seventy-five percent of the people in divorces and other cases represent themselves. Because of the high cost of legal services, this is a major trend and many courts are struggling to make it easier for people to represent themselves. However, some courts are not happy with people who do not use attorneys and refuse to help them in any way. For some, the attitude is, "Go to the law library and figure it out for yourself."

We write and publish self-help law books to give people an alternative to the often complicated and confusing legal books found in most law libraries. We have made the explanations of the law as simple and easy to understand as possible. Of course, unlike an attorney advising an individual client, we cannot cover every conceivable possibility.

***Cost/Value
Analysis***
Whenever you shop for a product or service, you are faced with various levels of quality and price. In deciding what product or service to buy, you make a cost/value analysis on the basis of your willingness to pay and the quality you desire.

When buying a car, you decide whether you want transportation, comfort, status, or sex appeal. Accordingly, you decide among such choices as a Neon, a Lincoln, a Rolls Royce, or a Porsche. Before making a decision, you usually weigh the merits of each option against the cost.

When you get a headache, you can take a pain reliever (such as aspirin) or visit a medical specialist for a neurological examination. Given this choice, most people, of course, take a pain reliever, since it costs only pennies; whereas a medical examination costs hundreds of dollars and takes a lot of time. This is usually a logical choice because it is rare to need anything more than a pain reliever for a headache. But in some cases, a headache may indicate a brain tumor and failing to see a specialist right away can result in complications. Should everyone with a headache go to a specialist? Of course not, but people treating their own illnesses must realize that they are betting on the basis of their cost/value analysis of the situation. They are taking the most logical option.

The same cost/value analysis must be made when deciding to do one's own legal work. Many legal situations are very straight forward, requiring a simple form and no complicated analysis. Anyone with a little intelligence and a book of instructions can handle the matter without outside help.

But there is always the chance that complications are involved that only an attorney would notice. To simplify the law into a book like this, several legal cases often must be condensed into a single sentence or paragraph. Otherwise, the book would be several hundred pages long and too complicated for most people. However, this simplification necessarily leaves out many details and nuances that would apply to special or unusual situations. Also, there are many ways to interpret most legal questions. Your case may come before a judge who disagrees with the analysis of our authors.

Therefore, in deciding to use a self-help law book and to do your own legal work, you must realize that you are making a cost/value analysis. You have decided that the money you will save in doing it yourself outweighs the chance that your case will not turn out to your satisfaction. Most people handling their own simple legal matters never have a problem, but occasionally people find that it ended up costing them more to have an attorney straighten out the situation than it would have if they had hired an attorney in the beginning. Keep this in mind while handling your case, and be sure to consult an attorney if you feel you might need further guidance.

Local Rules   The next thing to remember is that a book which covers the law for the entire nation, or even for an entire state, cannot possibly include every procedural difference of every jurisdiction. Whenever possible, we provide the exact form needed; however, in some areas, each county, or even each judge, may require unique forms and procedures. In our state books, our forms usually cover the majority of counties in the state, or provide examples of the type of form which will be required. In our national books, our forms are sometimes even more general in nature but are designed to give a good idea of the type of form that will be needed in most locations. Nonetheless, keep in mind that your state, county, or judge may have a requirement, or use a form, that is not included in this book.

You should not necessarily expect to be able to get all of the information and resources you need solely from within the pages of this book. This book will serve as your guide, giving you specific information whenever possible and helping you to find out what else you will need to know. This is just like if you decided to build your own backyard deck. You might purchase a book on how to build decks. However, such a book would not include the building codes and permit requirements of every city, town, county, and township in the nation; nor would it include the lumber, nails, saws, hammers, and other materials and tools you would need to actually build the deck. You would use the book as your guide, and then do some work and research involving such matters as whether you need a permit of some kind, what type and grade of wood are available in your area, whether to use hand tools or power tools, and how to use those tools.

Before using the forms in a book like this, you should check with your court clerk to see if there are any local rules of which you should be aware, or local forms you will need to use. Often, such forms will require the same information as the forms in the book but are merely laid out differently or use slightly different language. They will sometimes require additional information.

Changes in   Besides being subject to local rules and practices, the law is subject to change at
the Law   any time. The courts and the legislatures of all fifty states are constantly revising the laws. It is possible that while you are reading this book, some aspect of the law is being changed.

In most cases, the change will be of minimal significance. A form will be redesigned, additional information will be required, or a waiting period will be extended. As a result, you might need to revise a form, file an extra form, or wait out a longer time period; these types of changes will not usually affect the outcome of your case. On the other hand, sometimes a major part of the law is changed, the entire law in a particular area is rewritten, or a case that was the basis of a central legal point is overruled. In such instances, your entire ability to pursue your case may be impaired.

To help you with local requirements and changes in the law, be sure to read the section in Chapter 2 on "Legal Research."

Again, you should weigh the value of your case against the cost of an attorney and make a decision as to what you believe is in your best interest.

INTRODUCTION

Licensing, as an industry, has grown tremendously in the past decade. Patent and technology licensing constitute a large portion of the every-day technical industry. All types of software are routinely licensed in virtually every industry, as is music, photographs, text, and other artistic works. Likewise, character and brand-name licensing has boomed as entertainment conglomerates, sports teams, and even universities license lucrative characters, logos, and brand names. Today, in the United States alone, licensing is a multi-billion dollar industry.

Added to this is the trend of cutting costs and taking care of legal issues on one's own, instead of hiring an attorney. Individuals, freelancers, and small companies often try to deal with at least some legal matters themselves to avoid paying the typically high fees of legal counsel. At a minimum, there is a greater interest in understanding one's legal rights. And, to a great degree, this makes sense. While there certainly are problems that need professional legal assistance, many legal tasks can certainly be handled by yourself.

The end result is that more people than ever are involved with intellectual property transactions and arrangements in everyday business. And where there are business transactions, there must be contracts. Specifically, license agreements, nondisclosure agreements, joint venture contracts, assignments, and other legal agreements. Drafting, reviewing, and negotiating these agreements take special knowledge of licensing and an understanding of intellectual property, but it is possible to learn and master this knowledge.

• • •

This book is all about intellectual property licenses and agreements. It is a "How-To" guide to reviewing, writing, and negotiating most of the licenses and agreements necessary to turn intellectual property into profit. To the uninitiated, this admittedly sounds complicated, confusing, and perhaps even a bit frightening. After all, how often does something dubbed *intellectual* turn out to be straightforward and easy to understand? Luckily, the truth is very much the opposite.

This book explains how to do all of these things in an easy to understand manner, enabling anyone to master the basics—even with no prior knowledge or experience. Whether you are a business owner, a solo inventor or artist, or an employee or freelancer in a creative field who wants to better understand intellectual property, this book will be of benefit to you. This book is an introduction and guide designed to help the reader understand the basics, but know there are times when expert legal advice is needed. There are attorneys who specialize in handling intellectual property issues, and they are you best resource for complex or complicated matters.

We hope this book will de-mysteric otherwise difficult and often esoteric subject matter, so that you may better understand your rights, legal situation, and available choices. In the event you decide to seek legal advice in the area of intellectual property or licensing, as a result of reading this book, you will be much better informed. Being informed means asking better questions and being better able to understand the answers.

Guide to Using This Book

Who needs this book? The short answer is anyone involved with intellectual property. Basically, anyone using, selling, transferring, giving, or obtaining permission to use intellectual property may benefit from reading this book. Additionally, anyone working in a creative or inventive field—artists, writers, photographers, engineers, inventors, and so on—whether employees, independent contractors, or freelancers will benefit from a better understanding of intellectual property rights and the process of licensing and permission.

This book is unique in that it addresses licensing from the perspective of *both* licensor and licensee. Every type of license and intellectual property agreement—as well as each provision within these agreements—will be discussed from this dual perspective. Thus, an owner of intellectual property (the patentee, copyright, or trademark owner), as well as the person seeking to use intellectual property, will both benefit from this material.

As a quick reference, we have identified three broad categories of readers who may benefit from at least some of the parts of this book.

You own an intellectual property right. You own a patent, copyright, trademark, trade secret, or a combination of these intellectual property rights and you want to make money by giving someone else permission to use your rights. Such use can entail the manufacture and sale of a product, the publishing, sale, or display of an artistic work, the commercial use of a brand name, and so on.

You want to use someone else's intellectual property right. You want to use someone else's invention, artistic work, trademark or brand name, or confidential information to manufacture a product or for other commercial purposes. Also, you want to get permission (a quick, easy-to-use license) to use a copyrighted artistic work or a trademark for a one-time or limited commercial use.

You are an employee, independent contractor, or freelancer in an artistic or inventive field. You are an artist, photographer, writer, musician, inventor, or so on and want to better understand your rights in the intellectual property domain.

Even if you are not using, licensing, or otherwise dealing with intellectual property rights, you may still benefit from a better understanding of this very important field. There are numerous areas of law where knowledge of intellectual property issues and intellectual property licensing is helpful.

• • •

We would like to conclude this introduction with a short proviso, which will be repeated frequently in the chapters that follow. This book covers diverse (and hopefully fascinating) situations involving intellectual property licensing. It often does so by simplifying many of the numerous details which might arise in a real life scenarios. *Specific decisions involving your intellectual property and license may be affected by or even dependent on other areas of law—for example, employment law, trusts & estates, and so on—which are beyond the scope of this book.* Thus, depending on your specific legal situation, you may need to consult with an intellectual property attorney. Appendix C lists resources for such a purpose.

I | OVERVIEW TO INTELLECTUAL PROPERTY

In order to understand *licenses* and *intellectual property agreements*—topics that form the core of this book—you must first understand the fundamentals. You must know what *intellectual property* actually is. To illustrate, in a license, an individual or company (the *licensor*) gives someone else (the *licensee*) permission to use an intellectual property right. The licensor must understand how intellectual property operates in order to determine how to license effectively, as well as whether or not to license in the first place. Likewise, the licensee must also comprehend the nature of the rights being received in order to know what he or she can and cannot do.

This chapter covers the fundamental characteristics of intellectual property. It begins with an examination of the basics of the four main types of intellectual property: *patents*, *copyrights*, *trade secrets*, and *trademarks*. Since each of these rights has its own identity, functions in unique ways, and is protected by different means, we have to examine the individual features of each, separately. The chapter concludes with a brief section on the legal authority in the United States for all intellectual property rights.

Since the focus of this book is on intellectual property licenses and agreements, we shall examine only the foundation of intellectual property. For additional help, see the Appendices at the end of this book.

Basics of Intellectual Property

In simplest terms, *intellectual property (IP)* is the right to own a certain type of property. The property is not *real property,* like a house or acre of land; nor is it personal property, like a car or bank account. Rather, it is a property to new and original intellectual creations—specifically, new and original inventions, artistic expression, or other mental constructs.

Intellectual property is actually a general term for four basic types of rights: *patents, copyrights, trademarks,* and *trade secrets.* The first three are similar to each other in that they all protect a unique *creation.* Patents cover new and useful inventions; copyrights concern themselves with artistic expression; and, trade secrets protect business information. Trademarks, on the other hand, indicate *source.* They are unique words or symbols that indicate to consumers where a particular good, product, or service originates.

All intellectual property has an *owner* (or two or more owners, a situation that is referred to as *joint ownership*). The owners may be an individual or organization (i.e., a company, partnership, government entity, etc.), and in most situations, is the *creator* of the intellectual property. For example, if a new invention qualifies for patent protection, the inventor will typically be the one to receive the patent (though not always). As you examine each intellectual property right, you will better understand the link between creation and ownership.

Owning Intellectual Property

A question you may be asking yourself is how a mental creation such as an artistic work, mechanical invention, or brand name be *owned?* The answer is that intellectual property rights give their owner a set of *exclusive rights* to make, use, and/or sell the work, information, or artistic creation. Or, it allows businesses the exclusive right to market goods and services protected by brand names. An *exclusive right* means that only you, and nobody else, has that particular right. In other words, it is a type of *monopoly* for that right. This legally protected *monopoly* prevents everyone but the owner from taking advantage of and commercializing the intellectual property rights. This way, the intellectual property owner is able to *possess* and *control* his or her intellectual property.

Such government-granted exclusivity is also what makes intellectual property valuable. It is why licensing is such an important part of business practice. Because exclusivity eliminates all competition in a market, this can potentially translate to high revenue for the intellectual property owner.

Intellectual property differs from regular property in another significant way. Intellectual property either lasts for a limited time or must be protected and maintained in certain defined ways. Patents and copyrights, for example, are limited in duration. A patent is valid for 20 years, while a copyright typically lasts for the lifetime of its owner plus 70 years. After that, the patent or copyright is said to *expire* and pass into the *public domain* (where anyone may use it). On the other hand, trademarks and trade secrets may last indefinitely, but only if their owners meet specific legal requirements.

Infringement of Intellectual Property

As with all property, intellectual property is sometimes illegally copied and used. This is known as *infringement* (a theft of the intellectual kind). Infringement can take different forms. For instance, it is *copyright infringement* to photocopy a book and sell the copies and *patent infringement* to reconstruct a patented machine. But regardless of form, once an infringement takes place, the IP owner always has *legal recourse*. This may be a basic *cease-and-desist letter,* mailed to the suspected infringer. It may also be the initiation of litigation—the intellectual property owner's *last resort* for the enforcement of rights.

NOTE: *The discussion of intellectual property in this chapter applies only within the United States. Other countries have unique sets of laws regarding intellectual property.*

Using Intellectual Property

As an IP owner, you ultimately have four choices regarding your rights.

- ✪ You may choose to do nothing at all, which will have no effect on your rights (except that the IP owner must still maintain his/her intellectual property).

- ✪ You may choose to *commercialize* or market the intellectual property to the public—for example, manufacturing a product based on a patent or performing your copyrighted song.

- ✪ You may sell the intellectual property to somebody else (or transfer it for free). Legally, this is known as an *assignment*.

- ✪ You may permit someone else to use your intellectual property for a limited time in exchange for payment. This is known as a *license*.

The first two options do *not* require any intellectual property agreements when intellectual property is transferred (other types of agreements, however, may come into play). The third possibility, an *assignment*, is beyond the scope of this book. The last, a license, is covered throughout the book.

With the basics given, let us explore each of the four rights—patents, copyrights, trademarks, and trade secrets—in greater detail.

Patents: Protecting New and Unique Inventions

A *patent* is the right to a new, unique, and useful invention. This can be a machine, composition, manufactured article, or process. A patent is the government's *reward* to an inventor for creating something new and useful and disclosing this knowledge to the public. For example, if an engineer creates a new machine or a chemist synthesizes a new chemical compound, these may be eligible for a patent. The touchstone of patent protection is *functionality*—that is, performance of a *useful result*.

Of all the forms of intellectual property, patents are the most difficult to secure and the most complicated to protect. Patents are not granted automatically. An inventor who designs a new invention must first file a patent application. It is then scrutinized by the U.S. Patent & Trademark Office according to stringent criteria. The entire process is typically a long one, often lasting years. Even if a patent is granted, the precise scope of protection can be difficult to ascertain. In other words, proving that the invention has been infringed can be problematic. And even after all that, a patent may be found by a court to be invalid. This effectively terminates the patent right.

Legally, a patent gives its owner (also known as the *patentee*) the *right to exclude* everyone else from making, using, or selling the patentable invention. Further, it does not necessarily give the patentee the right to practice his or her own invention. This is because a patented invention may be made up of components or parts that are themselves patented (to make the overall device, one would need permission for use of the parts). A patent may also be obtained on an improvement to an existing patented device or process. In that case, the patentee would need permission to use the existing invention as well.

Types of Patents

There are actually three different types of patents: *utility patents, design patents,* and *plant patents.* The first, *utility patents,* are what people typically refer to when they talk about patents. Utility patents protect functional devices, processes, and material compositions and are by far the most common type of patent protection sought. *Design patents* come next in popularity. A design patent protects any new and original ornamental design on an article of manufacture (for example, a unique design of a lamp) and generally are easier to secure and understand.

Finally, *plant patents* are of primary importance to plant breeders and agricultural scientists. A plant patent basically protects newly invented or discovered varieties of plants that are reproduced asexually. The characteristics of plant patents differ significantly from utility and design patents. (Plant patents are beyond the scope of this book, but if you need more information regarding this type of protection, see Appendix A.)

It must be noted that regardless of popularity, all types of patents—and all intellectual property rights for that matter—are potentially extremely valuable to the owner. How intellectual property is valued is a subject we will return to frequently throughout this book (especially in the context of how companies make licensing decisions), but for now, suffice it to say that no form of intellectual property should be downplayed or ignored.

Patentable Inventions

Patents apply to *functional devices* or processes (i.e., those that accomplish useful results). Specifically, a patent may be granted for inventions in the following categories.

NOTE: *Some inventions may fall into more than one category.*

- *Machine*—a device that functions through the interaction of parts, such as an automobile or printing press.

- *Article of Manufacture*—a single object or multiple fused objects without movable parts, such as a wrench or a light bulb.

- *Composition of Matter*—a combination of chemical or other materials, such as a new form of plastic, a new fabric, or a drug treating hypertension.

✪ *Process*—a method of accomplishing a useful result through a series of steps; i.e., a method for strengthening a metal through chemical treatment.

✪ *Improvement*—an improvement on an already existing invention, such as a television set with a higher resolution or an easier-to-use vacuum cleaner.

One type of invention, commonly *copyrighted*, may in certain circumstances be patentable—namely, *computer software*. Typically, software is patentable if it is used to control something external to the software routine (such as an assembly line process) or if the program manipulates numbers representing real-world values (such as EKG signals). In other words, software is patentable if it is claimed in connection with a specific computer or machine. Most of the time however, look to copyright, at least initially, as the primary source of protection for software.

The last decade or so has seen tremendous growth in the range and types of inventions which qualify for patent protection. These include new organisms such as genetically-altered bacteria, sequences of DNA or RNA within a cell, biochemical compounds, and new methods for doing business, such as those related to e-commerce. This definitely gives one a sense that the boundaries of patent law are being pushed forward very rapidly.

Conception vs. Reduction to Practice

An important issue which arises with patents is the distinction between *conception* and *reduction to practice*. *Conception* is the point at which the inventor has mentally formulated the idea or concept for the invention. He or she has thought of the invention, mentally ran through some of its features, and most likely described this in some type of log or record. In contrast, *reduction to practice* is the point at which all, or most of the details of the invention have been worked out, and the invention has been shown to *work effectively*. Typically, this is accomplished by building a functioning *prototype* or writing a sufficiently detailed description.

To take a famous example, when Thomas Edison formulated the concept of a heated wire filament as a cheap and efficient source of light, he could be said to have *conceived* of the light bulb. But only after much experimentation and work, when Edison discovered the best materials and structure and built a working prototype of the light bulb, was the invention reduced to practice.

Both conception and reduction to practice are commonly associated with specific dates (or periods of time), which must be proven. Conception is typically demonstrated by reference to an inventor's notebook where much of the thinking and formulation of an invention is recorded in dated entries. The inventor may also file an *Invention Disclosure* with the *U.S. Patent & Trademark Office* (see Appendix E for more information), which serves to verify conception (but does not guarantee any patent rights). On the other hand, reduction to practice is demonstrated by a finished prototype or the filing of an actual patent application.

This so-called *statutory bar* is a one-year grace period that is unique to the United States law. If the inventor makes any kind of public disclosure of the invention, he or she must file a patent application within *one year* of the date of such disclosure, otherwise, the right to patent the invention is *forever* barred by law.

An inventor should also work diligently and carefully towards reducing the invention to practice for another reason. Because a patent right in the U.S. is based on a *first to invent* standard, there will sometimes be challenges from other inventors who claim an earlier invention date for the same invention (these challenges are resolved in a *patent interference* action). Overall, diligence in reducing an invention to practice, along with careful documentation will pay off in the long run.

To summarize, an inventor must be careful about properly documenting conception and reduction to practice of the invention; make sure there is no inadvertent public disclosure; as well as, beat all competing inventors in priority. All in all, quite a lot of responsibility.

Conditions for Patentability

Since we know that a patent is not granted to every invention, this implies the use of definite standards or criteria of patentability. Specifically, there are three:

✪   *novelty*;

✪   *utility*; and,

✪   *nonobviousness*.

Though there are other requirements for a patent (covered later), novelty, utility, and nonobviousness are the most fundamental and determine whether an invention has risen to the standard of a patentable invention.

Novelty means that the invention has to be *new*—that is, it must differ from already existing or publicly known inventions. In other words, the invention **cannot** have been previously described, disclosed, or patented in the United States or a foreign country.

The total of all existing inventions in a field that are similar to the invention one desires to patent, is known as *prior art* (the word *art* means field of invention). Before filing an application, the applicant typically conducts a *prior art search*, by searching databases of patents, publications, and other documents. Each particular invention located—whether described in a patent or publication—is known as a *prior art reference*. Upon filing the patent application, the applicant then has a *duty of disclosure* to disclose every prior art reference found.

Utility means that the invention must serve some useful purpose and not run counter to public policy. Though utility is generally the easiest condition of patentability to meet, it nevertheless can be grounds for rejection.

NOTE: *Scientific, mathematical, or theoretical knowledge are not subject to patent protection.*

Nonobviousness is typically the applicant's toughest hurdle. To qualify for a patent, the invention **cannot** have been *obvious* to someone who is skilled in the art or industry to which the invention belongs. In other words, even if an invention is new compared to the prior art, it may be rejected because it is not a large enough *leap* over what exists. Nonobviousness can sometimes be proven by demonstrating a market need for the invention and at the same time showing that no one else (besides the present inventor) has been able to fill it.

Aside from these three basic criteria, a patent must also contain a written description of the subject matter of the invention in sufficient detail to meet two additional requirements. First, such a description must be *enabling*. This means that someone of *ordinary skill in the art* must be able to construct or practice the invention with only a reasonable amount of experimentation. Second, the description must also reveal the *best mode* of the invention. This means that if there is more than one way to make or practice the invention (known as different *embodiments*), then the applicant must disclose what he or she believes to be the *best* one.

The standards and requirements discussed here reveal a common thread running throughout the application process. That is, it is the patent applicant's duty to reveal all relevant information. Otherwise, the patent may later be ruled *invalid* if it is ever the subject of a litigation. That terminates the patent right forever.

Components of a Patent

A patent (as well as the application, itself) consists of two main parts: *specification* and *claims.*

Specification. A detailed description of the invention, known as the *specification,* is usually accompanied by diagrams and figures. As discussed in the previous section, the specification must be both enabling and describe the invention's best mode. It is therefore incumbent on the patentee to understand everything about how the invention functions; the problem or market need the invention is intended to remedy; and, the other devices or methods in the invention's field.

Claims. These are sequentially numbered sentences that define the patent's scope. Simply put, the range of inventions that the patentee will be able to stop others from using, making, and selling is the patent's scope. The broader the claim, the more general it is. A claim to "a scooter with brakes," for instance, has a much broader scope than "a scooter with hand-brakes that are attached to handlebars located at the front end of the scooter."

The former claim, which is much more general than the latter, covers a great many variations on the theme of scooter-plus-brakes.

The actual number of claims varies from patent to patent, ranging anywhere from one to well over a hundred. But regardless of number, all claims serve the same function—to notify the public of what the patent covers.

Claims are also either independent or dependent. *Independent claims* state the invention without reference to another claim. *Dependent claims,* on the other hand, refer to a preceding independent claim and provide additional details.

The reason there is more than one claim in the typical patent is a simple one. Claims vary in their scope of coverage. The patentee wants to maximize the patent's scope, while at the same time minimize the risk that the patent will be *invalidated.* A patent reaches only so far as its broadest claim. If that claim is invalidated, the patent will then have another claim, which though narrower in scope, still offers protection for the invention. And so on for all the claims. For this reason, a patent's first claim is typically broadest in scope, with subsequent claims narrowing it bit by bit.

A final point about patent claims. Since each inventor uses his or her own unique terminology and phrasing, claims must be *interpreted* or *construed*, so that the claim and its scope may be clearly understood. *Claim interpretation* is a process that routinely occurs when a patent is the subject of a litigation. It is done by reading every word in a claim with reference to the patent's specification. If the meaning of a term or phrase in the claim is still unclear, outside sources (such as an industry expert) may be examined. However, the details of claim interpretation need not bother you here. It is just important to remember that the terms used in a patent should never be taken for granted.

Patent Application Process

As stated, an invention is not patentable simply by virtue of having been invented. A patent must be applied for and a variety of criteria and requirements must be met before the invention has even a possibility of being patented.

In the United States, the government agency in charge of patents is the *U.S. Patent & Trademark Office (PTO)*. As the federal agency which administers the patent and trademark laws, the PTO implements patent policy, disseminates patent information, and maintains patent-related databases. But most importantly, the PTO is responsible for *examining* patent applications and deciding whether or not to grant the patent.

The process of applying for a patent is known as *patent prosecution* (no relation to prosecuting criminals). It is a complicated process, complete with intricate rules and potential pitfalls. Except for the basics, it is beyond the scope of this chapter.

Applicants for a patent typically hire a *patent attorney* or *patent agent*, both of whom must be *registered* to practice before the PTO (by passing a specialized examination). However, it is legally permissible for inventors to prosecute their *own* application. This is known as prosecuting *pro se*. However, deciding whether to prosecute one's own application should not be lightly undertaken. Important factors to consider include the conceptual complexity of the invention and its potential for mass-marketing; the number of similar inventions in the field; as well as, the expense of hiring legal counsel that can be quite high.

The patent application, itself, contains several parts. Apart from the written description of the invention (the specification and claims), the applicant must also include a list of all prior art references found, a *declaration of inventorship*, and an *application fee*. The application, complete with all forms, is then mailed to the PTO. When it is received, it is post-marked and assigned to a specific *Patent Examiner*, who from that point on will be in charge of the application and will decide its patentability.

The examiner reviews the application; conducts a separate prior art search; and, responds to the applicant in an *office action*. The office action contains arguments challenging the novelty and/or nonobviousness of the invention (the examiner may also raise issues concerning the application's sufficiency). The applicant then files a *response* to the office action, in which he *amends* the claims, or revises the specification in order to overcome the additional prior art or rebut the examiner's arguments. The examiner then has the option of answering this in another action. The back-and-forth process continues until the Examiner either grants or rejects the application.

NOTE: *There is also an appeals process for rejected applications.*

An applicant for a patent also has the option of filing what is known as a *provisional patent application*. This is a preliminary application describing the invention without the claims section. This way, the inventor can get the earliest filing date possible and still take time to further refine the invention. However, a regular application must follow a provisional one within one year, otherwise the *provisional application* is deemed *abandoned*.

When the patent is granted an application, the application is said to be *allowed*. The applicant then pays an *issue fee* and the patent is officially *issued* as of a specific *issue date*. The newly issued patent also receives a *patent number*—i.e., U.S. Patent No. 5,146,634. The patent is then published and may thereafter be accessed by number, title, or an abstract summarizing the invention.

Once issued, a patent is only valid for a given period of time, known as its *term*. If the application was filed **after June 7, 1995**, the patent is for *20 years* from the date of *filing of the application*, or *17 years* from the date of *issuance*, whichever is longer. If, however, the application was filed **on or before June 7, 1995**, then the patent lasts for *17 years* from the date of the patent's *issuance*. Regardless of the length of the patent term, after expiration, the invention becomes part of the public domain.

The new patent owner must make payments known as *maintenance fees* to the PTO during the patent's term, in order to keep the patent in full force. Maintenance fees are due at three points during a patent's term, specifically, at three, seven, and eleven years from the issue date. Failure to pay these fees within the allotted time can result in the patent's termination.

After the patent issues, if the patentee manufactures or produces a product based on the patent, then each individual good should be *marked* with the patent number. This is known as *patent marking*. This serves as a type of public notice that a particular good is covered by patent.

Patent Infringement

To *infringe* a patent means to make, use, or sell (or offer for sale) an invention that is covered in a patent (which is still in force), without the permission of the patent owner. Patent infringement is either innocent or willful. *Innocent infringement* occurs when someone invents an invention from scratch, not knowing that it is already the subject of a patent. *Willful infringement,* on the other hand, is the result of direct copying. For example, an engineer sees a new machine he knows to be patented, but nevertheless reconstructs it in his laboratory (a process known as *reverse engineering*). Though both types of infringement are a violation of patent rights and may result in the payment of monetary *damages* to the patentee, willful infringement is much more severe.

If a patent owner suspects his or her patent is being infringed, the first step is to send the suspected infringer a *cease-and-desist letter* warning of a pending infringement. This is essentially a notice that the invention at issue is the subject of a patent and a demand to immediately halt the infringing activities. Cease-and-desist letters are typically drafted by attorneys and have an aura of authority about them for this reason. But until the alleged infringement is proven in court, the recipient of such a letter is not *legally* compelled to take any action.

If the infringer does not heed the demand, the patentee then has the option of initiating a lawsuit, in which compensation is typically demanded (i.e., *damages*) and a halt to the alleged infringement (an *injunction*). The patentee (as plaintiff) will attempt to prove infringement, while the alleged infringer (as defendant) will deny this fact and attempt to *invalidate* the patent. Of course, the plaintiff and defendant may settle the lawsuit by resolving the matter through some mutually agreeable arrangement (typically, payment of money with a licensing arrangement). The lawsuit will then be over by mutual consent.

If the lawsuit proceeds, both plaintiff and defendant have difficult tasks ahead of them. The plaintiff must *prove* that the defendant's device (or method) infringes the patent at issue. Infringement occurs by one of two means:

✪ literal infringement or

✪ doctrine of equivalents.

Literal infringement or *direct infringement* means that every feature of the infringing device or method is described in a claim of the patent. The *doctrine of equivalents,* on the other hand, allows for infringement even when there are differences between the infringing device and the patent, so long as these differences are insubstantial. In other words, the doctrine of equivalents prevents someone from copying a patented invention, making minor or insubstantial changes, and then claiming that the resulting device is not infringing.

The defendant, on the other hand, will counter the plaintiff's arguments of infringement, arguing that this new device is outside the scope of the patent's claims. At the same time, most defendants will also attempt to *invalidate* the plaintiff's patent. A patent granted by the PTO is *presumed valid.* This means there is no reason to doubt its validity. However, during a litigation, a patent will be reassessed under more strict standards. A patent may be found invalid for many reasons, but typically the argument will be made that the patent lacks novelty or is nonobviousness in light of the prior art.

The outcome of a litigation depends on a great many factors, not the least of which is the time and expense a party pours into its case. Much of the outcome will affect only the parties involved by payment of damages, an injunction, etc. However, it is important to remember that if a patent is found to be invalid, this will have an impact on the public as well. The invention may then be used by anyone.

Design Patents   As stated earlier, a design patent protects the *aesthetic* or *ornamental* appearance of an article of manufacture. The way the device functions or the details of its structure are irrelevant to a design patent. For instance, if someone designs a clock in the shape of a dolphin, this unique design may be the subject of a design patent. However, if patented, the design will protect similarly shaped *clocks*, not every object with a dolphin-shape. A design patent protects only *aesthetic* or *ornamental* designs. *Functional designs*, those which are essential for an object's function such as the shape of an airplane wing, are not covered by design patents.

The application process for design patents differs in important respects from that for utility patents. First, the requirements for a design patent are that the design be new, original, and *ornamental.* Second, the design patent application is much less expensive than a utility application, costing in the hundreds of dollars, instead of thousands. Third, a design patent application is much simpler than a utility patent, as there is no written specification section. Instead, the application consists of key drawings of the design depicting the extent of the protection—followed by *one* claim.

A design patent, like a utility patent, gives its owner the right to exclude others from using, making, or selling that design. Design patents are infringed when the design is substantially copied on a similar article of manufacture. In other respects, design patent infringement is dealt with in much the same way as infringement of a utility patent.

Design patents have a shorter life span the utility patents. Once issued, a design patent is valid for fourteen years from the *issue* date. But unlike utility patents, no maintenance fees are due on design patents. Design patents may overlap with copyright protection, as both types of intellectual property rights deal with aesthetic or artistic expression.

Copyright: Protecting Artistic Expression

A *copyright* is a right to own one's *artistic expression*, whether written, visual, or auditory in form. Of course, an individual may express himself or herself in many ways. For this reason, copyright extends over a wide variety of *works*, including books, articles, songs, photographs, sculptures, and so on. A copyright even protects *computer software*. (As stated earlier, software may also be patented.)

Unlike patents, a copyright arises *automatically* once a work is created. You do not need to register a work to receive a copyright (though registration is recommended). Basically, any original work created after December 31, 1977 is copyrighted as soon as it is fixed by its creator (also known as the *author*) in tangible form. This could be by being written down, tape recorded, or fixed in some other way in *permanent form*. Unlike a patent, the standards for copyright are fairly easy to meet. A work is copyrightable if it is *original* and *creative*. *Originality* refers to independent creation. The author of the work must come up with the work himself or herself without copying any existing works. The *creativity* a work must possess is of a minimal quality. That is, it has to be more than a mere list of facts, as in a phone book.

Copyright notice is also not required for a work to be copyrighted. Works often contain the symbol © or the word *copyright* followed by the year first published and the name of the owner. If a work is *published* (distributed to the public), this type of notice is *recommended*.

A copyright's *term* is much longer than a patent. Typically, copyrights are valid for the *life of the author, plus seventy years.* The copyright term begins the moment the work is fixed in tangible form, regardless of whether the work is published or registered. When the copyright term expires, the work becomes part of the *public domain* (as with patents), and may be freely used by anyone.

Idea vs. Expression

One basic principle relating to copyrights is that you cannot copyright an *idea*, only a particular *expression* of that idea. Although this rule has been the subject of much analysis in legal circles, it can be explained simply enough. The *idea* of a work is its concept or *essence*. This can often be described in a few sentences. The *expression*, however, is the entire development, with all details in place. The discerning reader might notice an analogy to patent law here—the copyright idea is similar to patent law conception, whereas copyright expression may be analogized to *reduction to practice*.

The distinction between idea and expression is most obvious in the case of written works. A story about a young man and woman from feuding families who fall in love and whose romance is discovered with tragic consequences is an *idea*. The particular play *Romeo and Juliet*, however, is an expression of that idea. It is of course possible to come up with a great many expressions for this idea. *West Side Story* is another such expression.

Types of Copyrightable Works

There are eight categories of works protectable under copyright law. Works are classified for registration and other purposes by the *U.S. Copyright Office.*

The categories of copyrightable works follow.

✪ *Literary Works*—all forms of written or textual works, including fiction and nonfiction books, newspaper and magazine articles, text advertisements, directories and factual compilations, and computer software.

✪ *Musical Works*—works which can be put down on sheet music, including songs, instrumental pieces, advertising jingles, etc.

✪ *Dramatic Works*—any work which is intended to be performed, including scripts, plays, screenplays, and operas.

✪ *Pantomimes and Choreographic Works*—dance and works of movement, such as ballet, modern and jazz dance, pantomime, and cheerleading routines.

✪ *Pictorial, Graphic, and Sculptural Works*—visual images and physical art, such as paintings, drawings, photographs, comics, statues, and designs on objects.

✪ *Motion Pictures and Audiovisual Works*—works of moving images and sound, such as movies and television shows, documentaries, commercials, and internet streaming videos.

✪ *Sound Recordings*—anything that can be recorded, including musical instruments, singing, spoken words, or other sounds.

✪ *Architectural Works*—designs of buildings, including the finished structure, plans, and sketches.

It is important to remember that copyright protects expression, not function. Nowhere is this more evident than in the case of articles of manufacture which possess unique designs. New and ornamental designs may be protected by design patents, but may also be copyrighted, if the design is separate from the functional part of the article. For example, a lamp with a uniquely-shaped vase as its base is copyrightable since its base is **not** essential for its functioning as a lamp. This is known as *conceptual separability*. This means, a useful object is copyrightable if one can *mentally separate* (rather than physically separate) the artistic elements from its functional ones.

Copyright Ownership

In most cases, the owner of a copyright is its author (remember that *author* is a general term meaning *one who creates* in copyright law). That is, the individual (or individuals) who creates the work is logically rewarded with ownership rights in the creation. As you recall, the owner may then *assign* or license the copyright. But the initial right of ownership belongs to the author.

An exception to this rule, however, is the *work for hire*. This is a work created by an employee within the *scope of employment*. In this case, the copyright in the work will automatically be owned by the employer, who will also be considered its author. Therefore, an employer does not need a written *assignment agreement* with his or her employees.

Copyright Rights

On the other hand, if the work is created by an *independent contractor*, the employer will have ownership if: (1) there is a written agreement in place specifying the work is a *work for hire* and (2) the work fits into one of several work-for-hire categories for independent contractor.

In practical terms, copyright ownership means you have certain *exclusive rights* with respect to your work. You, and only you, may sell, market, or publicize your work to the general public. This is true unless you license your work or your work is used pursuant to the *fair use* doctrine. (*Fair Use* is described later in this chapter.)

Specifically, copyright gives its owner six *exclusive rights*. These are the rights to:

1. *make copies of the work;*

2. *distribute the work to the public;*

3. *perform the work publicly;*

4. *display the work publicly;*

5. *prepare derivative works based on the copyrighted work; and,*

6. *publicly transmit the work (as in the case of sound recordings).*

NOTE: *A derivative work is a work which is based on or derives fro, a previous work. If someone takes the novel* Crime and Punishment *and turns it into a screenplay, the screenplay is a derivative work.*

The rights belonging to the copyright owner *exclude* everyone else from taking such actions with respect to the work (except as it relates to fair use). For instance, if you write an original article and post it on a website, no one may legally download the article and print it in a magazine. This would violate the copyright owner's right to reproduce or make copies of a copyrighted work. If you own a copyright in a song, no musician may, after hearing you perform it, go on to perform it also. That would constitute a very basic violation of the third exclusive right.

Each of the above rights is separable from the others. A copyright owner may, for instance, give permission to someone else to distribute his work, while retaining all other rights. This is a critical fact that must be kept in mind when drafting or reviewing any type of copyright license.

Fair Use of
Copyright

Fair use allows anyone to use a copyrighted work without permission from its owner, but only if such use is undertaken for certain defined purposes. These permitted uses include the following:

✪ scholarship;

✪ research or criticism;

✪ news reporting;

✪ other public interest uses; and,

✪ parody (humor).

Uses that are purely for profit are not considered fair use. The fair use doctrine is the one *exception* to the copyright owner's exclusive rights. Ultimately, a court would determine whether a use is a fair one in a copyright infringement lawsuit.

A determination of whether a use is a fair one also depends on other factors. One must consider not only the intended use, but also the *amount and substantiality of the portion used in relation to the copyrighted work as a whole*. If the use involves a relatively small portion of the original work, then it is likelier, all things being equal, that the use would be found to be fair use. Another critical factor is whether the use will ultimately compete with the original work in the same market. If it will, a court would likely find there was no fair use and conclude instead, that a copyright infringement took place. (We will examine *fair use* in greater detail as part of our discussion of permissions in Chapter 13 of this book.)

Copyright
Registration

As previously mentioned, registration of an original work is not essential for copyright protection. However, registration is *advantageous* for several reasons. First and foremost, it is a legal requirement for the filing of a lawsuit for copyright infringement and is a prerequisite to the collection of *statutory damages*. Second, it is a record of the creation of the work and may serve to prove priority of creation. Third, it is a type of nationwide notice to all potential creators that a particular work is already the subject of a copyright.

Analogously to the PTO, the *U.S. Copyright Office* (a division of the *Library of Congress*) handles all official transactions related to copyright law, from registration of works to implementation of copyright policy. However, unlike patents, copyright registration is a straightforward process and is virtually assured for most types of works. The registrant need only fill out a copyright registration form; enclose two samples of the work (the *deposit* requirement); a small fee (currently $30); and, send the packet to the Library of Congress.

NOTE: *There are different versions of the registration form for the eight categories of copyrighted works. Also, as technology moves forward, your specific category may be registered via computer. You may want tot check with the U.S. Copyright Office to determine if you can file your copyright electronically.*

If you are registering computer software, it is permissible to omit significant portions of the program when providing the deposit samples. This gives the programmer the opportunity to register the work before it is fully perfected and error-free.

Copyright Infringement
As you may recall from our discussion of patents, infringement takes place when someone other than the owner makes, uses, or sells a device (or process) that is identical or equivalent to the patented invention. For patents, it does not matter whether the infringer sees the invention and copies it or sits in his or her own laboratory and independently invents it. It is still patent infringement.

A copyright, on the other hand, is infringed only if someone directly *copies* the work. Independent creation of a similar, even an identical work, is not infringement. For instance, a songwriter is inspired and comes up with a tune that he believes to be original. Unbeknownst to him, that particular tune has already been composed by someone else (perhaps in a different style of music). The songwriter still may copyright the work and is not an infringer. Though the work is not new, it is original and deserving of a copyright just the same.

But assume you know your work has been copied. For example, if your work is famous and easily accessible, there is a greater chance that someone has seen and copied it. Sometimes the similarity between works is too great to be attributable to coincidence. For instance, a photographer notices pictures identical to his own, posted on various websites on the Internet. The first step in dealing with copyright infringement is similar to that for patent infringement—namely, the *cease-and-desist letter*. If the alleged infringer does not comply, the copyright owner also has the option of initiating litigation.

Copyright litigation follows the same general framework as patent litigation, with the standard of infringement in copyright law being *substantial similarity*. The plaintiff must prove not only that the accused work is similar to the copyrighted work in substantial respects, but also that the defendant *deliberately* copied the work. This is usually shown either by providing direct evidence of copying or by the mere fact that the defendant had *access* to plaintiff's work and the opportunity to copy. At the same time, the defendant will provide evidence that his work is dissimilar from the copyrighted work or that the defendant's use fell within the *fair use* exception. The defendant may also attempt to invalidate the copyright.

Trademarks: Indicating Business Source

A *trademark* is a name, logo, or symbol (a *mark*) that informs the public of the *business source* of a good or service. A business source is the individual, company, or organization that produces, manufactures, and/or markets a good or service.

The importance of a trademark lies in how easily consumers identify the mark with the features of the product it identifies. If you buy a soda marked *Coke,* you expect a familiar taste. If you purchase a Cadillac, you have a different kind of expectation: one of reliability, comfort, and luxury. A trademark is, in effect, shorthand for the qualities and reputation the product it represents. A good or service's reputation is known as *goodwill.*

Example: BIG MAC™ is an example of a well-known trademark. This specific trademark informs consumers that the hamburger that they are about to buy comes from and is produced by one company— McDonald's, Inc.® Therefore, whether the person is in New York or Hong Kong, the consumer knows that a "BIG MAC" hamburger comes from McDonald's ®.

Generally, a trademark serves two important functions. First, it prevents competitors from *stealing* the goodwill that a company has built up over the years, based on the qualities and reputation of that company's products. At the same time, a trademark ensures consumers are not *confused* by products or services that have similarly sounding names, but which really come from other sources. In fact, *likelihood of consumer confusion* is a critical concept in trademark law and is the legal standard of whether one mark *infringes* another.

Types of Marks   Besides trademarks, there are other types of marks that function in similar ways. These are *trade names*, *service marks*, and *trade dress*. A *trade name* represents companies instead of products—i.e., *McDonald's*, *General Motors*, or *Revlon*. Trade names function similarly to trademarks, but have unique registration rules.

A *service mark* identifies a service instead of a good—i.e., *Supercuts* for a chain of hair-cutting salons or *FedEx* for express mail delivery. Service marks function identically to trademarks.

Finally, *trade dress* is the unique appearance, design, or packaging of a good or service. It functions to indicate source. Examples of trade dress is the unique shape of the *Absolut* vodka bottle or the interior design of the *Hard Rock Café*. Trade dress is more complex due to additional, often complicated, rules.

(For the remainder of the book, when trademarks are discussed, trade names, service marks, and trade dress are included as well (unless stated otherwise).)

Acquiring a   Trademarks are similar to copyrights in terms of how rights are acquired. A
Trademark   given mark is not required to be registered in order to function as a trademark. Instead, the mark must be used on the good or service it represents, in ordinary commerce. In other words, an individual or company acquires the trademark right and becomes a trademark owner, simply by using the mark in commerce. This assumes there are no *confusingly similar* marks in the field. It is therefore more accurate to say that trademark rights are based on *first use*. In the event of a conflict between two similar marks, the *earlier use* will generally prevail.

There are *two criteria* that are important in the context of trademark use. The first is the *class of goods or services* (the type of good or service). Products or services can be said to *compete* with one another when they are roughly of the same type. A consumer who seeks a certain brand of furniture polish will not be confused by a similar name which is applied to, say, a CD player. Therefore, one must always ascertain the type of good or service for a given mark in order to evaluate it or compare it with other marks. Similar or identical marks may co-exist if they are within different classes of goods or services (since there will not be any consumer confusion).

The second criteria is the region or *geographical extent* of the use. Some marks are used throughout the entire nation—*Wal-Mart*™—or even internationally—*Sony*™. Others serve only one localized neighborhood—*Mike's Pizzeria* for a local pizza store. Therefore, if two marks are used in different neighborhoods, cities, or regions of the country (even for the same product or service), it does not matter how similar these marks are to each other. They may even be *identical*. Those two marks may then co-exist, with each trademark owner having full rights to their trademark within the region of use.

Trademark Distinctiveness & Strength

Trademarks are categorized according to their *distinctiveness*, and ultimately judged for registration purposes by their *strength*. A distinctive mark is one which consumers will easily remember and identify with the underlying goods or services. A distinctive mark is *unlikely* to be confused with other trademarks. This is important, since the standard for trademark infringement is the *likelihood of confusion* between the marks. For this reason, distinctive marks are *stronger* and will be easier to *federally register*. There are four categories of distinctiveness:

1. *arbitrary or coined marks;*

2. *suggestive marks;*

3. *descriptive marks; and,*

4. *generic terms.*

The first category, *coined or arbitrary marks,* are highest on the distinctiveness scale. They are words that are either completely fabricated (such as *Buick* or *Exxon,*) or which are ordinary, but bear no relation to the goods they represent (i.e., *Gateway* for personal computers or *Amazon* for online book purchasing). These types of marks may be federally registered *immediately* upon use.

Next on the distinctiveness spectrum are *suggestive marks*. These marks bear *some* relation to the goods represented, a tenuous one at best, and are used to evoke an image or idea in the minds of consumers. Examples are the mark *Obsession*™ for perfume, or *Banana Republic*™ for clothing stores. Though not as strong as arbitrary marks in an immediate sense, suggestive marks may nevertheless be inherently distinctive. The dividing line between an arbitrary and suggestive mark is sometimes a blurry one, so do not be troubled if you are unsure where a given mark fits.

The third type is a *descriptive mark*. These literally describe some characteristic of the good or service they represent. Examples are *Toys-R-Us*™ for a chain of toy stores and *American Airlines*™ for a commercial, nation-wide airline. Descriptive marks turn into strong marks if they become familiar to consumers through frequent use, giving them the chance to associate the name with the product. In that case, the mark will have acquired what is known as *secondary meaning*. This may result only after many years of use.

Lastly, there are the *generic terms*. These are words or phrases which refer to a class of goods. Some generic marks started out as arbitrary marks, only to become generic once their use became widely known. Common examples of these are *Thermos* and *Aspirin*. Generic terms are generally not protectable as trademarks for the simple reason that they identify a whole class of goods and cannot distinguish one particular good over another.

Trademark Registration   As we know, trademark rights begin with a mark's first use in commerce. However, as with copyrights, there are distinct advantages to registering a trademark. Trademarks may be registered either *federally* or on a *state* level, with federal registration being more far-reaching to state registration. The following discussion covers primarily federal registration, but some of the rules are similar. Trademarks which are left unregistered are known as *common law marks*.

There are compelling reasons to register a trademark. First, registration is a type of public notice that a trademark belongs to a given owner. Everyone is then presumed to know about it. Second, anyone who uses a confusingly similar mark after the mark has been federally registered will be deemed a *willful infringer*. This allows the trademark owner to demand higher damages in the event of litigation. Third, if the mark stays registered for more than five years, it reaches *incontestable* status and significantly strengthens the mark against all legal challenges.

As a first step to registration, a *trademark search* should be performed. This is done to uncover any similar or identical trademarks to your intended mark. As you might remember, a prior art search was also an important first step in obtaining a patent. In both the patent and trademark fields, a prior screening saves a great deal of trouble and expense down the line.

Trademark searches vary in their thoroughness (the number and types of databases searched), as well as expense. The most complete (and most expensive) searches are performed by a company called *Thomson & Thomson*. However, there are other searching services, most of which perform simpler searches at a discounted price. At the other end of the searching spectrum is a free search engine for federally registered trademarks on the U.S. Patent & Trademark Office website—the *Trademark Electronic Search System* or *TESS*. It often makes sense to start with a free search to get a sense of how *available* the desired mark is and then move on to a more detailed search if warranted. (You can find more information on trademark searching in Appendix A)

Once you complete the trademark search, assuming your mark is more or less unique, the remainder of the registration process is straightforward. A simple application must be filled out; a fee enclosed (currently $325); and, the packet mailed to the *U.S. Patent & Trademark Office*. Once the application has been approved by the PTO, the mark, together with its relevant information (applicant, goods or services, etc.) are published in the weekly *Official Patent & Trademark Gazette*. This gives any party thirty days to file an *opposition* to registration of the mark, upon setting forth specific reasons why registration should be denied. If an opposition is filed, the matter is settled by a proceeding before the *Trademark Trial and Appeal Board (TTAB)*. Assuming there is no opposition, the registered trademark issues with an official number and a registration date.

If an applicant has not actually begun using the mark, it can also be in an *Intent-to-Use (ITU)* application. This type of registration is based on the applicant's intention to use the mark in commerce at a future point. This must take place before the trademark's issuance. All other rules of trademark registration apply to an ITU application.

Once a mark is *federally registered*, the trademark owner identifies it with the symbol ®. (The symbol TM is used to denote unregistered or common-law marks). A mark can be a valid trademark even though unregistered (assuming the owner has *first use* rights to it). Therefore, these symbols are by no means the final word on trademark rights.

Trademark infringement may take various forms in a wide variety of circumstances. Two common scenarios are an individual or company sells, or attempts to sell, its own goods under another company's trademark and an individual or company uses a mark in the same class of goods or services and same geographical area in a way that is confusing to consumers.

A trademark owner may warn an individual or company of impending or ongoing trademark infringement with a *cease-and-desist letter*, reserving the right to bring a future lawsuit if the infringement continues. Trademark litigation involves much of the same dynamics as copyright or patent litigation, wherein the trademark owner, as plaintiff, will attempt to show *likelihood of consumer confusion* between the disputed marks. The defendant will attempt to invalidate the trademark at issue. Trademark litigation may also involve resolving a dispute as to priority of use between similar marks.

Trade Secrets: Confidential Business Information

A *trade secret* is any secret information used in business that gives its owner a *competitive advantage* over others. A trade secret can be almost anything—a secret recipe, a list of valuable customers, a new design for a machine, a new business method, etc. But it must be *commercially valuable* and must be *kept confidential* at all times. A commonly cited example of a trade secret is the formula for *Coca-Cola*—still a *secret* after all of these years. It is also important to note that secret does not mean that the information is completely unknown. It could, for instance, be known by someone, somewhere out there. What is important for its status as a trade secret is that the information not be known by *competitors* or someone who could be a *potential competitor*.

Though different in character from patents and copyrights, a trade secret is nevertheless considered intellectual property because it is a product of the mind. At some point, someone (acting alone or on behalf of an organization) had to have devised, gathered, or discovered the information and figured out how to use it for commercial gain. Like all types of intellectual property, a trade secret has an owner—namely, the individual or organization who devises or figures that the information is commercially advantageous. A trade secret may be assigned or licensed just like all other types of intellectual property.

Unlike patents and copyrights, trade secrets last *indefinitely*, so long as their confidentiality is maintained. Therefore, there is no *expiration date* to a trade secret. However, though trade secrets are strong in terms of longevity, they are *delicate* in that *any type* of disclosure effectively *terminates* a trade secret. This includes disclosure by: (1) *insufficient protection or mistake*—designs for a secret machine are accidentally misplaced and are found by a competitor; (2) *reverse-engineering*—a competitor figures out the secret information by examining the company's product; or, (3) *improper means*—the secret is discovered through corporate espionage. Though each of these actions terminates the trade secret, the last one at least entitles the owner to seek compensation. A lawsuit may be brought against the individuals responsible for improperly accessing the protected information.

Protecting a Trade Secret

A trade secret is protected and maintained by keeping it confidential *at all times*. A trade secret is not protected by an application process (as is a patent) or through registration (like a copyright), but rather, through the actions of its owner. The secret's exposure must be limited only to individuals within the organization and then, only to those individuals who have a *need to know* (this may involve computer security measures, marking documents with a "confidential" stamp, locking information in a vault, and so on). Confidentiality agreements should be used for all employees, consultants, accountants, and others who are exposed to the secret information (See Chapter 7).

Some trade secrets, by their very nature, can be used in the normal course of business without being revealed. For example, a secret, faster process to produce steel cannot be figured out by examining the product. The secret recipe for *Coca-Cola*—the secret ingredients—are not ordinarily discoverable. However, there are other trade secrets, that once commercialized without taking protective steps, will expose the secret itself. These types of trade secrets are typically protected by a *confidentiality agreement*. So, if a company possesses a valuable demographic analysis and desires to commercially market it, it must make sure its customers sign confidentiality agreements with respect to the secret information.

Trade Secret vs. Patent Protection

A trade secret may potentially overlap with patent protection (and sometimes with copyright, though patent overlap is more common). It often happens that a uniquely designed machine or a competitive business method, kept confidential as a trade secret, may also qualify for a patent. In that case, the two forms of protection must be reconciled.

The company must make a choice. Once a patent application is filed, the confidential nature of the trade secret is broken and the trade secret right essentially terminated. Patents and trade secrets each have their own distinct advantages, however, and a company should weigh the pros and cons of each form of protection *for its own unique situation*. For instance, trade secret protection may be significantly less expensive than the process of filing for a patent. On the other hand, if the trade secret, itself, involves very large-scale devices or machinery that is difficult to keep secret, a patent filing may very well be the simpler route.

Other Rights and Laws Related to Intellectual Property

Intellectual property is often discussed together with other types of legal rights, such as the rights of *publicity* and *privacy*, as well as the *law of antitrust*. Briefly stated, the *right of publicity* allows a famous person to commercially exploit his or her name, image, and likeness while the *right of privacy* protects someone from such exposure. In addition, *antitrust law*, which generally prevents companies from forming monopolies that can restrain competition and addresses certain aspects of the use of intellectual property.

Some of this is discussed later in the book, but it does not form its focus. As you can appreciate, understanding the subject of intellectual property often involves seeing it in a wider legal context.

Legal Authority for Intellectual Property

In the United States, most law, including intellectual property, originates with the legislative and judiciary branches of our government. The legislature, whether federal or state, puts forth general statutes and more detailed rules, typically categorized as *Code* and *Regulations*, respectively. Together, this is known as *statutory law*. The judiciary (the courts) interprets these statutes and regulations and puts forth what is known as *common law*. These are legal opinions resulting from litigation, in which the court interprets the relevant statutes in light the facts of the case. Together, statutory and common law form most of the *legal authority* available for a field of law.

With respect to patents and copyrights, legal authority has an ultimate basis in the *United States Constitution.* Article I, Section 8 of the Constitution states that "[t]he Congress shall have the power to promote the Progress of Science and useful Arts, by Securing for a Limited Time to *Authors and Inventors* the exclusive Right to their respective Writings and Discoveries" (emphasis added). This clause empowers Congress to draft specific statutes defining patent and copyright protection. The details of those statutes then define the outlines of the patent and copyright system.

The following is the legal authority for all the intellectual property rights we have been discussing.

Patent Law   Patents are the exclusive province of *federal law.* This means that there is one unified patent system across the whole nation, rather than state-by-state rules. The *statutes* of patent law are contained in the following:

✪   *United States Code* (U.S.C.), Chapter 35, Sec. 1—376; also known as the "U.S. Patent Act." These are the most general and fundamental rules of patent law (the index reveals the topics covered);

✪   *Code of Federal Regulations* (C.F.R.) 37, Sec. 1, elaborating most of the sections in the U.S. Code in greater detail; and,

✪   *Manual of Patent Examining Procedure* (*MPEP*), currently in its eighth edition, which sets forth virtually all patent prosecution rules.

NOTE: *Unless you are prosecuting your own patent, it is unnecessary to read the MPEP. However, if you are, please approach this manual with great caution—it is extremely technical.*

In addition, the *U.S. Patent & Trademark Office (PTO)* has a wealth of patent and trademark related information, including: forms, regulations, prior art databases, information on recent legal changes, and so on. Their website is:

www.uspto.gov

Apart from the statutes, there exists *patent common law,* interpretations of patent statutory law. This can be more complicated to locate since patent court cases are spread throughout much of the federal court system. However, with the creation of the *U.S. Court of Appeals for the Federal Circuit* (or simply, the *Federal Circuit*) in 1982, much of the judicial system's patent legal authority is concentrated in this court's legal opinions. Aside from the United States Supreme Court, the Federal Circuit is the ultimate judicial authority on patent law.

Copyright Law   Like patent law, copyright law is federal and there is one nationwide copyright law system. The statutes of copyright law are contained in:

- ✪ *U.S.C.*, Ch. 1–13, Sec. 17 (also known as the Copyright Act of 1976), which are the most general and rules of copyright law and

- ✪ *C.F.R.*, Title 37, Sec. II, elaborating most of the sections in the U.S. Code in greater detail.

The *U.S. Copyright Office* has information on all aspects of copyright law, as well as forms for registering works, databases, and guides to regulations and policy. Their web site is:

http://lcweb.loc.gov/copyright

Court cases dealing with copyright law can be found in any federal court. There is no specialized court dealing with copyright disputes.

Trademark Law   Trademarks are protected *both* under *federal* law and *state statutory* and *common law*. Federal statutes can be found in:

- ✪ *U.S.C.*, Ch. 15, Sec. 1051—1127 (also known as the *Lanham Act*), which are the most general federal statutes of trademark law and

- ✪ C.F.R., Title 37, Sec. I, which elaborate more detailed rules pertaining to trademarks.

Trade Secret Law   Trade secret law is generally the province of *state statutory* and *common law*. States pass specific statutes on trade secrets and court cases interpret these rules. However, the federal *Uniform Trade Secrets Act (UTSA)* has been passed as a model for the rules of trade secret protection. Currently, forty-two states have enacted statutes similar to the UTSA.

The U.S. Patent & Trademark Office (PTO), aside from handling patents, has a division devoted to trademarks. The website is:

www.uspto.gov

This includes free online trademark searching (Trademark Electronic Search System or TESS) as well as a wealth of guidelines, rules of practice, and forms. Trademark court cases may be found throughout the entire federal and state court system.

(See Appendix A for additional resources on patents, copyrights, trademarks, and trade secrets, including helpful websites, general reference books, and more technical professional guides.)

2 NATURE OF AGREEMENTS

Now that you have an understanding of intellectual property, you are ready to explore the basics of *license agreements*. However, it is important to examine the nature of agreements, or contracts, more generally. You have to know how they are entered into and the manner in which they are enforced. The next several sections of this chapter will do just that.

Defining Agreements

Legally speaking, an agreement is a promise or set of promises between two or more people to perform an action (or several actions). Alternatively, an agreement can also be a promise to refrain from doing something. The individuals, companies, or organizations who enter into an agreement are known as the *parties*. A corporation is considered a separate legal entity with the power to enter into a contract as a party. In theory, there may be any number of parties to an agreement, but very often there are only two or three.

NOTE: *Agreements are also referred to as* contracts. *These two terms are often used interchangeably, though it is customary to say* license agreement, *but not* license contract.

For our purposes, the most significant point about agreements is that they are *legally binding*. This means that with a valid agreement, the parties are *legally required to* perform the obligations stated in the agreement. If a party does not carry out or perform its obligations as stated in the agreement, it is said to be in *breach* (default) of that agreement. Such a *breach* often brings with it legal and financial repercussions. The breaching party may be taken to court by the other party and forced to either pay monetary damages, or to perform its legal obligations, or both.

Types of Agreements

There are a great variety of agreements that are seen in everyday life, whether in business or in our personal lives. The following are *some* of the more common ones.

✪ *Sales Agreements.* Agreements which involve the sale and purchase of goods in business or major assets such as a automobiles, houses, or land.

✪ *Leases.* Agreements which allow someone use of a property—an apartment, land, an automobile, etc.—in exchange for periodic payments.

✪ *Development Agreements.* Agreements in which one party requests or *commissions* a work from someone else that involves the creation or development of the work.

✪ *Service Agreements.* Agreements that involve the performance of a service; consulting for a company; or, acting as an agent for a writer or an actor.

✪ *License Agreements.* Agreements in which legal permission is granted to someone for a specified purpose.

For the remainder of the book, however, we will be focusing on licenses and other intellectual property-related agreements such as assignments and confidentiality agreements. (See Appendix E for more information about these other types of agreements.)

Written vs. Oral Agreements

In theory, agreements may be either written or oral. The vast majority of agreements, especially those in business, are written. Further, certain types of agreements *must* be in writing or they will be *invalid*. Common examples of these are contracts for the sale of goods for more than $500, agreements for purchase of land, and contracts which cannot be performed in less than a year.

However, it is *strongly recommended* that regardless of the type of agreement you enter (no matter how simple), that it be in writing. And where intellectual property is concerned, the writing requirement is even more important. There is almost no way to keep track of all the detailed decisions, terms, and provisions that go into a licensing transaction or arrangement without a written document.

Legally speaking, what counts as a *writing*? In our age of faxes, emails, and other electronic communications, this is indeed a very important question. Does a letter written from one party to another constitute a written agreement? What if the letter is faxed? Or emailed? As you can appreciate, the electronic nature of modern commerce has raised some interesting legal issues with respect to contracts.

While it is always best to have a signed, *hard* copy of an agreement, courts in some states have determined that the *writing* requirement may sometimes be satisfied *electronically*. For example, take the case of online sales. If you have a *reproducible record* of the contract's terms and a record of the other party's response, then the writing requirement has been satisfied. Likewise, a *digital signature*, a type of electronic authorization to a communication, has also been interpreted as a valid assent to a contract.

Agreement Terms & Conditions

Agreements contain a series of provisions known as the agreement's *terms* or *terms and conditions*. The agreement provisions set forth the *transaction* between the parties, as well as all the promises, rights, and obligations of the parties. These are all set forth in a series of paragraphs, each one of which typically has a heading which summarizes the content of that paragraph.

An agreement, regardless of what kind it is, is a *self-contained* document. This means that everything in the agreement must be defined and understood by reference to the information in the agreement. This includes the parties to the agreement, their exact obligations, every term and condition, and so forth. In addition, every important word or concept used in the agreement that is not self-explanatory must be defined. Frequently, an agreement will contain a *definitions* section that will define all important words. Alternatively, a *schedule* or *exhibit* may be added to the agreement for the purpose of more precisely delineating or defining the agreement's terms.

Most agreements will last for a limited time. Such duration is known as the agreement's *term*. Some agreements, however, last indefinitely. Their term is said to be *perpetual*. For the first category, an agreement's term can vary widely. Some agreements will last only weeks, while others can run for many years. However, a term of one year is customary in many business transactions. After the agreement ends or *terminates*, the parties are usually no longer bound by the agreement.

NOTE: *The word* term *is used here to mean the duration of the agreement as well as a particular provision within the agreement as in* terms and conditions. *Such dual use is customary, so please keep this distinction in mind in the chapters which follow.*

Agreements also typically have *termination* conditions that specify the specific conditions under which one or more parties may *terminate*, or end the agreement before the expiration of its term. There are several different *types* of termination conditions. For example, an agreement may usually be terminated if the other party breaches—that is, fails to perform under the agreement. An agreement may also set forth a termination for convenience or for a failure to perform according to given business standards.

Negotiating Agreements

Legally speaking, a contract or agreement results from two separate actions: *offer* and *acceptance*. An *offer* is a putting forth of a proposal which amounts to: "I will do X for you, if you do Y for me, under the following conditions…" An *acceptance* is another person's assent to the terms of the offer. In addition to offer and acceptance, a valid agreement must also contain *consideration*. This means that something of value must be *bargained for* in the agreement. In other words, a simple promise to do something for someone else is not, by itself, a legal contract.

The process of offer, acceptance, and the presence of consideration occurs naturally in everyday business. There is no need to further analyze them. A more relevant discussion is the way agreements are *negotiated*.

Many agreements, including the majority of intellectual property licenses, are negotiated before they are signed. Negotiation is the process whereby each party tries to gain the best terms for itself. This can include money, performance of services, guarantees, compensation for breach, and many others. Each party will put forth terms and provisions that are subsequently expanded, deleted, and/or otherwise revised, until an agreement is reached between the parties. The length of time the parties will negotiate can vary, greatly. Some agreements are negotiated during a phone call. Others may undergo many months (or years) of on-again off-again negotiation, until the parties are finally ready to sign.

Proper negotiation between parties is often referred to in legal circles as *negotiation at arms-length*. This is another way of saying the negotiation is legitimate, and not merely for show. For a negotiation to be *arms-length*, the parties must be completely separate entities, owned by different parties, with separate interests. Mere legal separation is often insufficient. For instance, a company and its *wholly-owned subsidiary* are separate entities from a corporate perspective. But since they are *commonly owned,* a negotiation between them may not be considered a legitimate, arms-length transaction. Whether an agreement is negotiated (or a transaction conducted) at arms-length is often important for other legal reasons, especially in corporate law.

There are, of course, agreements that are signed without having been negotiated. This is especially true of agreements between consumers purchasing products, renting or leasing property, borrowing money, and the companies that supply these goods and services. We have all signed leases for apartments (or sales agreements for home purchase) without even reading the legal terms, let alone negotiating them. However, when the parties to an agreement are companies or individuals with highly tailored requirements or where significant sums of money are concerned, negotiation is an expected and commonplace occurrence.

In coming to an agreement, the parties may also decide specific terms by reference to similar agreements in their field or industry. This is commonly known as a *Standard of the Industry*. For example, suppose you are a software company in need of an agreement to cover a license of your software product. A good place to start would be a review of licenses of software companies of similar size, in licensing arrangements of similar complexity. A great many provisions are *handed down*, with some variation in details, from one contract to another in this manner.

Example: In many cases, companies will arrive at a fee for a license by reference to the *standard* payment in their industry. For example, a software company develops a new software program that keeps track of stock market trades. Before marketing the software, the software company will want to predict how much it will make from licensing its software to traders and financial institutions. There will likely be a standard range of fees that are paid for similar software products in the securities industry.

In a negotiation, one party may have greater *bargaining power* than the other. Bargaining power refers to a party's overall strength in market position and/or the general desirability of that party's intellectual property, product, or service. Stronger bargaining power places that party at an advantage relative to the other, enabling the stronger party to better dictate the terms and provisions of the agreement. For instance, companies who license software from *Microsoft* have most likely discovered the full extent of the latter's bargaining power. Much to the chagrin of their customers and suppliers, companies with dominant market positions often refuse to revise the terms of their agreements, relying instead on their *standard* agreements to fit all situations.

The negotiation process, itself, can also contain intermediary points before the final agreement is signed. One intermediary document that may be entered into during negotiation of a final agreement is the *letter of intent*. This is a relatively short agreement that summarizes the parties' intention to enter into a final, full-scale agreement sometime in the future (an agreement to agree). A letter of intent will typically summarize the overall points of a future agreement between the parties. However, letters of intent are generally not legally binding on the parties. If any of the parties backs away from the deal, the other party will generally not be able to claim breach (unless the letter of intent specifically states that it is, in fact, binding).

Once an agreement is signed and dated by all the parties, it is said to have been *executed*. This means that the parties have consented to be legally bound by the terms and conditions present in the agreement. These legal obligations will last for the duration stated in the agreement, known as the *term*. Once an agreement has been executed, a party may not rescind or cancel its obligations stated in the agreement, unless this right is explicitly stated in the agreement. (See termination clauses in Chapter 5.)

Enforcing Agreements

Agreements are, in a sense, self-created law. When two or more parties enter into an agreement, they, in effect, create their own *private,* legal relationship that may be enforced in a court of law. This enables individuals and companies who do business with one another to structure enduring relationships so that terms remain the same. As there is generally a great deal of fluctuation in the business world, it is advantageous to attempt to structure stable contractual relationships. This enables businesses to make economic and financial calculations, thus better planning for the future.

The law that governs the interpretation and enforcement of agreements or contracts, is known, simply enough, as *contract law.* Contract law applies to *all* agreements, but is specific to the state where the contract is performed. Thus, if a party does not perform its obligations under an agreement, the other party may sue the nonperforming party. The court will then interpret the contract according to legal rules and regulations of the state. There are, however, commonalities of law among all states. Some of these will be discussed in the next two sections: *breach* and *remedies.*

In addition, certain *kinds* of agreements are subject to other federal and state laws. For example, residential leases are governed by landlord/tenant laws of which every state has a different version. Such law will supersede or pre-empt, at least some of the provisions a landlord or tenant would normally be able to include in a lease. In other words, while a landlord and tenant have the freedom to write any terms in their lease, they cannot put in provisions which contradict landlord/tenant rules in that state. Similarly, agreements for the sale of tangible goods are governed by the *Uniform Commercial Code (UCC)* that applies nationwide.

Breach of Contract

If a party to an agreement does not perform his or her obligations as defined in the agreement, the situation is known as *breach.* Sometimes parties to an agreement will distinguish between a *breach* and a *material breach.* A material breach is a breach that has a *substantial (material)* effect on a party's financial or legal situation. This differs from a breach whose consequences are minor or easily repairable. Usually, parties will *not* be too concerned with nonmaterial breaches, but will be quite vigilant in responding to *material* ones.

To illustrate this point, take the case of a software license that allows the licensee to make one back-up copy of the licensed software program. If the licensee makes two copies, this is a breach, but *not* a material one. If, however, the licensee duplicates the software numerous times and starts distributing it to persons outside the license, that breach is definitely *material*.

NOTE: *A breach of the agreement—whether material or not—will occur if there is nonperformance under any of an agreement's provisions. Since a typical agreement puts forth many terms and obligations on the part of each party, the parties must be careful to obey each and every term of the agreement and not take actions explicitly forbidden them.*

Another important point is that a material breach of even *one provision* in an agreement *may* result in *termination* of the *entire* agreement and loss of all rights (or benefits) for the breaching party. The specifics of this will depend on what the agreement explicitly states with respect to termination. However, many agreements have termination clauses allowing for the non-breaching party to terminate an agreement if it is materially breached. This is especially important in the context of license agreements. A licensee (the party who is using someone else's intellectual property) must remember not to use the intellectual property in ways that are not authorized by the license, as this would typically constitute a material breach. A material breach could lead to termination of the license. (See *Chapter 5: Main Terms* for more information.)

Remedies Available for Breach

If a party breaches an agreement, the nonbreaching party may initiate a lawsuit. Depending on the harm suffered, the nonbreaching party may receive *remedies* for such breach. There are two potential types of remedies for the majority breaches of an agreement: *monetary damages* and *injunctive relief.*

Monetary damages. Monetary damages are exactly what the name implies—that is, financial compensation to make up for the loss suffered by the nonbreaching party. There are several varieties of monetary damages which may be awarded by a court. The specific type of damages a court will award will depend on many factors, including: the nature of the legal claim, the amount of financial or other harm suffered by a party, and even the behavior of the parties to the lawsuit.

Some of the more common types of damages are the following.

✪ *Direct Damages* (also known as *Compensatory Damages*). These are the most common type of monetary damages for contract breach. Direct or compensatory damages is a sum of money that would put the non-breaching party in the position it would be in if the contract *had been* properly performed.

Example: A seller and buyer sign a sales contract in which the buyer promises to pay $ 1,000 for certain merchandise. The buyer later breaches the agreement by not paying the seller, though he does receive the merchandise. The seller sues for contract breach. The typical remedy for such breach would be to compensate the seller the $1,000 he would have received had the buyer performed his obligations.

✪ *Consequential Damages.* These are damages that flow not from the actual breach of contract, but from the consequences or results of such breach. This commonly includes lost profits and lost business. For example, take a case of two companies that enter into a very important contract. If one of the parties breaches the agreement, the other (non-breaching) party is likely to not only suffer direct losses from nonperformance of the contract, but also lost profits from business that depended on having the contract fulfilled.

✪ *Punitive Damages* (also known as *Exemplary Damages*). These are damages awarded by a court to the winning party as a type of *punishment* for the other party's behavior. The behavior must be *outrageous* or *egregious*. Though courts do not award punitive damages in situations of ordinary contract breach, punitive damages are more common in litigation involving intellectual property. For example, damages paid to a patent owner for patent infringement can be tripled if the infringer is found to have acted *willfully*. (See Chapter 1 for more information on patents and infringement.)

Attorney's Fees. This is an award by a court of the legal costs that a party pays to its attorneys for the litigation. Attorney's fees are not typically awarded in the event of contract breach, unless the contract specifically provides for recovery of such fees. However, some federal and state laws provide for the winning party's recovery of attorney's fees in certain cases.

Sometimes it is important to distinguish direct damages from all other damages, including consequential, punitive, attorneys' fees, as well as others. Later, Chapter 7 discusses the significance of the distinction between direct damages and all other types of damages.

Injunctive relief. Aside from monetary damages, there are circumstances where a court may also award *injunctive relief* to the party suing for contract breach. This can mean that the court will stop that party from taking certain actions. In the area of intellectual property agreements and licenses, this type of remedy often takes the form of a *preliminary* or a *permanent injunction.* A *preliminary* injunction is sought at the very start of the litigation process, while a *permanent* injunction, if granted, is given at the very end of the litigation, as part of the plaintiff's overall remedies.

Example: A small photocopy shop located near a college campus sets up a service for the students where it photocopies whole textbooks (without permission from the textbook publishers) and sells the copies at a significant discount. The textbook publishers learn of this activity and sues the owner of the photocopy shop. At the start of the litigation, the publishers go to the judge and ask for a preliminary injunction to halt these sales, pending the lawsuit's outcome. Afterwards, if the publishers win, they can also get a permanent injunction prohibiting such activity in the future.

3 | ESSENTIALS OF A LICENSE AGREEMENT

Now that you know what an agreement (contract) is, generally speaking, and have explored some of the basics of their negotiation and enforcement, it is time to introduce the license agreement. Because an intellectual property license is a specific type of agreement, the overall legal framework for contracts—contract law, rules, and regulations—will also apply for license agreements.

A license is defined as permission to use intellectual property granted by its owner (the *licensor*) to someone else (the *licensee*) so the latter can use those rights according to the terms of the license. (The licensee does not, however, receive ownership of the intellectual property.) That use might entail either the licensee's outright use of the rights, or the manufacture, sale, or other distribution of a product based on the intellectual property. For the privilege of using the intellectual property, the licensee typically pays the licensor a fee, usually referred to as a *royalty*. Royalties and other payments are discussed in Chapter 6.

Licenses vary greatly in content, form, and style. First and foremost, they vary depending on the intellectual property right involved. A software license looks quite different from a trademark merchandising license, because the *type* of intellectual property right granted—copyright or trademark—is different.

NOTE: *Another way of understanding a license is by reference to the licensor's rights. A license is essentially a promise by the licensor not to sue the licensee for intellectual property infringement. This is due to the fact that intellectual property is essentially the owner's exclusive right to use. Anyone else using these rights without permission—that is, a license—infringes these rights.*

A typical license agreement is made up of many provisions covering a wide range of areas, but will almost always contain certain *essential* parts. In addition, licenses invariably contain business provisions that address the business arrangement between licensor and licensee, as well as numerous legal provisions protecting the two parties. Licenses can be referred to as *license agreements* or sometimes as *intellectual property licenses*. These are different names for the *same* thing.

The five basic parts of a license agreements are:

1. introduction and definition of parties;

2. license grant;

3. term;

4. payment; and,

5. the parties' signatures.

It is a significant point, worth repeating, that virtually all real-world license agreements will contain a great many more provisions then the basic ones discussed in this chapter. As a quick glimpse, some of these additional provisions include: representations and warranties, ownership, breach and cure, limitation of liability, indemnification, and confidentiality. As you can see, a license agreement can get very complicated. However, a thorough understanding of these basic parts will provide the groundwork necessary to understand the complexities, as well as to creatively draft your own agreement.

Introduction and Definition of Parties

Defining the parties is the first step in entering into any licensing transaction, as well as the first step in drafting the actual license agreement.

The parties are the persons (companies, corporations, or organizations) who will be entering into the license and agreeing to be legally bound by all of its terms and conditions. All licenses have *at least* two parties—the *licensor* and the *licensee*. The *licensor* is the owner of the intellectual property rights and the party authorizing use of the intellectual property in question. The *licensee* is the party *receiving* the permission and the rights. Though there may be other parties, the licensor and licensee are always the main parties to the license agreement.

The parties to a license must be carefully defined, both in terms of who they are and to what extent they are covered by the license.

License Grant

The *license grant* is the very heart of the license agreement. In a license, the owner of intellectual property gives someone else permission to use the rights, for a limited time and under enumerated conditions. The *license grant* section summarizes the intellectual property transaction that is taking place between the parties (i.e., the permission to use the intellectual property rights).

However, the license grant provision is, itself, made-up of separate parts, each one addressing important legal issues. Each of these separate parts are discussed in greater detail in future chapters. But for simplicity, think of the license grant as answering three separate, though interrelated, questions.

1. What rights is the licensor granting?

2. Is the grant exclusive or nonexclusive?

3. What can the licensee do?

Rights Being Granted

The answer to this question defines that license type. Is the licensor giving the licensee permission to use a patent, a copyright, a trademark, or a trade secret? Or a combination of these rights? The rights being granted must be clearly stated and defined in the license.

Exclusive or Nonexclusive Rights

This is a critical distinction that must be noted in every license and stated explicitly in the *License Grant* section. All licenses are *either* exclusive or nonexclusive, but never both. The following elaborates this distinction:

Exclusive. This means that the licensee is the *only* person, or company, who may use the intellectual property rights being granted. In other words, the licensor is forbidden from making any more license grants during the term of the license.

Nonexclusive. This means that the licensee may, at its discretion, license the same intellectual property rights to other parties in separate licenses. In other words, the licensor *may* give permission to other people (in separate license agreements) to use the intellectual property in question. The licensor may grant additional nonexclusive licenses as often as it wants, but is not obligated to do so.

Rules for the Licensee

Every license specifies a precise set of *rules* for the licensee's use of the intellectual property rights. Will the licensee use the intellectual property to manufacture, sell, and/or distribute a product? Or will the license just allow the licensee *use* of the intellectual property rights? It is up to the parties to decide and this is often a critical issue of negotiation.

For example, a software license may state that the licensee—a large corporation—may use a software program only within its organization (or a certain department), for its own internal purposes (i.e., it cannot distribute or resell the program), and may not make copies, except as a back-up.

A patent license may grant the licensee permission to use a patent in order to manufacture a certain type of product and then sell these products within a given territory.

The license grant section may also contain other information regarding the license and ownership of the intellectual property. Overall, the license grant section conveys a great deal of legal information in a very compact manner.

If this all sounds a bit confusing, do not worry. Reviewing the sample license beginning on page 47 will provide a good example of what this provision looks like.

License Term

The *term* of the license is the length of time the agreement is in effect. At the end of the license's term, the license is said to *terminate* or *expire*. After termination of the license, the parties will no longer be bound by the license's provisions. Of course, after termination of the license, the parties are free to renew the agreement for yet another term (or a successive number of terms). With this renewal, they are free to renegotiate and change any of the license's terms and conditions, as long as there is consent on the part of both parties to do so.

Along with the term, the parties will usually insert one or more conditions under which one or more of the parties may *terminate* the license before the expiration of its term. (Such termination conditions will be examined in more detail in Chapter 4.)

NOTE: *The word* term *means both the duration of the license as well as its specific provisions. You should keep in mind the specific context of the word's use.*

Payment Provisions

Though an intellectual property owner may give away use of his or her intellectual property for free, in the vast majority of cases, the licensee will pay for use of these rights. Given that money is the reason for licensing in the first place, this is quite an important issue. If you are the licensor, you will want to know how much money you will be making from the license. If you are the licensee, you will want to know how much the license will cost you.

There are two forms of payment for a license:

✷   a fixed *lump-sum payment* or

✷   *royalties.*

Fixed payments, as the name implies, stay the same, whereas royalties depend on the sale of a manufactured product based on the intellectual property. Which of these will be chosen in a given license depends on the type of license, the licensee's authorized actions as well as other business considerations. (These and other payment provisions are explained in Chapter 6.)

Parties' Signatures

This is by far the simplest of the provisions of a license and might seem a bit obvious to discuss. However, it is critical. Each and every party to the license agreement must signify consent to the terms and conditions of the license agreement with a signature. Every signature is also dated. The date of signature does not have to match the date of the license agreement. In addition, the name of each signor, his or her title, and the name of his or her organization (if the party is a business) is also provided underneath the signature. In signing a license agreement, anyone with the legal authority to represent and legally bind the company in contract may sign the license.

The parties to the license agreement may sign the agreement *separately*—that is, one party signs and forwards the original to the other for their signature. Some licenses may state this explicitly—namely, that the agreement may be signed in counterparts. Either way, so long as the signature of every party to the agreement is present, the license agreement will be considered a binding contract.

Sample License Agreement

The following is a *simplified* license between two fictional companies. This specific license involves a software product, and as such, contains certain language unique to *software* licenses. A break-down and analysis of each of its basic provisions is given. Remember, the emphasis here is on seeing the overall form of a license agreement, not on learning the details of its often numerous terms and conditions. (A thorough examination of all license provisions will be provided in Chapters 5 through 8.)

Sample Agreement

This Software License Agreement ("Agreement") is made and entered into this August 1, 2003 ("Effective Date"), by and between Soft Systems, Inc., a New York corporation with offices at 121 W. 57th Street, New York, NY ("Soft Systems") and Pinnacle Financial Co., a Delaware corporation with offices at 200 Main Street, Kansas City, MO ("Pinnacle").

WHEREAS, Soft Systems has developed and owns all rights to a software program known as the E-Z Financial Database ("Software") and more fully identified in Exhibit A;

WHEREAS, Pinnacle desires to use the Software for its own internal business purposes;

NOW, THEREFORE, in consideration of the mutual promises contained herein, the parties agree as follows:

1.   License Grant. Soft Systems grants to Pinnacle a nonexclusive license to use the Software for its own internal business purposes, without the right of sublicense, subject to the terms and conditions of this Agreement. Pinnacle shall not copy or otherwise duplicate the Software except for one (1) copy for back-up purposes, and shall not transfer, sell, or otherwise distribute the Software to any third party. All rights not specifically granted to Pinnacle shall be reserved to Soft Systems.

2.   Term. This Agreement shall commence on the Effective Date and continue for a period of one (1) year, unless terminated according to this Agreement. This Agreement may be renewed for additional one (1) year periods, at the mutual consent of the parties.

3.   Termination. Soft Systems may terminate this Agreement if Pinnacle materially breaches any provision, subject to a thirty (30) day cure period. Upon termination, Pinnacle shall return all copies of the Software to Soft Systems.

(continued...)

> 4. Fees. During the term of this Agreement, Pinnacle shall pay Soft Systems a royalty of $ 5,000 per year. Payments shall be made every quarter for the duration of the term.
>
> IN WITNESS WHEREOF, the parties have executed this Agreement as of the date first written above:
>
> SOFT SYSTEMS, INC. PINNACLE FINANCIAL CO.
> (Licensor) (Licensee)
>
> _____ _____
> Name   Date Name   Date
>
> _____ _____
> Title Title

License Commentary

Remember that these are the *bare minimum* terms of a license agreement. Virtually all license agreements contain many more details regarding the business provisions of the license, as well as numerous legal provisions. So please do not use this bare bones as a form for your license.

Definition of the Parties

The first part of any license agreement is the *introductory* paragraph. In the sample license, we are referring to the following paragraph:

> This Software License Agreement ("Agreement") is made and entered into this January 1, 2003, by and between Soft Systems, Inc., a New York corporation with offices at 121 W. 57th Street, New York, NY ("Soft Systems") and Pinnacle Financial Services, a Delaware corporation with offices at 200 Main Street, Kansas City, MO ("Pinnacle").

The introductory part of a license agreement achieves four important goals:

✪ the license agreement itself is identified—that is, is it a technology, software, trademark license, and so on;

✪ the license agreement is dated;

✪ the parties are introduced and identified; and,

✪ abbreviated names for all the parties—as well as for the license agreement itself—are provided, which will be later used throughout the agreement.

Let us examine each of these four goals in turn:

The license agreement itself is identified. In the very beginning, it is explicitly stated that the agreement is a "software license agreement." While this may seem an obvious point, it is a very important one. As is often the case, parties will enter into more than one agreement with each other and it is necessary to clearly label each one.

The license agreement is dated. It might be a bit obvious to state that every business document should be dated. However, with license agreements, this becomes especially important since the term (duration) of the license is often measured by the date first written in the agreement.

The official date of a license agreement is usually given the name Effective Date. In the introductory paragraph the effective date is described by the following:

...is made and entered into this August 1, 2003 (the "Effective Date")...

Later in the license, you can refer simply to the "Effective Date" as the official start of the license or for other purposes. The date of the license agreement does not have to match the dates of each of the parties' signature.

The parties are introduced and identified. Every party to the license agreement must be separately introduced, address stated, and if a corporation, the state of incorporation. Or, in the alternative, the address of its principal offices can be stated. This not only makes it clear who the party is, but by specifying location, removes any confusion if there is another business with an identical name.

Delineating the exact nature of the licensor and/or licensee can sometimes be tricky. For example, parties which are companies can have parents, subsidiaries, or be affiliated with other companies. Even within a company, the license may be confined to a certain department or a specified group of users.

Abbreviated names are given. Abbreviated names for the parties, the licensed property, and the agreement itself are very convenient, since all of these are likely to be referred to throughout the agreement.

Recitals Immediately after the introductory paragraph defining the agreement and the parties, a license will often contain several additional statements known as the *recitals.* This section summarizes the parties' intentions, introduces the subject matter (or property) of the license agreement, and states that the parties are agreeing to all the terms that follow.

In the sample license agreement, the following is the recitals section:

> WHEREAS, Soft Systems has developed and owns all rights to a software program known as the E-Z Financial Database ("Software") and more fully identified in Exhibit A;

> WHEREAS, Pinnacle desires to use the Software for its own internal business purposes;

> NOW, THEREFORE, in consideration of the mutual promises contained herein, the parties agree as follows:

As you can see, each party's overall *intention* or *desire* to enter into the license is stated. In addition, the licensed intellectual property (frequently referred to as the *licensed property*) is often introduced and defined, sometimes with reference to an exhibit or attachment. Of course, the recitals for each license will vary, as different licenses will contain different provisions.

While recitals are not an absolute requirement for a license, they are somewhat of a custom in the world of licensing. It is best that you know what they are since you might run into them in license agreements you will be reviewing. Of course, if you are not using recitals in your license, you *must* define any term requiring definition (in our sample license, "Software" is such a term) elsewhere in the license.

Regardless of whether you use recitals in your license, the last sentence should be included as follows:

> In consideration of the mutual promises contained herein, the parties agree as follows:

This sentence not only stresses that all parties are agreeing to the terms and conditions that follow, but also clearly divides the introduction of the agreement from its main body. Such division is important if the agreement is ever litigated, since courts tend to separate the main body from the introductory paragraphs and focus on the main body in interpreting the agreement.

License Grant   The following provision in the above license is the license grant section:

> License Grant. Soft Systems grants to Pinnacle a nonexclusive license to use the Software for its own internal business purposes, without the right of sublicense, subject to the terms and conditions of this Agreement. Pinnacle shall not copy or otherwise duplicate the Software except for one (1) copy for back-up purposes, and shall not transfer, sell, or otherwise distribute the Software to any third party. All rights not specifically granted to Pinnacle shall be reserved to Soft Systems.

Just as a well-drafted license grant provision is supposed to do, the three basic questions covered earlier in this chapter are answered.

1. What rights is the licensor granting?

    Answer: Rights to the Software.

2. Is the grant exclusive or nonexclusive?

    Answer: Nonexclusive.

3. What can the licensee do?

    Answer: Use the Software solely within its own organization.

In addition, other restrictions on the licensee's actions are provided as well as other information regarding the specific grant of rights.

NOTE: *The term Software was previously defined in the recitals. However, if it were not so defined, the License Grant Section would be a good place to define it.*

License Term   As previously stated, the term of the license is its duration. In the above sample license, the *term* provision is the following:

> TERM. This Agreement shall commence on the Effective Date and continue for a period of one (1) year, unless terminated according to this Agreement. This Agreement may be renewed for additional one (1) year periods, at the mutual consent of the parties.

The term provided here is one year. In addition, the license states that the term may be renewed at the consent of both parties. The presence of the statement regarding renewal is not absolutely necessary (since parties always have that right), but may become important if the parties agree to an auto-renewal provision.

> TERMINATION. Soft Systems may terminate this Agreement if Pinnacle materially breaches any provision, subject to a thirty (30) day cure period. Upon termination, Pinnacle shall return all copies of the Software to Soft Systems.

According to the termination conditions provided, the licensor, *Soft Systems*, may terminate the license only for licensee's *breach*. (A violation of one or more of the license's conditions.) It may do so, only if the licensee is provided a thirty day period to *cure* such breach.

Payment Provisions   Like the other terms of the above sample license, the payment terms have been simplified:

> FEES. During the term of this Agreement, Pinnacle shall pay Soft Systems a royalty of $ 5,000 per year. Payments shall be made every quarter for the duration of the term.

These terms are for the most part self-explanatory. Much more information about payment follows in Chapter 6.

Parties' Signatures   The last provision is always the parties' signatures. This is, for the most part, self-explanatory. An authorized representative of each party signs and dates, and also provides his or her title underneath such signature.

The following sentence is important to insert before the actual signature lines in a license agreement:

> **IN WITNESS WHEREOF, the parties have executed this Agreement as of the date first written above:**

This statement stresses that the fact that the parties have agreed to all of the terms and conditions of the license and are signing the agreement with this knowledge. It also re-emphasizes the *official* date of the license agreement.

The very phrase "IN WITNESS WHEREOF" is not critical, but is a matter of custom. If the recitals are placed in the agreement, then you should use this phrase as well.

4 | BUSINESS DECISIONS

The licensor must ask whether he or she should license in the first place. And for the licensee, it is whether to enter into the license agreement. In the majority of cases, these decisions will be made for monetary reasons. Sometimes, however, the decision to license is decided, for other reasons, such as the license's infringement of an intellectual property right.

Should You License?

Why *should* you enter into a license agreement? If you own intellectual property—a patent, copyright, trademark, or trade secret—is it preferable to commercialize these rights yourself? Alternatively, is it simpler to sell (to assign) these rights to another party in one complete transaction? Conversely, if you are a potential licensee, why not develop your own intellectual property—or purchase it outright—instead of licensing someone else's?

In most cases, whether to license intellectual property is a business decision made by each party. It is as simple (or sometimes as complicated) as determining whether the potential revenues from licensing will exceed its costs and/or be more profitable than the alternatives. The licensor and licensee must each make a separate analysis. The licensor will weigh whether licensing fees or royalties will exceed the costs of investing to commercialize the intellectual property itself. The licensee will make similar judgments with respect to its own costs and profits.

Licensing vs. Producing It Yourself

There are situations when licensing must be undertaken in order to avoid infringement. Though this, too, is a choice on the part of the potential licensee, it involves a different type of analysis.

Licensing is frequently an attractive option because commercialization of intellectual property is difficult, expensive, and often requires specialized knowledge. Developing a patent or copyright into a commercially successful product requires great investment of resources and costs. In addition, since the outcome is never guaranteed, trying to market intellectual property is often fraught with risk. Therefore, for most intellectual property owners, it will be far easier and less risky to license intellectual property, than to commercialize it directly.

At the same time, there are companies that have the manufacturing, marketing, or other resources, but lack the idea, brand, or invention. These companies will make ideal licensees. One can see the licensing transaction as an efficient *division of labor*. A licensor typically has the idea, invention, artistic work, or brand, but lacks the manufacturing or marketing resources. The licensee usually has the manufacturing capabilities (depending on its size), but no intellectual property. Thus, a solo inventor who receives a patent will very often license the invention to a company with a factory (to make the product) and a sales force (to sell it).

But licensing applies in other situations as well. Sometimes an intellectual property owner does have the resources to turn his or her intellectual property into a commercially successful product, but desires not to do so for a variety of reasons. Maybe the IP owner can make more money by producing other products. Or perhaps the owner lacks particular knowledge regarding a certain market and seeks to learn more about it before manufacturing and marketing a product. Regardless of the reason, this type of situation is ideal for a licensing arrangement.

Example: A large corporation such as IBM owns many patents that it chooses not to develop into products, but instead offers to license to others. This is yet another example of how a license *channels* intellectual property to the party most desirous (and willing to assume the risk) of commercializing it.

In short, if you are the *intellectual property owner* and are looking to manufacture and market a product based on your intellectual property, there are many excellent reasons to license. This is especially true if you are licensing to a licensee who is an established and well-known company. Some of these important business advantages are:

- ✪ licensee's effectiveness to reach new markets;

- ✪ licensee's possession of effective manufacturing and distribution capabilities;

- ✪ licensee's established customer base; and,

- ✪ name recognition of licensee.

There are times that two or more parties will each want to use technology that belongs to the other. In this unique situation, the parties will enter into what is known as a *cross-license*. As the name implies, each party licenses its intellectual property to the other, so that each is both a licensor and licensee.

Licensing vs. Selling Your IP

If you own intellectual property, is it more beneficial to sell your intellectual property in lieu of licensing it? It is a given that an intellectual property owner always has the option of selling his or her intellectual property (*assignment*). However, while an assignment is much simpler than a license, it has its own drawbacks.

The difficulty with a sale of intellectual property is often in the setting of a *fair* price that the buyer and seller will agree on. Since the intellectual property oftentimes has not yet been commercialized or used in a significant way, it is hard to know how much money it will ultimately make, and therefore how *valuable* it is.

Another drawback to selling—as opposed to licensing—intellectual property has to do with the *permanence* of a sale. Once a sale is made, there is no going back. There are no *refunds* in the world of intellectual property. And this is risky for both parties. For the intellectual property owner, the risk is that he or she could be giving up intellectual property that could later turn out to be very valuable. For the intellectual property *purchaser*, the risk is that he or she is buying something that may later prove to be less valuable than the purchase price.

An intellectual property license has an advantage over a sale. In this respect, a license has the advantage of allowing both licensor and licensee to *test out* the commercial potential of intellectual property and see whether it meets with each party's expectations. However, that being said, there most certainly are situations where a sale (or purchase) of intellectual property makes financial sense for both parties.

Licensing to avoid Infringement

There are situations when licensing is undertaken almost by necessity. This happens when an individual or company starts making, using, and/or selling a product or artistic work that is *already covered* by someone else's intellectual property.

If the intellectual property owner discovers what is believed to be infringing use, he or she may then threaten a lawsuit unless the infringing party either: (1) *stops the infringing uses* or (2) *enters into a license with the owner.* The owner is saying, in effect, either pay me for the right to use my property or stop using it.

This scenario often takes place with patent rights, but may also occur with trademark and copyrights, as well. Sometimes, if an intellectual property owner sues an alleged infringer and the lawsuit ends up in court (as opposed to being settled), a court may even impose the equivalent of a license on the infringing user. In patent law, this is known as the *reasonable royalty* measure of damages.

If the intellectual property owner makes this kind of demand, the alleged infringer does have several choices. He or she can:

✪ *continue using the intellectual property, and face a possible lawsuit;*

✪ *stop all uses of the intellectual property; or,*

✪ *enter into a license with the intellectual property owner.*

Continue using the intellectual property and face a possible lawsuit. Even if you choose this option because you believe the owner is mistaken (or is bluffing), it is risky and potentially very costly. This is especially the case where valuable intellectual property is involved. In general, defending against a lawsuit is a very costly endeavor, even if you win. And in the event you *are* found to be infringing, you risk the possibility of paying very high monetary damages, in addition to your legal costs. Finally, the intellectual property owner may be able to obtain a *preliminary injunction* from a court before the lawsuit even begins (and a *permanent injunction* afterwards), and thus may stop your use of the intellectual property, regardless.

However, that being said, it is also possible that the intellectual property owner will not pursue a lawsuit against you, even if you continue your *alleged* infringing uses. After all, a plaintiff (the suing party) in any lawsuit bears the expenses of initiating the litigation and so must weigh the costs and benefits. Sometimes, it simply will not be worth the effort.

For these reasons, it is often hard to predict what will happen in the abstract, without reference to the details of a particular situation. Therefore, if you plan to pursue this course of action, it is strongly recommended that you consult with an experienced intellectual property attorney.

Stop all uses of the intellectual property. Again, this could be costly, depending on the intellectual property involved and the nature of the infringing use. Once production or manufacture is set up and begun, it may be costly to stop production and switch to *noninfringing* alternative. However, there are times where halting your planned uses and finding an alternate means is very simple and inexpensive. Examine all the financial and legal aspects of your specific situation and weigh this choice versus taking a license.

Enter into a license with the intellectual property owner. If the alleged infringer does choose to enter into a license with the owner, he or she may do so for a variety of reasons. He or she may believe the intellectual property owner is correct and has a valid claim. Or, while there is not enough conclusive evidence, it would be too costly and time-consuming to try to litigate the issue. Either way, you may not have a great deal of bargaining power if you enter into a license under this kind of threat. Sometimes, this may be your best bet to deal with such an alleged infringement. Once again, an intellectual property attorney may help you make this kind of determination.

NOTE: *If you receive any kind of cease and desist letter from an intellectual property owner, consult with an intellectual property attorney. An attorney will assess the merit of the alleged owner's claim, as well as the likelihood that your actions are actually infringing. The attorney will then be able to advise you as to your best available options, given your financial and legal situation.*

Business Issues to Consider

Once you have made the decision to enter into a license, whether you are the licensor or license, you now have a whole new set of business decisions to make, legal issues to consider, and a license agreement to draft and negotiate. During each phase, you will be dealing with a wide variety of important issues. Along the way, many decisions you make will be quite significant. These decisions will have a great effect on whether your license is well-drafted and will effectively serve your needs.

License agreements are made up of a series of terms or provisions, typically written out in paragraph form, with section headings. For the sake of convenience, these provisions have been grouped into three broad categories:

1. *The Main License Terms*—These are the general business issues that provide the overall structure to your license, including definition of the parties, the license grant, payment, term, termination, and so on.

2. *Legal Protections*—These are provisions that *cover* the parties, both financially and legally.

3. *Standard Terms*—These are additional, miscellaneous legal terms that are fairly consistent across many licenses.

The business provisions *define* and *structure* the overall licensing transaction. In thinking and writing out a license's business terms, each party will clarify its intentions and pinpoint the exact nature of the transaction.

When trying to make your overall licensing decisions, it helps to consider all the separate business issues. In this respect, it is often helpful to think of the business terms as the answers to a series of questions.

The basic *business* questions that should be answered by both licensor and licensee are:

✪   Who are the parties to the licensed?

✪   What intellectual property will be licensed?

✪   What can the licensee do?

✪   Will the license be exclusive or nonexclusive?

- ✪   What will the payment be?

- ✪   What is the license term?

- ✪   How can the license be terminated?

- ✪   Will any services be performed?

Who Are the Parties?

As stated in the previous chapter, when entering into any business relationship, it is an important first step to know with whom you are doing business. With respect to license agreements, it also becomes important to precisely *define* all the parties to the license. However, due to the complexities of many business transactions, this is not always as straightforward as it seems.

The two main parties to a license agreement are, of course, the licensor and licensee. But it is not enough to know who the licensor and licensee is in an ambiguous way. Both parties must be accurately defined. If you are the licensor, you have to define the companies, departments, affiliates, and/or individuals who will be receiving your intellectual property. Deciding this may depend on other business terms and conditions. Properly defining the parties and resolving the legal issues with this point is covered in the next chapter.

NOTE: *When entering into discussions with potential licensees, the licensor should be very careful about disclosing any trade secrets, ideas for future development, or any other confidential information. Often, this is done by having the other party sign a confidentiality (nondisclosure) agreement, before any important information is exchanged or business transacted.*

Who is a Potential Licensor or Licensee?

Whether you are a licensor or licensee, you should be conducting extensive research to learn as much as possible about the market for your intellectual property. This involves gathering information about not only the market itself, but also on the companies and individuals that comprise it. Among the key questions that need to be addressed are:

✪ *Size of the Market*—Are you in a specialized niche or a fairly broad market?

✪ *Key Players in the Industry*—What individuals or companies have licensed in your field, or have taken licenses?

✪ *Licensing Practices*—How is the intellectual property generally licensed? What is the *standard of the industry?*

For many licensors and licensees—especially those doing business for the first time—another potential difficulty involves a very basic emotion: trust. How will you know whether the individual or company you will be dealing with will make timely payments, deliver the licensed property (or other materials), and generally fulfill its obligations under the license? And how do you know whether a party is financially sound and will stay in business for the duration of the license?

This too involves doing one's homework, both in terms of a party's legal *track record* as well as the party's overall financial shape. You can use legal databases to search for federal or state legal cases involving the party. Researching the financial aspects of a company is also possible for a relatively modest cost. Financial sources that help paint an overall financial picture include *Dun & Bradstreet* and *Standard & Poor's* analyses and companies' 10K's, 10Q's, and annual reports. Much of this information is available in business or law libraries or on-line.

Which Intellectual Property will be Licensed?

Which Rights Do You Own?

The *license grant* provision is pretty much the heart of the licensing transaction and the license agreement. After identifying and defining the parties to the license, the next issue is deciding upon and structuring the nature of the license grant.

In some cases, a licensor will need to take a preliminary step before deciding what rights to grant. This is especially true for companies (or individuals) who own a large number or a wide variety of intellectual property rights.

For the licensor, a prior step to deciding what to license is knowing what intellectual property is actually possessed. This may sound a bit counterintuitive. After all, how can someone be unaware of what he or she owns? However, ownership of intellectual property can often be quite complicated. If, for example, you own several patents, numerous copyrighted works, or registered (or unregistered) trademarks, you will probably need accurate records to keep track of your rights.

Remember that owning intellectual property is very different from owning *physical* property. The former involves development or acquisition, registration (in some cases), and subsequently, proper maintenance, payment of fees, and record keeping. And if one owns multiple intellectual property rights, keeping accurate track of these rights is an especially important process.

Which Rights Should Be Licensed?

For many companies, an efficient way to keep track of its intellectual property is with an *Invention Disclosure Form* for patents and a *general disclosure form* for other types of intellectual property. Further, to fully map out the entire inventory of its intellectual property, a company may conduct what is known as an *Intellectual Property Audit*. This type of audit is similar to its financial counterpart, except the investigation is of the exact nature and scope of the intellectual property owned by a company.

The intellectual property being licensed can take a wide variety of forms. For example, your licensed intellectual property could be any of the following (including combinations of these):

Patent.

- ✪ a patented invention—new and unique machine, device, material, or process (including some software);

- ✪ a patent application, which has *not yet issued*; or,

- ✪ a developed product based on a patent.

Copyright. Any artistic work, such as a novel, article, musical composition, work of art, photograph, painting, drawing, sculpture, or most software.

Trademark. A word, phrase, or logo—either federally or state registered, or unregistered.

Trade Secret. Confidential information used in business, such as a client list, technical designs or specifications for a machine or process, or software.

It is worth noting that regardless of the exact type of the invention, product, artistic work, or information, it is always intellectual property rights—patent, copyright, trademark, and/or trade secrets—that are being licensed.

Remember that a licensor can license more than one form of intellectual property. In many cases, licensing a combination of IP rights will actually be more advantageous for both parties. In fact, the presence of more than one type of intellectual property in a license may increase the overall value of the license. This is especially the case if one of the licensed intellectual property rights is generally recognized by the public. For instance, a patented product, not yet marketed, that is packaged with a *well-known* trademark may be a lot easier for the licensee to commercialize.

Some common licensed combinations of intellectual property rights include:

- ✪ *Patent and Trade Secret*—a patented device or machine together with technical information protected by a trade secret.

- ✪ *Copyright and Trademark*—a copyrighted design, character, or picture together with the licensor's trademark.

- ✪ *Patent and Copyright*—software which is protected by patent, as well as copyright.

NOTE: *There are several points worth noting if you are licensing a patent. A licensor may license a* patent application *that is still pending—that is, one that has not yet been granted. However, once a patent has been granted, it may be legally licensed only if the patent is still in force—in other words, still within its 20-year term.*

Regardless of the type of right or rights granted, everything must be carefully defined and spelled-out in the license. The next chapter will discuss these details and nuances of drafting this *License Grant* provision.

What can the Licensee Do?

Use-Only vs. Make and Sell Licenses

You have decided on the intellectual property rights that will be licensed. Or, if you are the licensee, you have identified the types of rights you need. You now have to consider what the intellectual property will be used for and the extent or scope of such use. The issues to be examined include:

✪ *use-only* vs. *make and sell* licenses and

✪ restrictions on the licensee.

Typically, the licensee receives intellectual property rights for the purpose of either:

✪ *using the rights itself* or

✪ *making and selling a product based on these rights.*

For convenience, we refer to these two categories of licenses as *Use-Only* and *Make and Sell Licenses.* This distinction is a very important one since it defines the most central aspect of the license.

NOTE: *The terms* Use-Only *and* Make and Sell *are not technical legal names for these types of licenses. We use these terms to help make this key distinction absolutely clear.*

Use-Only Licenses. If the license falls into the first category, the licensee may only use the intellectual property and nothing more. A common example of this type of license is the standard software license. The licensee receives rights to use a software program solely within its organization and only for its own internal business purposes. It may not further reproduce or distribute the program outside the company.

Make and Sell Licenses. On the other hand, a license could be given to make, sell, and/or otherwise market a product based on licensed intellectual property. This *Make and Sell* License will look very different from the *Use-Only* license. For one thing, you will need to define a *licensed product* in the license agreement. Additionally, payment for this type of license will typically be a percentage of the income (a royalty) made by each sale of the manufactured product. Many other differences exist as well, which will be discussed in greater detail.

Though we have used the term *Make and Sell*, this does not always mean that manufacturing and selling must occur together. This type of license could also be to manufacture a product only, or alternatively, to sell a product without the right of manufacture. It is up to the parties to decide the exact terms of the license. However, if the licensor grants a particular licensee the right of manufacture only, it will have to enter into yet another, separate license agreement with the sellers. (This is sometimes referred to as a *distribution agreement*).

Restrictions on the Licensee

The licensor can define (or restrict) the licensee's actions in many ways. These include:

- ✪ the geographical territory in which the licensee may sell the licensed product (Europe, New York State, North America, etc.);

- ✪ the specific market the licensee may target (residential, industrial, wholesale, etc.); and,

- ✪ the right of licensee to sublicense its rights—that is, to license to other parties. (Sublicensing will be addressed in the next chapter.)

Regardless of the type of license—*Use-Only* or *Make and Sell*—licensors and licensees have conflicting interests when it comes to the licensee's permitted actions. In most cases, the licensee will prefer a generalized license grant—the broader the better. This will give the licensee free reign to use intellectual property in as many ways as possible. It is also important for the licensee to think about how business needs may evolve in the future and whether the license grant will cover those needs. Once again, a broader license grant will be more advantageous for the licensee.

The licensor, on the other hand, will usually want to narrow the license grant to specific uses on the part of the licensee. If a licensee demands broader rights, then the licensor will often want more money to compensate for a broader grant.

Will the License be Exclusive or Nonexclusive?

Every license agreement is either *exclusive* or *nonexclusive* (but never both.). An *exclusive license* means that the licensee has a *monopoly* on using the licensed rights for the term of the license. In contrast, a *nonexclusive license* allows the licensor to license the same rights to other companies or individuals in separate agreements. Every license agreement must explicitly state whether it is exclusive or nonexclusive. That means regardless of the type of license you enter, you must decide between an exclusive and nonexclusive grant.

In general, *licensees* prefer to receive *exclusive* rights to intellectual property. This is especially true of the licensee if making and selling a product based on the licensed rights. In this case, the licensee will most likely be investing considerable costs in developing and marketing the product. An exclusive license will eliminate competition for the licensee, allowing it a broader market, and hence more revenue. This will also be worth more to the licensor.

Licensors, on the other hand, generally prefer to make their licenses *nonexclusive*. This will ensure that they can make subsequent grants of the same intellectual property to other licensees and possibly make more money.

That being said, there are times when an exclusive license makes sense for *both* licensor and licensee. This often occurs in the area of *merchandising*—that is, the license of an image, logo, brand, or design which will be placed on a manufactured article such as clothing, toys, luggage, and so on. An exclusive license may sometimes make more financial sense. One exclusive license with a large, well-placed manufacturer may bring the licensor more licensing revenues than many nonexclusive licenses with smaller licensees. Once again, the particulars of the market and the needs (and bargaining power) of the parties will be determinative.

What will the Payment be?

For obvious reasons, this is a very important question for both parties. Each party is, of course, trying to maximize profits and minimize costs that will arise from a licensing arrangement.

There are different ways to structure payment of a license, but overall, payment provisions break down into two basic types:

✪ *fixed payments* and

✪ *royalties*.

If the licensee is only using the intellectual property (without making and selling a product), fixed payments are typical. On the other hand, if the licensee is making and/or selling a product based on the licensed intellectual property, the more popular method of payment is by royalties. Royalties are typically a percentage of income derived from sale of the licensed product. There are also licenses where the licensee makes fixed payments, on a per-year basis. These payments are fixed, but are paid for as long as the license lasts.

An *exclusive* license may also include other provisions that play a role in structuring the overall payment. These are royalty advances, guaranteed annual minimums, and many others. All of these provisions are ways of reducing the financial risk for a licensor and giving the licensee an incentive to sell as many licensed products possible. Figuring out the payment provisions and addressing all financial concerns in a license can sometimes be a complicated endeavor.

What is the Term of the License?

The next issue which must be decided is the *term* of the license—in other words, how long will the license agreement last. Determining the right term for a license is important for both parties. This is because each party's obligations and commitments under the license will be fixed and unchangeable for the duration of the term. If the situation turns out not to be advantageous for one of the parties, it is stuck with the license.

Example 1: If a licensee must pay $5,000 per quarter for a software license, it must continue to make these payments throughout the license's entire term, regardless of its own financial situation.

Example 2: If a trademark owner licenses a trademark in an exclusive license to last five years, it will be stuck with one licensee (for better or worse) for the entire five-year period.

(Both of these examples assume there are no termination conditions in the license.)

In *Make and Sell* licenses, the licensor and licensee will likely have different views as to what the term should be. A licensee will generally seek a longer term, so it can take more time to recover its initial investment. A longer term will also give it the opportunity to make as much money as possible from the licensed intellectual property. A licensor, on the other hand, will probably want a shorter term. It will first want to see if the licensee's product is successful, and, in the event it is, have the option of increasing the royalties due under the license.

In a license where the licensee merely receives the right to *use* the licensor's intellectual property, the licensee does not make an initial investment and hence may try to negotiate for a shorter term. This will give it more flexibility to test out the licensed product and get rid of it, if the licensee is not satisfied.

How can the License be Terminated?

Along with the term of the license, the parties must also decide whether the license agreement may be *terminated* before its expiration, and if so, under what conditions.

NOTE: *Remember that termination means by one party only. If licensor and licensee both wish to terminate the license at the same time, they can always do this, regardless of whether there are any termination conditions in the license agreement.*

As discussed earlier, termination conditions in the license work hand-in-hand with the license term. This makes sense since early termination effectively shortens the license term. For instance, if one or both parties have the right to terminate the license at any point during its term, the license term as stated will have less of an impact on the parties.

In a typical license, each party generally desires for itself, a broad right to terminate the license (and simultaneously wants to limit the other's termination right). The more conditions under which a party can terminate a license, the more flexibility and control that party has. In this sense, the *right of termination* is a type of power.

Termination conditions can be quite varied and are often tailored to the diverse license agreements that exist. However, most can be categorized into three different groups. These are:

1.   termination for material breach;

2.   termination for failure to meet given business standards; and,

3.   termination for convenience (*at will* termination).

Termination for Material Breach

Termination for material breach is virtually a standard condition for most license agreements. In most licenses, the licensor and licensee are each able to terminate the license if the other party materially breaches any of its obligations.

Example: Suppose a software licensor promises to technically support and correct errors in the licensed software. If the licensor does not provide this support, nor does it correct software errors, then this will constitute a material breach and the licensee will likely have the right to terminate the license.

Termination for breach conditions are usually stated with a *cure* provision. This gives the breaching party a chance to solve the problem (within a given amount of time) before the other party may terminate. For example, in the above scenario, the software licensor might have thirty days to provide the required support, after being notified by the licensee.

A license that allows for termination for material breaches only, could be characterized as a fairly strict license. Once such a license is signed, there is no way for one party to leave the licensing *relationship* before its natural expiration. Therefore, there is a certain amount of risk involved in signing this kind of license.

Termination for Failure to meet Business Standards

A license may also contain termination conditions for a party's—usually, the licensee's—failure to meet agreed upon standards. Such standards typically involve the licensee's sales of a minimum amount of its manufactured product. This type of termination condition is frequently inserted into a license in order to reduce the licensor's risk and to provide an incentive to the licensee to maximize sales.

Example: A private university, which owns a trademarked logo and design. As licensor, it gives an exclusive license to a manufacturer (the licensee) to make and sell a clothing line—sweatshirts, sportswear, etc.—with the logo and design. In a sense, the licensor is taking a chance on this one manufacturer. If the latter does not make a sufficient effort into making and selling its products, the royalties the licensor will receive may not amount to much. A termination for failure to meet certain business standards is one way to address this concern.

Termination for Convenience

At the opposite end of the spectrum from a license with no termination conditions is one where licensor or licensee (or both) have the right to terminate at any time for any reason. This is known as an *at will termination*, or a right of *termination for convenience*. This is the *broadest* type of termination right. If one party has this kind of termination right, it has a significant advantage over the other. If both parties have this right, the license will be considered quite flexible, as either party can basically *leave* the license at any time. The rationale behind a termination for convenience is to reduce risk for one or both parties.

It is important to point out that a license can contain any combination of these termination conditions. However, a party's overall right to terminate is measured by the *broadest* of its termination rights. Therefore, if a party may terminate for breach as well as for convenience, then the much broader *termination for convenience* will define that party's right.

In addition to termination conditions, the license will also contain certain obligations (mostly for the licensee) that will survive the termination of the license. These are known as *post-termination obligations*. Additionally, the license will specify that certain of its provisions will continue indefinitely (or for a given amount of time) after the license agreement's termination. These are the *surviving provisions*.

Will any Services be Performed?

The primary purpose of a license is to allow someone, the licensee, to use intellectual property. But along with such use, the licensor and/or licensee may also agree to perform certain services along with, or as part of, the licensing transaction. In some cases, such service obligations will increase the value of the intellectual property or the license as a whole. In certain industries, the performance of services will be expected as common practice. For instance, certain types of software and patent licenses will typically contain maintenance provisions to install, repair, and/or maintain the licensed property.

Service provisions can vary from straightforward to complicated, depending on the type of intellectual property, the complexity of the license arrangement, and the particular needs of the parties. In some cases, service means nothing more than answering the licensee's technical questions. In others, it could mean an ongoing obligation to maintain, repair, and provide future versions of a product. If service obligations are stated in a license, they become part of that party's obligations under that agreement. This means that failure to provide the required services may result in material breach of the license.

Payment for any services in a license agreement can be made *separately* or can be added to the overall payment for the license rights. This will be a matter for the parties to negotiate, given the standards in their industry, as well as their prior agreements (if any). The licensee may even expect *free* technical maintenance or other services from the licensor. As with other terms of the license, the relative bargaining power of each party will determine fees as well as other financial considerations.

5 | LICENSE AGREEMENT: MAIN TERMS

Now that you have dealt with the overall business issues that go into a license, you are ready to draft these provisions, as well as consider the legal terms in your license. For most, this is usually the murkiest and most difficult of any of the parts of a license agreement. While most people find it possible to understand the business issues of a contract, they often do not understand the legal terminology. However, legal terms are vital to a well-drafted license. Every license agreement will contain at least *some* legal provisions, and more often than not, will contain more legal than business terms.

The legal terms of a license agreement delineate the legal rights, obligations, and responsibilities between the parties to the license. Details about the licensed property, warranties each party makes regarding what it is offered, and other rights and obligations are addressed by the legal provisions. Legal terms also deal with the possibility of the agreement's breach and the chance, however remote, of future litigation between one or both of the parties. Such litigation can be between a party (or both parties) to the agreement and a third party, as well as between the parties themselves.

Because there is such a diversity of legal terms, it is helpful to break them down into different categories. Most terms can be grouped into one of the following categories:

- ✪ main terms;

- ✪ legal protections; and,

- ✪ standard legal terms.

This chapter will deal with most of the *main terms* of a license. (Legal Protections are discussed in Chapter 7 and Standard Legal Terms in Chapter 8.)

License provisions that determine the overall *structure* of the license agreement are:

- ✪ definition of the parties;

- ✪ the license grant;

- ✪ license term and termination; and,

- ✪ payment.

In addition, there may be service provisions and other legal terms that are important to the specific intellectual property being licensed or the product being produced by the licensee.

Defining Terms and Using Schedules and Exhibits

Before we get to the main provisions in the license, an important topic with respect to writing a license agreement (or any agreement, for that matter) must be discussed. This is the issue of defining all the important terms in the license. (In this section, *term* means a specific word or concept, not an entire provision of an agreement.).

Defining Important Terms

Defining terms in your license is important. Any term whose meaning is not fully clear (*unambiguous*) from its use in the license should be defined. The result of not taking the time to carefully define the important terms in your license can be confusion and misunderstanding between the parties. This may even lead to legal problems down the road. What is not properly defined during the negotiation and drafting phase of a license may end up being argued and even litigated afterwards.

Among the terms that should be defined in your license are terms relating to:

- ✪ *The Licensed Intellectual Property*—such terms could include *licensed property, licensed materials,* and/or *licensed product.*

- ✪ *Payment*—this could include such, terms as n*et sales, expenses, royalty period,* among others.

- ✪ *Technology*—if your license involves technology, software, or technical information, you may need to define terms such as *software, updates, module, release,* and similar concepts.

- ✪ *Service*—this includes terms such as *error correction, customization, advertising services, marketing responsibilities,* or other terms relating to services performed by either party.

- ✪ *Corporate and Business Structure*—depending on the nature of the licensor's and licensee's business and the complexity of your license, you may need to define terms such as *affiliate, facility, purchase order,* and so on.

There may be other important terms that need to be defined in your license.

Most often, you will have the choice of defining your key terms in several places within the license agreement. If your license is relatively simple and straightforward, you could define the term in the section or paragraph where it is actually discussed. However, if your license is more complicated, you may need a separate *definitions* section.

For example, terms relating to the intellectual property being licensed—such as *licensed property* or *licensed product*—can be defined:

- ✪ in the recitals;

- ✪ in a separate definitions section;

- ✪ in the license grant provision itself; or,

- ✪ in an exhibit or schedule (discussed later in this section).

Likewise, other terms such as payment, corporate, or service-related terms can be defined in a separate *definitions* section, in an attached schedule, or in the provision that discusses the term.

Using Schedules and Exhibits

Oftentimes, instead of defining key terms directly in the license agreement, you may want to make reference to an exhibit or schedule. Such an *exhibit* or *schedule* will contain the actual definitions or descriptions.

For example, the following clause may frequently be found in the *license grant* provision of a license:

> Licensor grants to licensee the right to use the Licensed Materials listed in Schedule A, attached hereto and incorporated herein.

The *Schedule A* is attached to the completed license agreement as a separate page (or pages). To continue with this example, such a schedule would contain a definition of *licensed materials* that could be in the following *sample* form:

Licensed Materials:

• U.S. Patent No. 4,345,123;

• Licensor's proprietary process to increase the flexibility of rubber, by the following steps: [list process];

• The U.S. trademark "FlexTreat."

NOTE: *The attached hereto and incorporated herein language, illustrated in the above example, should follow the first mention of a particular schedule or exhibit. There is no limit to the number of attachments that may be added to a license agreement. Any additional attachments should be numbered consecutively—such as Schedule 1, 2, 3… or Exhibit A, B, C, and so on. An attachment does not need any special heading except its identifying name—for example, "Schedule A."*

Using an attachment with a license agreement has two distinct advantages. First, it is often easier to list and describe intellectual property, an invention, or information, in an attachment rather than in the body of the actual license. This is especially true if the intellectual property involves more than one form of licensed property. A schedule or exhibit can also consist of a copy of an issued patent or registered trademark, a diagram, blueprint, or schematic, as well as other documents that can, themselves, run many pages.

If, by any chance, there is a conflict between a provision in a license agreement and what is stated in an attachment, the attachment will take precedence (unless otherwise indicated in the license agreement). In other words, if your license agreement says one thing, and the attachment another, any court interpreting the agreement will be guided by the attachment. Make sure your exhibits, schedules, and attachments are consistent with the terms of your main license agreement.

Defining the Parties to the License

If you are a licensor and are planning to enter into a license with an *individual* or a *relatively small business* as licensee, you have pretty much completed the task of *defining* the licensee. If, however, your licensee is a larger company with different departments, affiliated companies, and/or foreign branches, the task may be a bit more complicated.

Larger companies often will have subsidiaries or may, themselves, be *subsidiaries of a parent company*. In addition, they may be *affiliated* with other companies. Typically, Company A is considered to be affiliated with Company B if one controls more than 50% of the stock of the other or they are within the same common control.

You should explicitly state in your definition of the licensee whether any subsidiary, parent, or affiliate companies are to be included. For example:

> This License Agreement is made this 30 day of March, 2003, by and between ABC Co. ("Licensor") and XYZ Co., including all of its affiliated companies and divisions ("Licensee").

If you are the licensor and are licensing to an individual, it is clear that there is only one user. If, however, the licensee is a *company*, with potentially numerous users, you may have to decide on who will and will not have access to your licensed property. If a company is defined as the licensee, and assuming nothing is said to the contrary, all employees of that company will generally be assumed to be included. But there may be other users aside from employees. These may include consultants and independent contractors who work for the company, including financial consultants and auditors.

NOTE: *If you are a licensor and are licensing any type of trade secret, you will need additional protections providing for the confidentiality of your licensed property or information. Such protection will prevent disclosure of the trade secret outside the organization.*

Determining the Beneficiaries to the License

Aside from precisely defining and delineating the licensee (and licensor), both parties will have to consider possible *beneficiaries* to the license or to the rights stated in the license. There are three ways that parties, other than the original licensor and licensee may end up as part of the license (or as users of the licensed intellectual property):

1.   sublicensing;

2.   assignment; and,

3.   corporate successors.

Sublicensing   *Sublicensing* is a right given by the licensor to the licensee so that the latter can further license the intellectual property. In other words, the licensee will be a *licensor* with respect to new parties who will receive a license.

NOTE: *According to current law, the right to sublicense must be explicitly stated in the license agreement. In the absence of such a statement, a licensee will not have this right. Despite this, however, many licensors will state that their license grant does not include the right of sublicense. This is based on the principle that it is always better to spell things out in a license then leave things open to interpretation.*

Assignment   An *assignment* of intellectual property is a transfer of ownership. An assignment of an agreement is closely related. When a party assigns an agreement, it is actually transferring its own rights and obligations under the agreement to someone else. In an assignment, a new party *steps into the shoes* of one of the original parties to the agreement. Any party to an agreement may potentially have the right to assign the agreement, but this has to be addressed in the license.

Corporate
Successors   Aside from sublicensing and assignments, another way your license may be transferred to other entities is through *corporate successorship*. Companies may be bought outright in asset purchase or stock purchase transactions or may be merged with other business entities. Though corporate successors is briefly discussed in Chapter 8, a detailed consideration of corporate successorship is beyond the scope of this book.

Drafting the License Grant

The license grant needs to be examined in terms of those three interrelated questions first introduced in Chapter 3.

1. What intellectual property is being granted?

2. Is the license grant exclusive or nonexclusive?

3. What can the licensee do with the intellectual property?

Remember that the license grant is the heart of your license agreement. It must be written precisely, using accepted legal language, and with as much brevity as possible. At the same time, the license grant must address all key business and legal issues that typically arise with this provision. So to avoid future problems in your license, make sure to read through and thoroughly understand this section. Review it as many times as necessary.

Determining the Extent of the Licensed Property?

A license agreement is an *authorization* to use intellectual property. However, the type of intellectual property being licensed will vary greatly from license to license. The subject of a license can be:

✪   an intellectual property right: a registered—or pending—patent or trademark;

✪ a finished product or process covered by a patent;

✪ an artistic work protected by copyright; or,

✪ information protected by trade secret. (The license may also grant any combination of these.)

The intellectual property, invention, artistic work, or information being licensed is typically given the name *licensed property* or *licensed materials*. Regardless of its nature, the licensed property must be carefully described. Products or artistic works should be described sufficiently to be identified. If the license involves a patent or registered trademark, the patent or registration number should be specified. In addition, the patent can be attached as a schedule or exhibit to the license.

The licensor may gain extra assurance by adding a provision stating the license is being granted *subject* to all the terms and conditions stated in the license agreement. This way, it is specifically stated in the license that the licensee's right to use the licensor's intellectual property is conditioned upon its *proper* use of that property. In other words, if the licensee does not perform its obligations under the license, it will be in breach and subsequently lose all rights to the licensed property.

Ownership and Proprietary Rights Clauses

The licensor will often *explicitly* state that it owns and *retains ownership* of the licensed property. This is especially true of software and other *technical* licenses. (See Chapters 10 and 11.) This type of provision provides extra protection to the licensor. It also provides clarification to the licensee that the licensor is not parting with any ownership rights to the licensed property (in other words, there is no assignment of any kind). A common phrase which conveys this is the following:

Licensor shall own all rights, title, and interest in and to the licensed property.

If this type of ownership statement is not stated in the license, the licensor will still own the licensed property. But adding this type of statement will certainly help, in the unlikely event that there is some confusion about ownership.

Another popular variation on the ownership theme is the *Reservation of Rights Clause*. In this type of provision, the licensor states that it retains all rights that are not explicitly granted to the licensee. Once again, this provides extra assurance to the licensor by emphasizing a licensee may carry out only those actions specifically authorized in the license, and no others.

A standard *Reservation of Rights* provision will look like the following:

> All rights in and to the licensed property not specifically granted to the Licensee in this Agreement are hereby reserved to the Licensor.

(The *in and to* language used to the Licensed Property is frequently used in contract drafting to cover every possible way of reading the contract.)

These types of ownership clauses are also important in the context of other intellectual property agreements. For instance, if two companies are entering into a joint venture or an agreement for the development of a final work, they may find themselves exchanging technology, trade secrets, or other works.

Exclusive or Nonexclusive

The next issue that must be addressed in the *license grant* provision is whether the license is to be *exclusive* or *nonexclusive*. You simply state that your license grant is exclusive or nonexclusive. For example:

> Licensor grants to Licensee an exclusive right to:

Every license is either exclusive or nonexclusive, but not both, with one exception. This is the situation where an exclusive license requires certain business conditions to hold for the license to remain exclusive. For example, a licensor may require that the licensee sell a certain number of products. If the licensee fails to meet these goals, the license will then turn into a *nonexclusive* license. This type of condition is similar to conditions that allow for termination of a license for licensee's failure to meet certain goals.

A licensor may make only one exclusive license grant of his or her intellectual property (unlike a nonexclusive license grant, where the same property may be licensed again and again in other agreements). However, an exclusive license grant is exclusive only to the extent of the *scope* of the license agreement. In other words, even an exclusive license grant may be made multiple times if the territory or market is different in each license or if the licensees are allowed to do different things.

Example: Suppose a patent licensor grants a licensee exclusive rights to make and sell a product based on the licensed patent. The terms of the license state that the licensee can sell such products only in the United States. This license is therefore exclusive for the territory of the U.S. only. The patent owner may still license the same patent to other licensees to sell products anywhere outside of the U.S.

Finally, if you are the licensor and are entering into an *exclusive* license, you must address another important point. This is, whether you, as the intellectual property owner, will be able to use your own intellectual property. Some courts have interpreted an exclusive license to mean *absolute exclusivity*—that is, even the licensor cannot use its own intellectual property. Therefore, you and the licensee should agree on whether the exclusive grant is to mean absolute exclusivity. A simple one-line statement can be added at the end of the *license grant* provision to address this point.

Deciding the Scope of the License

The last part of the license grant provision involves answering the question: What can the license do? This itself can involve the consideration of many sub-issues and considerations. Some of the important ones are examined below.

Use-Only Licenses

As we have previously stated, a license can give the right to a licensee to either directly use the intellectual property or make and sell a product based on such intellectual property. The former, *use-only licenses*, are the simpler of the two. In this type of license, the nature of the use is typically specified as licensee's *internal business purposes*. For example:

> Licensor grants to Licensee the nonexclusive right to use the Licensed Property for its own internal purposes.

This makes it clear that the license is for *use only*. But there is still a lot of open and somewhat *ambiguous* territory that would be preferable to explain. Thus, the licensor may want to enumerate specific restrictions on the licensee. For example, if the licensee receives the right to use a software product, the license would state that the licensee may not copy or reproduce the software, sell or distribute it outside the licensee's organization, or modify or make derivative works based on it. Narrowly-drawn restrictions remove any doubt as to what the licensee can and cannot do.

Make and Sell Licenses

For *make and sell licenses*, on the other hand, there are additional issues that must be considered. In the majority of these licenses, the licensee receives the right to make a product based on the licensed intellectual property. Such product is referred to as the *licensed product*. Sale of the licensed product will usually be limited to a certain territory.

It is possible that, during the term of the license, the desired territory for the license will change. In that case, the parties should attach a schedule with a defined *licensed territories* that could either note the details up-front or which may be amended by the parties from time to time.

NOTE: *On the issue of territory, it is important to remember that once you are entering into a license with a territory outside of the United States, you are dealing with a foreign country's laws. There are regulations and other restrictions in each nation applicable to goods, information, and persons. These laws are also subject to changes in international policies, so one must frequently update this information. In addition, certain types of technical data are regulated by the U.S. Department of Commerce (and other agencies) and U.S. persons are prohibited from distributing it in foreign countries. These areas, however, are beyond the scope of this book.*

Due to the similarity of the words, it is important to keep the distinction between licensed property and licensed product clearly in mind. Licensed property is the intellectual property that the licensor owns and is licensing to the licensee. Licensed product is the product manufactured and/or sold by the licensee, based on the licensed property.

Putting It Together

Finally, to bring together the various provisions and concepts just discussed, the following example is of a typical license grant provision (for a *Make and Sell* license):

> Subject to the terms and conditions of this Agreement, Licensor grants to Licensee a limited, nonexclusive right, without right of sublicense, to the Licensed Property in order to manufacture and sell the Licensed Product in the territory of North America. Licensee shall not reproduce, distribute and/or modify the Licensed Property or any part thereof. Licensor shall at all times retain ownership of the Licensed Property. All rights not specifically granted to the Licensee hereunder are hereby reserved to the Licensor.

Your specific license grant will need to take into account all the specific details of your licensing transaction and hence, may be longer (or shorter) than the example provided here.

License Term and Termination

After the license grant, the next important issue that must be addressed by the parties is *term* of the license. Along with the license term, the parties must decide under what conditions the license agreement may be terminated by one or more of the parties. The term and termination conditions of a license work together as a unit.

License Term   The *license term* provision in a license agreement is typically straightforward and simple. The start of the term can also be defined as the date of the license agreement, or a different *effective date*. (See Chapter 3 for a review of effective date.) In addition, the term provision will usually refer to any termination provisions present in the license.

One example of such a term provision that uses on *effective date* of the license as the official start of the license term is the following:

> This Agreement shall commence on the Effective Date hereto and shall continue for a period of one (1) year from the Effective Date of this Agreement unless terminated earlier, as provided herein.

The license term provision may also state that the license may be renewed or provide for an automatic renewal provision. An example of this is as follows:

> This Agreement shall commence on the Effective Date and shall continue for a term of one (1) year, unless earlier terminated, as provided herein. This Agreement shall automatically renew for successive one (1) year terms, unless either party gives notice to the other of its intention not to renew the agreement not less than thirty (30) days prior to the expiration of the then current term.

This provision clearly indicates that despite the agreement's automatic renewal, either party may terminate the agreement upon thirty days notice.

Termination Conditions

The right of a party to terminate the license is a very important right. Most often, a party will have this right only in the event of certain conditions. Generally those termination conditions are:

- ✪ for a party's material breach;

- ✪ as a result of a party's failure to fulfill business standards;

- ✪ for convenience; and,

- ✪ as a result of a party's bankruptcy.

The first three are examined in this chapter, while the last is discussed in Chapter 7.

Termination for Breach/Cure Provisions

Termination for Breach provisions are found in nearly all license agreements and are fairly standard in form. Simply stated, this type of provision allows a party to terminate the license for the *material breach* of the other party. In a sense, such termination is one *penalty* for a breach of the license.

There are potentially many types of *material breaches* that typically trigger termination of a license. Some of the more common ones are:

- ✪ licensee's failure to make royalty payments or pay the fees owed under the license;

- ✪ licensee uses the licensed intellectual property in an *unauthorized* manner—that is, in a way that exceeds the scope of the license; or,

- ✪ the licensed property infringes the rights of a third party.

Typically, these type of provisions are mutual, providing that both licensor and licensee may terminate for the material breach of the other. In addition, an opportunity to *cure* (that is, to fix) such breaches is usually provided. (See Chapter 2 for a discussion of material breaches).

An example of this kind of provision is as follows:

> Either party may terminate this Agreement for the other party's material breach of any provision of this Agreement, provided that the breaching party is allowed a thirty (30) opportunity to cure such breach.

In other words, once a party discovers that the other is in material breach, it should notify the breaching party as soon as possible. After receiving such notice, the breaching party will then have thirty days to repair or cure such breach.

However, you must be careful with respect to cure provisions. Certain types of breaches should not be allowed an opportunity to cure. This is because certain breaches result in damage to the other party that cannot be fixed in any meaningful way. For instance, if the licensor licenses valuable trade secrets to the licensee and the latter reveals this to another business, this will constitute a material breach. The licensor will lose its competitive business advantage due to loss of this trade secret. At this point, it does not really matter what the licensee does. The secret information has already been revealed. There is nothing that can reverse the trade secret owner's loss. *Breach of confidentiality* is but one example of a breach that should result in immediate termination without the opportunity to cure.

Termination of a license for material breach will *not* foreclose other legal remedies for the non-breaching party. In other words, the party that terminates the license may still come after the breaching party for money damages or injunctive relief. (See Chapter 2 for a discussion of damages.) Sometimes this principle is even explicitly stated in the license after the *termination for breach* provision. For example:

> Termination of this Agreement for material breach by the non-breaching party shall not be construed as exhaustive of all legal remedies available to such party.

Termination for Failure to Fulfill Business Standards

Unlike a termination for material breach, this type of termination condition is found mainly in exclusive licenses where the licensee manufactures and sells a licensed product and the licensor receives royalty payments for such sales. It makes sense that if the licensor grants such a license, it will want to insist on the licensee for example, a certain level of sales. If the specified standards are not met, the licensor will then have the right to terminate the license.

A variation on this type of termination condition involves the licensee's production of the *licensed product*. This type of termination states that if the licensee-manufactured products do not meet certain quality standards set by the *licensor*, the latter will have the right to terminate the license agreement. This type of provision is especially important with trademark and merchandising licenses. The specific standards with all of these types of conditions are up to the parties to decide (based on their specific needs).

Termination for Convenience

As previously stated, this type of termination condition is the broadest of all. If a party has this type of termination right, it will have great flexibility in leaving the licensing relationship. This will have an effect on the other party's long-term business planning. For this reason, you should carefully consider whether to agree to this right for the other party. In most cases, a licensor will offer this type of termination right to the licensee as an incentive to take the license.

An example of a *termination for convenience* provision is as follows:

> Licensee may, upon thirty (30) days prior written notice to Licensor, terminate this Agreement for any reason at any time throughout its Term.

A *mutual termination for convenience*, which gives both parties the flexibility of termination at any time, is possible as well.

Post-Termination Rights and Obligations

When a license terminates, the licensee will no longer have the right to use the licensed intellectual property. At that time, the licensor's obligations also cease and the parties will no longer be bound by the terms of the license. Depending on the license, however, there may be additional things that happen upon termination. Most often, the licensor will likely insist on certain *post-termination* obligations on the part of the licensee.

Typical post-termination obligations on the licensee include the following:

❂ *Return of Licensor's Materials.* This includes the licensee's return and/or destruction of all licensed and confidential materials belonging to the licensor that were provided to the licensee under the license. Such materials will also include all copies made by the licensee.

❂ *Payoff of Amounts Owed.* Depending on whether the termination is early, and is for breach, convenience, or otherwise, the licensor may require the licensee to pay off all amounts upon termination.

❂ *Sell-Off of Licensee's Inventory.* If the license involves the manufacture and sale of a licensed product, the licensor may give the licensee a certain period after termination to sell its remaining inventory. After that, the licensee will have to destroy all remaining products.

✪ *Providing Inventory Summary or Accounting.* With licenses involving manufacture and sale of a licensed product, the licensor may request an accounting of licensee's remaining inventory or other similar information.

The licensor may, in turn, have requirements of its own. Typical post-termination obligations on the part of the *licensor* include *return of licensee's materials.* This means that any confidential or proprietary materials that licensee has provided to the licensor should be returned to the former.

Aside from these, the parties may also need other post-termination obligations to address specific concerns. This will depend on the type (and complexity) of the license as well as the specific circumstances of the parties.

NOTE: *Unless otherwise specified, post-termination obligations typically continue beyond when the agreement ends, regardless of whether the license expires naturally or is terminated beforehand (according to the license's termination conditions). If you want to distinguish between obligations that persist after the end of a license term and those that are triggered only with early termination, it must be explicitly stated in the license.*

Survival Clause

Closely associated with post-termination obligations is the *survival clause.* This is a separate provision, often found at the end the license agreement, that lists the terms of the license that will survive the license's termination. For example, they may want the confidentiality provision to apply indefinitely. Other provisions that normally survive license termination are:

✪ restrictions on licensee's use of the licensed property;

✪ all confidentiality provisions;

✪ most representations and warranties;

✪ legal protection of the intellectual property;

✪ indemnification and limitation of liability provisions (see Chapter 7 for more information); and,

✪ choice of law provisions and other miscellaneous terms.

6 LICENSE AGREEMENT: PAYMENT PROVISIONS

This chapter addresses a topic of utmost concern to both the licensor and the licensee—*money*. For the licensor, money is what licensing is all about. In most cases, the intellectual property owner will decide *whether to license in the first place* based on money—that is, the revenue the license is expected to accrue. For the licensee, payment for the license is one of the costs of either using or commercializing the licensed intellectual property. The licensee will typically weigh these costs against profits from the sale of its product.

Pricing the License, Fairly

Before we discuss how to draft the various payment *provisions—royalties, guaranteed minimums, advances, royalty statements*, and so on—we need to consider a more basic question. How do the parties actually arrive at a specific price for the license? And, whatever the specific dollar amount, is this typically a fair price for the licensing transaction?

Like other issues in the license agreement, this is determined by numerous factors, mostly business in nature. Some of these are predictable and subject to one or both parties' control, while others may not be. There is not a formula for how license payments are arrived at in a given case, but review of the material in this chapter as well as careful analysis of your own situation, will help you arrive at the best and most accurate *price* for your license. If this is your first time entering into a license agreement, it may be harder to predict in advance what the overall payment will be. After gaining more licensing experience, predicting payment becomes a bit easier.

Following are among the factors important in determining the payment for a license.

- ✪ *Commercial value of the intellectual property.* The *demand* for the property. For *make and sell licenses*, this is one of the most important factors in determining the overall *price* for the intellectual property.

- ✪ *Exclusive or nonexclusive license.* Again, for *make and sell licenses*, an exclusive license is worth more to the licensee than a nonexclusive one.

- ✪ *Bargaining power of the parties.* As with any negotiation, a larger or more market-dominant party will be able to command a higher rate (as licensor) or will be able to get away with paying less (as licensee).

- ✪ *Similar licenses in the industry.* Otherwise known as the *standard of the industry*, other licenses in the same field and industry will help the parties determine what the payment will be in their specific case.

- ✪ *Prior licenses between the parties (if any exist).* If the parties have entered into licenses in the past, this may be an important factor on current payment terms.

- ✪ *Scope of the license grant.* Most favorable license provisions for the licensee may result in a higher price for the license.

- ✪ *Services provided by a party.* As for instance, the licensor's obligation to provide maintenance would likely increase the value of the license.

There will likely be other market and economic factors that will affect the final royalty rate or payment for the license. After considering the factors and determining a fair price, you are ready to address how that price will be paid. There are two basic ways payment can be made for a license: fixed payment and royalties.

Other important factors are whether the intellectual property or product is a break-through technology (or a very unique artistic creation) or is a standard product; the number of competitors in the market; whether the market for the product is expected to expand or decline in the near future; as well as, the overall state of the economy.

Fixed Payments

A *fixed payment* is, as the name implies, a fixed dollar amount that the licensee pays to the licensor for the license. Fixed payments can be paid up-front (for example, right after signature of the license agreement), in installments, or annually. But regardless of how it is set up, we are referring to this as a *fixed payment* to distinguish it from a *royalty*. The latter, as you will find out in the next section, is a percentage of sales of a manufactured product.

Example: EasyPics Co. maintains a database of unique (and copyrighted) pictures, graphic designs, and other artwork. If an individual or company wants to reproduce any of these pictures (i.e., on a website or in a brochure), they must enter into a license with EasyPics. The license will likely require the user to pay a fixed payment for the rights to use the pictures. It may be a yearly fee or a one-time payment.

Fixed payments are typical of *use-only licenses*. The licensee does not produce or manufacture a product based on the intellectual property. Hence, since there is no product that will be sold on the market, it makes the most sense for the licensee to pay the licensor a fixed amount for the license. This amount is frequently a *per-year* amount if the license is intended to be renewed on an annual basis.

It is important to note that even a *make and sell license* can also be paid for through fixed payments. An advantage to structuring the license with a fixed payment is *predictability*. That is, the licensor and licensee know what the price of the license is.

Example: John owns a patent on a unique underwater camera. He licenses his patent to AquaCo., a sports company, to manufacture and market the invention. However, because John is not sure how well the manufactured camera will sell, he agrees to a one-time fixed payment instead of royalties (based on sales of the cameras). In arriving at a specific dollar amount, John estimates what he would have received from a *fair* royalty for the license over a given period of time.

If your license is structured as a fixed payment, you will definitely save a lot of time in drafting your license agreement. Fixed payment terms are far easier to draft, review, and analyze than royalty provisions. A fixed payment provision essentially states that the licensee pays the licensor a given dollar amount for the license (or a dollar amount per year), and that is it. Specific payment details need to be included, but generally speaking, licenses with fixed payments are easier to figure out and draft than those based on royalties.

A one-time, fixed payment provision is pretty straightforward:

> For the license granted herein, Licensee shall pay Licensor a sum of $10,000, which shall be due within thirty (30) days of signature of this Agreement.

The following is an example of an annual payment provision for a license with a renewable one-year term:

> Throughout the term of this Agreement, and for any subsequent renewed terms, Licensee shall pay Licensor a sum of $ 1,000 per year for the license, which shall be due within thirty (30) days of signature, or the date of renewal.

Here is yet another provision in the context of a (hypothetical) software transaction, setting forth payment by installments:

> Licensee shall pay Licensor a total sum of $ 10,000 for the Software, payable as follows:
>
> • An advance payment of $ 2,500 immediately upon execution of this Agreement;
>
> • $ 2,500 upon customization and acceptance of the Software; and
>
> • the remaining $ 5,000 upon 6 months of use of the Software.

The term of the license becomes important when you try to decide between a one-time sum and yearly payments. If your license term is a fairly short duration—a year or two—and is intended to be renewed, it is best suited for an annual fee. On the other hand, if the license is to last for a longer duration (or indefinitely), a one-time payment makes more sense.

Royalties

When the licensor gives the licensee the right to manufacture, create, and/or sell a product based on its intellectual property, the parties will often set up payment by *royalties*—that is, a type of payment that depends on the product's sales. Since royalties *depend* on the sale of a product, a royalty-based license (especially an *exclusive* one) can almost be described as a type of *partnership* between licensor and licensee. The licensor will want to give the licensee every incentive to sell as many products as possible.

Compared to fixed payment, royalties can be somewhat complicated and requires careful financial analysis and consideration. The next two sections cover the *basics* of royalties intended for licenses that are relatively straightforward. On the other hand, if your license involves complicating factors such as a complex royalty schedule, a foreign party, and so on, you may have to review additional reference material or even consult with an intellectual property attorney.

Royalties: Fixed Sum vs. Percentage   A royalty is a payment to the licensor based on the number of *licensed products* sold by the licensee. The more products sold—the more money the licensor will taken in from the license. There are two types of royalties: *a fixed sum per product* and *a percentage of sales*.

A *fixed sum per product* royalty states that for every licensed product sold by the licensee, the licensor will receive a given amount. The important thing for both parties to understand is that with the fixed-sum approach, the licensor's royalty remains the same regardless of ups or downs in the product's actual market price. This may be an advantage or disadvantage for a party depending on what happens to the price of the product.

The *percentage of sales* royalty is the more popular approach. It states that for every product sold by the licensee, the licensor will receive a percentage of the final sale price. The percentage is known as the *royalty rate*.

The actual royalty rate in a given license will depend on the intellectual property involved, the type of license, and will also vary from field to field (i.e., a royalty rate for a patent in the chemical industry will differ from a patent for sporting equipment). That being said, royalty rates can range from about 1–2%, at the very lowest, to 12 percent, or even higher. You must thoroughly research the market for your intellectual property right to determine the royalty rate most suitable to your license.

Royalty provisions can, however, get more complicated than this. The rate itself can be made to vary based on volume of sales (so that the more licensee sells, the higher the rate becomes), the type of licensed product, and so forth. Therefore, just specifying one royalty rate is not always the whole story. You will see some examples of these types of complex royalties in the material and in the sample license agreements later in this book.

Royalties are typically calculated on a quarterly basis and are paid on this schedule. However, your specific business needs may require a different calculation and payment schedule

Net Sales   If the parties are using a *percentage of sales* royalty, they must decide whether to structure the royalty as a percentage of *gross* or *net sales*. *Net Sales* are usually defined as the selling price of the product minus common business expenses such as taxes, shipping costs, returns, and so on.

The actual deductions that are included in your *Net Sales* definition will vary from license to license, and will depend on your industry, field, and other business circumstances. Though it is certainly possible to structure a royalty based on gross sales of the licensed product, it is more common to see royalties calculated based on net sales (the remaining material in this chapter will assume this).

The following is a standard royalty provision which ties together the above principles (the royalty is based on net sales and calculated on a quarterly basis):

> Throughout the term of this Agreement, Licensee shall pay Licensor, a royalty of 5% for each Licensed Product sold by licensee, based on the Net Sales of such Licensed Products. Royalties shall be calculated on a quarterly calendar basis, and each royalty payment shall be due within thirty (30) days after the end of the preceding quarter, for example on the 1st day of January, April, July, and October.

"Net Sales" shall mean Licensee's gross sales, as indicated by customer invoices, minus any discounts, returns of any Licensed Products, and/or value added taxes.

Advances and Guaranteed Minimums

A license can involve financial risk for both parties. The licensee may incur great expense in commercializing a product that does not sell, while the licensor may be locked into a relationship with a licensee that either is not fulfilling its license obligations or is just not selling enough products to the licensor's satisfaction. Both *advances* and *guaranteed annual minimums* are ways for the licensor to reduce this risk. Both provide a strong incentive to the licensee to make as many sales of the licensed product as possible.

Advances and guaranteed annual minimums are important to consider when you are entering into an *exclusive* license. An exclusive license states that only that licensee gets the right to use the intellectual property in question and/or manufacture and sell a licensed product. This means the licensor is entirely reliant on the licensee to produce a licensing income. The longer the term of the license agreement, the longer the licensor will be locked into that relationship with the licensee. Advances and guaranteed annual minimums will ensure that the licensor will receive some money from the license.

An *advance* is a sum of money forwarded by the licensee to the licensor at the start of the license term, but before any sales are actually made. Once sales are made, the actual royalties are subtracted from the advance amount until the advance is *paid up*. In other words, the advance is *recoupable* from the future royalties that are to be paid to the licensor. If the royalties never reach the amount of the advance, the licensee will have to absorb the loss. Advances are generally *nonrefundable*, but parties sometimes state this fact explicitly just to be on the safe side.

NOTE: *You may see an advance referred to as an* up-front *payment or an* initial fee. *However, licensing terminology needs to be kept straight. Advances are* recoupable *from future royalties, while other types of fees or fixed payments may or may not be. For example, a license could provide for an initial fixed fee and royalties thereafter. There may also be separate payments for maintenance or installation or other types of services. All of these details need to be carefully spelled out in your agreement.*

A *guaranteed annual minimum* sets a per-year *minimum* amount that the licensor receives from the licensee, regardless of the actual amount of royalties. If royalties in any one year are lower than the minimum or if there are no royalties at all, then the licensor will receive the guaranteed amount for that year. If, however, royalties are higher than the minimum, the licensor should receive the higher amount.

Sublicensing

If the license gives the licensee the right to sublicense—that is, the right to make further licenses to others—the parties will need an additional payment provision addressing this right. Generally, if the licensee sublicenses any of its rights, the licensor will receive a percentage of the licensee's sublicensing revenue. A *standard of the industry* percentage in many cases is 50%. The following standard clause addresses sublicensing royalties:

> Licensee shall pay Licensor 50% of all revenues from any sublicense of the Licensed Property, as permitted hereunder.

NOTE: *If you are the licensor and are providing the licensee with the right to sublicense, it is not enough to merely insert this sublicensing payment clause in your license. You also need to have additional provisions relating to the sublicensing grant, and in many cases, additional protections for the intellectual property when it is sublicensed.*

Other Royalty-Related Terms

In addition to the above provisions for the calculation and payment of royalties, most licenses involving royalties also contain some of the following provisions:

Royalty Statements

A *royalty statement* is a written document that the licensor submits to the licensee, usually on a quarterly basis, stating how many sales of its licensed products were made. In addition, royalty statements set forth additional information on the sale price of the license products, as well as deductions related to the calculation of *net sales*.

The following is *one* example of a royalty statement provision (for quarterly royalties) under the license:

With each Royalty Payment, Licensee shall provide Licensor with a written royalty statement in a form agreed upon by the parties. Such royalty statement shall set forth the number of Licensed Products sold and description, gross invoice, amount billed customers, discounts, allowances, returns, and royalty paid. Licensee shall provide such royalty statements to Licensor regardless whether any sales were actually made during the quarter.

Basically, the parties can agree on the specific form and content for the royalty statements, as well as the frequency such are due.

Audit Provision   If the licensor is to receive royalties for its license, the licensor must continually monitor whether accurate payment is made throughout the license's term. Errors are possible (and unfortunately, so is fraud) in such statements. Some type of recourse to verify the accuracy of licensee's statements and royalty payments becomes imperative.

Therefore, along with receiving royalty statements, the licensor will usually insist on a provision allowing for inspection of the licensee's financial records. This is known as an *audit provision*. This generally gives the licensor the right to check for errors and discrepancies between the royalty statements and actual sales and royalty payments. If a large enough discrepancy is found, the licensee may be required to pay a penalty. In exchange, the licensor generally promises to limit the frequency of such inspections, as well as to keep all of licensee's information strictly confidential. Usually, audit provisions are intended to apply for the term of the agreement, as well as a limited amount of time thereafter.

The following is an example of a standard audit provision:

During the term of this Agreement, and for a period of __ years thereafter, Licensor shall have the right to inspect Licensee's books, records, documents, and all other materials and information relating or pertaining to this license and Licensee's payment of the royalties hereunder. Licensor shall conduct such inspections only during business hours and not more than once in any calendar year, and provide two (2) days notice to Licensee before such inspection.

In the event that such inspection reveals a discrepancy of more than 5% between what Licensor was owed versus Licensee's actual payments, Licensee shall immediately pay the difference and shall further reimburse Licensor for all reasonable costs of such inspection.

> Licensor shall keep all information obtained from such disclosures strictly confidential and shall not disclose any confidential or proprietary business information belonging to Licensee, unless agreed to by Licensee in writing or required by law. Notwithstanding the preceding, such confidential or proprietary information may be used in any legal proceeding based on Licensee's failure to pay the royalties due hereunder.

Finally, most license agreements have a provision which imposes a penalty on the licensee for late payments. Typically, this involves charging a per-month percentage—i.e., 1.5% per month—as a type of *interest* on the payment due until the amounts are paid. An alternative is to use a *prime rate plus x percent* (per annum) formula. Such a *late payment* provision will hopefully ensure prompt payment of all monies due under the license.

The following is an example of a simple *late payment* clause:

> Any late payments made by Licensee under this Agreement shall incur a charge of 1.5% per month of the outstanding amounts, calculated from the due date until payment is made.

NOTE: *Laws in certain states may regulate the maximum amounts of interest one party may charge another. You may want to insert the phrase* or the maximum rate permitted by law *after the rate.*

Additional Business Terms

Finally, the parties may include any of a number of business provisions that address issues in their economic and business relationship. Some of these may act as an incentive for a party to enter the license, while others are more in line with a type of protection for one or both parties.

These business provisions are optional. They are certainly not required, nor are they always advantageous. Depending on the circumstances, they may benefit the licensor, the licensee, or both parties equally. The terms provided here are fairly standard and may need to be revised to fit the unique circumstances of your case.

Most Favored Nations Clause

A *most favored* or *most favored nations clause* has nothing to do with nations. It is a promise by the licensor that the terms it is offering to the licensee will be equal to or better than those offered to other licensees. Most favored nations clauses are only provided in a nonexclusive license.

A licensee often benefits from a most favored nations provision since this type of guarantee will help it stay competitive within its market. For example, if a large software developer/licensor provides its software product to many companies in a specific industry, a given licensee will want at least equal prices and terms as other companies. However, whether a licensor will want to grant this type of guarantee is a separate question. Quite often, the relative bargaining power of the parties will go a long way in determining the presence or absence of a *most favored* clause.

The following is an example of a fairly standard *most favored nations clause*:

> Licensor guarantees that the license fees herein are the lowest of all same or lower than those charged to any other licensee who is licensing the same Licensed Property under similar terms and conditions. If, at any time hereafter, Licensor offers a licensee license to any third party on more favorable terms, conditions, or prices, Licensor shall, at the same time, offer the same terms, conditions, and prices to Licensee.

Noncompete Provision

A *noncompete* or *noncompetition provision* is essentially a promise by a party not to compete with the other, usually for a limited amount of time, and/or within a given market or territory. It could also be a more general promise made by both parties not to compete with each other. This type of provision is often desired by a party to prevent the other from entering its market or creating or developing a product which competes with the former's products.

A standard noncompete clause might look something like the following:

> During the term of this Agreement, and for a period of three (3) years thereafter, Licensee promises not to compete with licensor in [insert Licensor's specific product market.

The party promising not to compete should generally be very careful about making this type of contractual promise, given that this will restrict its future actions. In some cases, additional language needs to be specified to the provision to make sure it is not unduly restrictive and limits the party's future economic possibilities.

NOTE: *In some states, courts will not enforce an open-ended, general noncompete clause unless it is qualified in terms of time and/or a specific market.*

7 LICENSE AGREEMENT: LEGAL PROTECTIONS

This chapter addresses the legal *protections* commonly found in a license agreement. Here, protections mean a group of provisions that protect the licensor, licensee, as well as the intellectual property. Specifically, these provisions revolve mainly around issues of liability, minimization of financial risk, and the possibility of litigation—both between the parties and with third parties.

Following is a quick breakdown of these legal protections.

- ✪ *Representations and Warranties*—important promises and guarantees by each party of the licensed property, as well as its authority or future performance.

- ✪ *Indemnification*—a party's promise to reimburse the other party if the former breaches its stated warranties.

- ✪ *Limitation of Liability*—a stated monetary limit to a party's liability in the event that a party breaches the license agreement.

- ✪ *Insurance*—requirement on the part of licensee to maintain insurance sufficient to cover potential losses from potential lawsuits by third parties.

✪ *Protection of the Intellectual Property*—a variety of provisions that require the licensee to place proper notices on the licensed products and take other steps to maintain the licensed intellectual property.

✪ *Third Party Infringement*—a provision that spells out how the parties may take legal action in the event a *third party* infringes the licensed intellectual property.

✪ *Confidentiality*—a provision that states that all information and materials belonging to a party are confidential and must be not be disclosed by the other party.

✪ *Force Majeure*—a provision relieving a party of liability for delays or nonperformance stemming from factors beyond its control.

✪ *Bankruptcy*—a termination of the license provision if a party becomes bankrupt or is unable to operate a business.

✪ *Injunction*—a provision stating that in the event one party breaches certain critical provisions, the other party may get a court order preventing further breach.

Representations and Warranties

Present in virtually all license agreements, the *representations and warranties* section of a license agreement consists of a very important set of promises. Certain types of warranties will be made by each party of the license to the other. In other types of warranties, only one party will provide a promise. Overall, the representations and warranties section will vary depending on the type of license involved, as well as the relative bargaining power between the parties. All of these issues are examined below.

The representations and warranties state what each party is *guaranteeing* its intellectual property and/or future performance under the license. If any representation or warranty later turns out not to be true, the warranting party may then be liable for material breach of the license. Thus, each party to a license relies on this section as a type of assurance of the quality, not only of the intellectual property, but also of the license as a whole.

Two overall types of representations and warranties will be discussed. They are mutual corporate warranties and typical licensor's warranties.

Mutual Corporate Warranties

Corporate warranties are standard in most licenses; are provided equally by both licensor and license; and, are generally not a point of negotiation. These types of warranties basically ensure the right of each party to enter into the license agreement, as well as the absence of legal impediments to performance under the agreement. Therefore, neither party should have any difficulty with making these warranties. If one of the parties to a license has a problem providing any of these warranties, the other party should consult with an intellectual property or a corporate attorney.

The following is an example of a fairly comprehensive and *mutual corporate warranty* provision:

> Each Party to this Agreement warrants that: (i) it has full right, power, and authority to enter into this Agreement; and (ii) this Agreement does not contravene or otherwise conflict with any other agreement entered into by that Party.

Licensor's Warranties

The licensor will typically provide several key warranties with respect to the intellectual property it is licensing. This will provide as much assurance as possible to the licensee that the intellectual property it receives is valid and, just as importantly, does not infringe anyone else's rights. This translates to an assurance that the licensee will be able to use the intellectual property without the *threat of litigation* from others. The licensee will typically insist on this type of warranty as a *licensee's* major concern is that it be able to use licensed property *without interference*.

The licensor's warranties revolve around the general principle that a licensor can license only that which it actually possesses. In most licenses, the licensor will at least make the following warranties:

> Licensor is the legal owner of all right, title, and interest to the licensed property;
>
> The licensed property, and its use by licensee, will not infringe or otherwise violate any intellectual property right of any third party, including without limitation patent, copyright, trademark, or trade secret; and,

Licensor has not previously encumbered, assigned, conveyed, or otherwise transferred its right, title, or interest in the licensed property, and has not granted a license to any third party to use the licensed property.

In general, with respect to the licensor's warranties, the licensee generally wants these to be as broad and unconditional as possible. The licensor, on the other hand, will want to narrow and limit as many of these warranties as possible. The resulting language may often be a negotiated *compromise* between these opposite intentions based on the parties' overall bargaining power.

If the licensor is licensing a *technical* product, such as software, data, machinery, or other functional product or process, the licensor may also be expected to warrant its *performance or accuracy (for data)*. This type of warranty can be limited or quite broad, depending on the complexity of the license and the parties' needs. Depending on the type of license, however, the licensor may seek to *disclaim* most of these *performance* warranties. This means that the licensor explicitly notifies the licensee that it is not responsible for these warranties. This will often arise with software licenses.

For example, a very broad *disclaiming of warranties* provision would read as follows:

NOTWITHSTANDING ANY OF THE PROVISIONS OF THIS AGREEMENT, THE LICENSED PROPERTY IS PROVIDED "AS IS." LICENSOR MAKES NO WARRANTIES, EXPRESS OR IMPLIED, WITH RESPECT TO THE LICENSED PROPERTY, INCLUDING WITHOUT LIMITATION ANY WARRANTY OF MERCHANTABILITY OR FITNESS FOR A PARTICULAR PURPOSE.

NOTE: *As you can see, this provision is capitalized and boldfaced. It is recommended that you do the same with any provision in your license that disclaims warranties or representations. Disclaiming of a warranty by one party must be conspicuous and easily visible to the other party.*

Indemnification

The word *indemnification* means reimbursement. When one party agrees to indemnify the other under certain conditions, it is saying that it will reimburse that party for its money losses (damages) if those conditions occur. This is known as an *indemnification* or *hold harmless* provision.

In most cases, a party to a license will promise to indemnify the other if sued by a third party. Specifically, the lawsuit must arise from a breach of a warranty made by the party promising to indemnify. This makes sense given the way a license works. If a party warrants certain things under the license, it should stand behind those warranties. The promise to indemnify is a party's way of guaranteeing its warranties.

Example: In a trademark license agreement, the licensor warrants that its licensed trademark does not infringe any third party rights. The licensor also promises to indemnify the licensee for losses suffered as a result of a breach of this warranty. But unknown to licensor, the trademark that is licensed has actually been previously registered by a completely separate third party. If that third party sues the licensee for infringing its trademark, the licensor will have to indemnify (reimburse) the licensee for any money damages suffered as a result of this lawsuit.

As you can see, indemnification provisions frequently work together with the representations and warranties provisions in the license agreement The licensor typically promises to indemnify the licensee for lawsuits based on breach of its warranty. An indemnification provision states that the licensor will indemnify the licenses in the event of a lawsuit against the licensee that is based on the licensor's breach of its warranties. An example of this type of provision is as follows:

> Licensor will indemnify and hold harmless the Licensee, from any and all third party claims, liabilities, damages, and/or costs, including without limitation reasonable attorneys' fees, arising from the breach of its warranties in Section __ of this agreement.

If the licensee is providing warranties of its own, its indemnification provision should guarantee those specific warranties. The licensee may also be asked to indemnify for material breaches of licensor's intellectual property. The licensee's representations and warranties will vary from license to license

In general, indemnification provisions vary greatly depending on the intellectual property, industry, as well as the type and complexity of the license. If your specific case is complicated or if the opposing party to your license puts forth an indemnification provision that is different from the examples provided here or in the sample license agreements, you may need to consult an intellectual property attorney.

Limitation of Liability

When a party is said to be *liable* for something, that means that the party is legally responsible for that thing. If the party fails to perform, a court may enforce an obligation. Most of the time, this means the liable party will end up paying monetary damages. A *limitation of liability* provision in an agreement means that the agreement sets a limit to what a party (or parties) will be required to pay in the event of a breach and subsequent lawsuit to recover money damages for that breach.

Many things can go wrong during the performance of a licensing agreement, even with the parties' best intentions. In case things do go wrong, that party will want to minimize its exposure to potential losses resulting from a lawsuit. Think of the limitation of liability provision as an additional form of insurance against potential loss.

NOTE: *Limitation of liability provisions provide limitations to damages resulting solely from lawsuits of the* parties to the agreement. *Another person or company outside of the agreement (a third party) may always sue you if they have a legitimate claim. Since they are not part of the agreement, they have not agreed to any of the provisions contained in that agreement.*

There are two types of limitations of liability, and it is important to understand both kinds. Whether you are licensor or licensee, it is recommended that you put both of these in your agreement. They are the monetary amount and the type of damages.

Monetary Amount   A limitation of liability provision will limit the *total amount of money* that a party may be liable for in the event of breach of the agreement. For example, if the licensor limits its liability under the license to a given amount, it will never have to pay more than the amount if it is sued by the licensee.

Here is one version of the provision that sets as its monetary limit the royalties paid in a one-year period:

> In no event shall licensor's total liability hereunder exceed the amounts paid by licensee under the license in any one (1) year.

Alternatively, the liability limitation may specify a precise number:

> In no event shall licensor's total liability hereunder exceed ten thousand ($10,000) dollars.

The exact limit amount (whether "amounts paid under the license" or by an precise number) will have to be decided (and is often negotiated) by the parties. If a specific dollar amount is set, it should reasonably correspond to the value of the license.

It is also possible to have a limitation of liability, but to exempt certain types of breaches from that provision, thus indicating that certain types of breaches merit a potentially much higher award. For example, a *licensor* may want to state that its liability will not exceed a certain amount, except in the event of the licensee's breach of the restrictions on intellectual property or confidentiality. A *licensee*, on the other hand, may leave liability open for breach of the licensor's warranty that the intellectual property does not infringe any third party's rights. Both of these types of exemptions provide extra assurance to the party making it, that they will be properly compensated in the event of a serious breach.

Types of Damages   As discussed earlier in this book, if one party sues another, there are potentially different types of damages the latter may incur. One type is *direct damages* that is meant to compensate a party for the losses suffered as a result of the other party's breach. For example, if the licensee does not pay the $50,000 owed under the license, direct damages are recovery of the $50,000. However, there are potentially other types of damages, such as *consequential, punitive,* and *incidental,* among others. This is an area where a lawsuit may result in extraordinarily high awards against one of the parties to the license. The solution is a limitation of liability provision for *types of damages* as well as the amount.

A typical limitation of liability provision that limits *types of damages* might read as follows:

> In no event shall the Licensor be liable for any indirect, incidental, special, consequential, or punitive damages, including without limitation lost profits, even if it has been advised of the possibility of such damages.

It is important to point out that during negotiation of the license agreement, if one party introduces a limitation of liability provision (whether for money amount or type of damages or both), the other may insist on a similar provision protecting itself. Thus, many of these provisions end up covering both parties more or less equally, resulting in a *mutual* provision.

Insurance

An insurance provision provides additional assurance to the licensor that in the event of a lawsuit by a third party, both parties will be financially covered. Insurance provisions are optional, but can cover different types of losses. For example, if the licensee is making and selling a physical product, the insurance provision should protect against lawsuits resulting from customers who are harmed by defective products. One example of this type of provision is as follows:

> Licensee shall, for the Term of the Agreement, obtain and maintain at its own cost and expense a standard Product Liability Insurance in the amount of $_____ naming Licensor as an additional insured. Such policy shall provide protection against any and all claims, demands and causes of action arising out of any defects or failure to perform, alleged or otherwise, of the Licensed Products or any material used in connection therewith or any use thereof. The policy shall provide for ____ days notice to Licensor from the insurer by Registered or Certified Mail, return receipt requested, in the event of any modification, cancellation, or termination thereof. Licensee shall furnish Licensor a certificate of insurance from this policy within ____ days after execution of this Agreement.

Protection of the Licensed Property

In most intellectual property licenses, but especially ones involving patent, trademark, or merchandising rights, the license will contain provisions obligating the licensee to protect or maintain the licensed intellectual property. The main goal of these agreements is to secure the licensee's cooperation in maintaining the licensed intellectual property. This most often involves providing appropriate notice on any licensed products, and providing documents and information related to registration, payment of required fees, and renewal. However, these provisions may also state that the licensee shall not *interfere with* or take steps to *undermine* licensor's intellectual property. The specific form of such protections vary with the intellectual property right being licensed.

Make and sell licenses also typically contain provisions protecting the quality and standards of the licensed products manufactured and sold by the licensee. This can include: requirements to adhere to quality control standards, submissions of the licensed product samples to the licensor, licensor's right to inspect licensee's production facilities, as well as others. Such protections are found most often in *make and sell licenses* for patents and trademarks, as well as in their merchandising. Since consumers associate the licensed products with the intellectual property, and vice versa, these types of provisions ultimately protect the intellectual property as well.

Third Party Infringements

In the earlier discussion on indemnification, the scenario where someone outside the license agreement (that is, a third party) sues the licensee for intellectual property infringement was covered. But what happens if the third party is the one who is infringing the licensed intellectual property? For instance, during the term of the license, the licensee or licensor may discover that a third party is infringing the licensed intellectual property. How will the licensor follow up on this and what role will the licensee play in any litigation?

A provision often titled *Third Party Infringement* or *Third Party Lawsuits* addresses this issue. Clearly, the licensor, as owner of the intellectual property at issue, has the responsibility and authority to follow up in protecting the intellectual property. In *nonexclusive* licenses, for example, the licensee's role may consist of notifying the licensor if it has reason to believe any infringement of the licensed property is occurring. However, with *exclusive* licenses, the situation may be a bit different. An exclusive license agreement, while falling short of an actual joint venture or partnership, does produce common interests between the licensor and licensee. It is in both parties' interest to ensure that the licensed intellectual property is not infringed by any third party. As with indemnification provisions, these types of provisions vary depending on the license and can get complicated.

Confidentiality

Confidentiality is typically an important provision in your license agreement. Each party entering into a license usually must provide certain information and materials to the other. Depending on the type of license, these can include technical information and materials (data, blueprints, specifications, etc.), financial data, marketing information, and so on. Likewise, through the natural course of performance of a license, a party may gain access to another party's information and materials, even when such are not actively disclosed.

Oftentimes, the economic value of this information to an individual or company lies in its secrecy. Disclosure of such information, also known as *proprietary information*, to business competitors or the public in general could be of detriment to its owner. This is also true for other types of information such as marketing plans, financial data, customer lists, the identity of certain projects, and so forth. Much business knowledge these days consists of such proprietary materials and information.

Confidentiality Provision

A *confidentiality* provision in the license agreement is designed to protect the parties and the value of their information. In it, one or both parties agrees not to disclose any information or materials that it receives from the other party. The provision may be more broadly worded to apply to all information and materials belonging to a party related to a particular subject.

A nondisclosure provision is oftentimes mutual. It will apply identically to licensor and licensee. However, typically a licensor will start with a one-sided confidentiality provision protecting its licensed property. As part of its negotiation, the licensee may then make the provision mutual or define its own information to be kept confidential.

The following is a basic *mutual* confidentiality provision found in many licenses:

> The parties acknowledge that proprietary materials or information may be disclosed by one Party to the other, including without information trade secrets, technical, financial, and marketing materials or information shall constitute (*Confidential Information*). Each Party promises not to disclose or otherwise disseminate any Confidential Information belonging to the other Party, without the prior consent of the other Party.
>
> Confidential Information shall not include any information which is: (i) in the public domain or becomes public knowledge, through no fault of the recipient; (ii) received, without any breach of confidentiality, from a third party lawfully in possession of such information; (iii) independently derived without reference to the Confidential Information of the other Party, as evidenced by supporting documentation; or (iv) required by law, regulation, or a valid court order to be disclosed, provided that the disclosing party gives prior notification to the other party.

Unlike some other terms in the license agreement, confidentiality provisions are generally not limited in terms of time and place. Each party will have a duty not to disclose the other's confidential material. This duty extends *everywhere* and at all times. A confidentiality provision should survive beyond the term of the license and is typically included in the *Survival Clause* of the license agreement. This means that even after termination of the license, each party still has a continuing obligation *not* to disclose the other's confidential information.

The parties may also specify that the confidentiality provision will last for the *term of the agreement* plus a given number of years afterwards—most often, between three to seven years. This type of survivability is often found in industries where information becomes obsolete within a relatively short amount of time. This is especially true, for example, of technical information in the software and Internet industries. However, certain types of information needs to be protected in perpetuity (forever), and you must take this into account in your license agreement.

Separate Confidentiality Agreement

Sometimes, one or both parties will want to sign a separate *confidentiality agreement* that covers information and material to be exchanged between the parties. A separate confidentiality agreement accomplishes the same result as a confidentiality provision within a license agreement. However, the coverage of a separate agreement may be potentially greater, since a general confidentiality agreement between two parties could be made to apply to all transactions between them, not just licenses (depending, of course, on the exact terms of the confidentiality agreement).

If the parties are involved only in a licensing transaction and the license is fairly standard and straightforward, a confidentiality provision in the license agreement is probably sufficient. However, if the parties are working together to develop something or if the parties are undertaking any kind of joint venture, a separate agreement addressing confidentiality is probably a good idea.

Force Majeure

A *force majeure* provision is one that relieves a party of an obligation under the agreement, if the breach is due to an external event beyond that party's control. The triggering events can vary, but the intent of this provision is to protect the party from adverse events over which it has no direct or indirect control.

Example: A software license states that the licensor must provide an update to a software program and deliver it to the licensee by a certain date. However, a fire occurs before this date, destroying the licensor's offices. The licensor is prevented from preparing and shipping the update. If the license agreement contains a general force majeure provision, the licensor would not be in breach of the license.

Force majeure provisions are oftentimes *mutual,* applying equally to both parties. However it is certainly possible for the licensor or licensee to insist on force majeure just for performance of its own obligations.

The following is a typical *force majeure* clause in a license agreement:

> Neither party shall be liable for any loss or delay resulting from any event which is beyond its reasonable control, including without limitation acts of God, flood, fire, natural disaster, war or military hostilities, or labor stoppage, provided that the party claiming force majeure promptly notifies the other party as soon as such event occurs.

Bankruptcy

What happens if, during the term of the license, the licensee has difficulty meeting its obligations under the license as a result of bankruptcy or other financial difficulties? The licensor may not want to remain in a licensing arrangement with a licensee whose business future is uncertain. This is especially true if the license calls on the licensee to manufacture and sell a product based on the licensor's intellectual property. Alternatively, what if the licensor is unable to meet its license obligations due to financial hardships.

The presence of a *bankruptcy provision* in the license will address these concerns. A *bankruptcy provision* generally states that if the *licensee* (or sometimes, if either party) becomes bankrupt (as the term is defined in the agreement), the *licensor* may immediately *terminate* the license. As with the other termination conditions, this gives the licensor an extra assurance that it will not be tied to a license with a company without the financial means to carry out its obligations under the license. A bankruptcy provision may apply to one party only or both, depending on how it is negotiated.

A bankruptcy provision protecting the licensor could look like the following:

> Upon prior written notice, Licensor may immediately terminate this Agreement if the Licensee: (i) becomes insolvent; (ii) files for bankruptcy or petitions under insolvency law of any jurisdiction; (iii) expresses an inability to pay the sums due hereunder; (iv) proposes any liquidation, dissolution, or financial reorganization with creditors; or (v) has a trustee, receiver, custodian, or similar agent appointed to it.

This provision covers several different variations on bankruptcy and is therefore quite broad. This is because the definition of bankruptcy may vary from state to state, as well as be triggered by different events.

Injunction

An injunction allows the plaintiff (the party bringing the lawsuit) to actually *prevent* the activities which are found to be unauthorized and illegal. In the context of intellectual property licenses, injunctions are typically obtained for the *unauthorized* reproduction or distribution of the licensor's intellectual property or a party's confidential information. Since injunctions can *only be granted by a court of law,* licensors sometimes seek to guarantee their right to an injunction in the agreement itself. In other words, if the licensee uses the intellectual property (or confidential information) in an *unauthorized* manner, the licensor will *automatically* be able to get an injunction preventing further unauthorized use.

The following is one example of the above provision:

> Licensee acknowledges that a violation of any provision relating to Licensee's use of the Licensed Property or of Licensor's confidential information shall constitute irreparable harm to Licensor, and entitle Licensor to obtain, in addition to all its legal remedies, immediate injunctive relief in any court of law.

Make sure that the language in this section is consistent with your previous definitions and provisions in your license.

8 | LICENSE AGREEMENT: STANDARD TERMS

Typically found at the end of the license agreement, the standard terms provisions are oftentimes grouped under a single section. The section heading could be some variation of the following titles:

- ✪ miscellaneous terms;

- ✪ standard terms; or,

- ✪ general provisions.

It is also possible that these terms or provisions may not be grouped under one general heading at all, but simply be present towards the end of the agreement. Some of the provisions discussed below may even be placed throughout the license depending on the topic being discussed, so it is important to look for them throughout the license agreement.

The provisions themselves cover a wide variety of topics related to the license agreement itself, such as whether the license may be assigned; notices between the parties; what happens if a section of the agreement is invalid; and, how the license should be interpreted in the event of litigation. Since many of these provisions are often virtually identical across a wide spectrum of license agreements, they are sometimes referred to as *pro forma* or *boilerplate* provisions (many of these provisions are in fact found in other legal contracts, not just in licenses).

It must be stressed that the fact that these terms are labeled *standard* or *miscellaneous* does not mean that they are unimportant. Quite the contrary, these provisions have important repercussions on the parties.

Following are some of the more important of the standard legal provisions discussed in this chapter:

- ✪ assignment;

- ✪ successors;

- ✪ choice of law/jurisdiction;

- ✪ alternative dispute resolution;

- ✪ notices between the parties;

- ✪ severability/waiver;

- ✪ entire agreement;

- ✪ modifications;

- ✪ relationship between the parties;

- ✪ headings; and,

- ✪ counterparts.

Not every license will contain all of these standard provisions. However, as a general rule, more *complicated* or *longer-term licenses* or those with more *valuable intellectual property* require more legal protections.

Assignment

An *assignment* can be located anywhere in the license agreement, though it is frequently found under the standard legal terms. The assignment provision is very important and should be carefully considered by both parties to the license.

When a party assigns a license agreement, it is actually transferring its own rights and obligations under the agreement to a third party. A new party will *step into the shoes* of one of the original parties to the agreement. In most agreements, parties prefer not to be silent on the issue of assignment. This means that in general, an agreement should spell out whether or not parties have the right of assignment.

In general, the licensor should think carefully about whether the licensee should have the right to assign the license agreement. If the licensee can assign the license, it may result in a completely *new party* entering the picture. Though any new party would be legally bound to follow the obligations under the agreement, this new party introduces a level of uncertainty to the relationship.

Therefore, many license agreements will contain the following provision prohibiting such assignment (except with the licensor's consent):

> The Licensee shall not have the power to assign this Agreement without the prior consent of the Licensor. Any assignment made without such consent shall be void.

One compromise between licensor and licensee on this issue is keeping the prohibition on the licensee's assigning of the agreement, but also prohibiting the licensor from *unreasonably* denying the licensee's request to assign. In other words, if the potential assignee (the party which *receives* the license agreement) is a viable business, in good financial condition, and it is able to fulfill its business and legal obligations under the license just as the original licensee would, there would be no business reason for the licensor to object. Thus, under such circumstances the licensor would be legally *required* to permit such assignment.

This version of the assignment provision can be stated as follows:

> Licensee shall not assign this Agreement without the consent of Licensor, which consent shall not be unreasonably withheld.

Of course, as with all issues in a license agreement, the licensor and licensee may work out a different compromise with respect to assignment. If the licensee is a large company with one or more affiliates, another compromise provision would allow the licensee to assign only to its affiliates, but to no other party. An example could be stated as follows:

> Licensee may not assign this Agreement without the consent of Licensor, provided that Licensee may assign this Agreement without such consent to an Affiliate of Licensee.

NOTE: *If this language is used, the term affiliate should be defined elsewhere in the agreement.*

If the *licensee* has sufficient bargaining power, it may insist on a no assignment provision on the part of the licensor. In that case, the *licensor* will be the one prohibited from making an assignment, while the licensee will be allowed to make such assignment. The parties may also compromise and make no assignment *mutual*, as in the following:

> Neither party may assign this Agreement without the consent of the other party.

Successors

If a party to the license is a company, you may have to consider the possibility that it may be acquired by or merged with another business entity. A *successors* provision deals with these eventualities. Often, one can find successors language along with the assignment provision, under the miscellaneous terms. For example, the following general language states that the license agreement *will be binding* on all types of successors:

> This Agreement shall be binding upon and shall inure to the benefit of both Parties, and their heirs, administrators, successors, and permitted assigns.

If either party is a company, the possibility of a corporate successor may be an issue. A discussion of the details of corporate successors is beyond the scope of this book. However, one example of a simple provision by which any *successor* to the licensee (that is, a purchaser of the licensee's assets) will *acquire* the license agreement:

This Agreement shall not be assigned by Licensee unless in connection with a transfer of substantially all of the assets of the Licensee, or with the consent of the Licensor.

Choice of Law and Jurisdiction

Once a license agreement is signed, each party hopes that the other will perform all of its obligations and that the license transaction will be free of problems. However, even with the best of intentions, sometimes a dispute between the parties still arises. Some of these disputes unfortunately end up with one party suing the other in a court of law.

In the event of such a lawsuit, two provisions present in the majority of license agreements—often in the same section or paragraph—may become important. These are the choice of law and jurisdiction provisions. Each is a distinct provision, but the two are closely related.

Choice of Law   You learned in Chapter 1 that much of the law covering intellectual property rights is *federal* in nature. Federal law has *nationwide* application. That is, regardless of where the parties are located (as long as they are in the United States), they will be subject to the same legal rules and regulations.

However, *contract law*, the law governing the interpretation of contracts is state, rather than federal-based. This means that every state in the U.S. has its own rules and regulations relating to contracts. Depending on the details of the case, a court in a given state may apply the law of its own state or the law of another state in order to resolve conflict.

A *choice of law* or *governing law* provision enables the parties to a license to choose under which state's law the agreement will be interpreted in the event of a lawsuit.

The following simple statement should suffice to cover the parties' choice of law provision:

This Agreement shall be governed in accordance with the laws of the State of [insert State], without regard to its choice of law or conflicts of law provisions.

NOTE: *The phrase "without regard to its choice of law or conflicts of law provisions." Without going into a complicated analysis, this essentially states that the laws of the chosen state will apply at all times, regardless of whether those very laws necessitate application of another state's law. This phrase is not critical to a choice of law provision, but it is available to use to cover all bases.*

Choosing a State. You may be asking which state's law should you use in your license agreement. Oftentimes, this may not make much of a difference, since many states have similar provisions with respect to the interpretation of contracts. In many cases, a party will simply designate its home state as the state law of choice.

However, some states treat certain types of contracts more favorably than others. It is beyond the scope of this book to offer an analysis of each state's laws, but you can do further research regarding specific contract laws in each state. Alternatively, you can check with an attorney regarding the laws of a specific state, if any issues arises with this provision.

Jurisdiction   The issue of *jurisdiction* (sometimes referred to as *personal jurisdiction*) deals with the location (state) in which a lawsuit is brought. In theory, a lawsuit may be brought in any state, even one in which the plaintiff (the person suing) or defendant (the person being sued) does not reside. However, not every state will have *power* or *authority* over the defendant. There are numerous, diverse rules (which vary from state to state) specifying when the defendant may be sued in a given state.

To get around these complicated rules, a party (or both parties) can *consent* to jurisdiction in a particular state. This way, if a lawsuit is brought against the party in a particular state, the lawsuit is guaranteed to take place there. For example, the following provision in a license ensures that if the licensor sues the licensee (for whatever reason) in New York State, the licensee will be forced to litigate there:

Licensee consents to the jurisdiction of the federal and state courts of the State of New York.

However, if the licensee is the one to sue the licensor, the licensee may bring the lawsuit anywhere, and hence this provision will not be applicable.

Alternatively, a *mutual jurisdiction* provision applying to both parties can be formulated thus:

> All disputes under this Agreement shall be resolved in the federal and state courts of the State of [insert State], and the Parties hereby consent to the jurisdiction of its courts.

Jurisdiction is very important in situations where licensor and licensee reside in different states. This is especially true if these locations are spread far apart. For example, in the event of a lawsuit, it would be very difficult for an individual or owner of a small business residing in New York to go to court in California or even in Virginia. This is the case whether the party is plaintiff or defendant. If the license agreement states that both parties consent to the jurisdiction in California, then the New York resident has no choice but to use the California courts.

NOTE: *In some licenses, an additional provision entitled* venue *is included. Venue is just a more specific way of localizing the place in the event of future litigation. For example, "All disputes under this Agreement shall be resolved in the federal and state courts of Manhattan county, New York State, and the Parties submit to personal jurisdiction in such courts."*

Alternative Dispute Resolution

In addition to choice of law and a jurisdiction provisions in the license, the parties may also seek to resolve any disputes that may arise between them through *alternative dispute resolution (ADR)*. Typically this includes arbitration or mediation.

Arbitration is essentially a fast, inexpensive, and simplified litigation. Its speed, inexpensiveness, and simplicity are also the reasons for its popularity. In an arbitration, an arbitrator (who is akin to the judge) is appointed and an arbitration proceeding is held where each party presents its claim. The arbitrator's final judgment is *binding* on the parties, and can only be overturned upon a showing of clear abuse.

Mediation consists of a neutral party (the mediator) advising both parties as to how they can resolve the dispute without the mediator's word being in any way binding on the parties. Therefore, mediation is more along the lines of an attempt at a compromise rather than a formal procedural process. Some parties attempt mediation and failing to reach a resolution, enter into arbitration.

NOTE: *The presence of an arbitration or a mediation provision in the license will ensure that either an arbitration or mediation proceeding will be entered into even if only one party to the license desires to do so. If both parties desire to undergo an arbitration or mediation proceeding, they can always do so, regardless of whether there is are any provisions in the license addressing this issue.*

An arbitration or mediation provision is not always necessary or even recommended. Depending on your type of license, your specific business needs, as well as the nature of the potential dispute, you may benefit more from court litigation than using ADR. One clear advantage of arbitration or mediation is that these proceedings are less expensive and typically speedier than full-blown litigation in a court of law. If you are an individual or small company with limited financial means, arbitration or mediation may thus be an attractive option.

If you decide to put an arbitration or mediation provision in your license agreement, keep it within standard or accepted format. The largest and most popular arbitration organization used by parties is the *American Arbitration Association.* It is frequently referred to in an alternative dispute provision. However, arbitration/mediation provisions vary from the very simple to the complex. The very simple ones are one or two sentence provisions, as for example, the following:

> The parties agree to submit any disputes arising from this Agreement to final and binding arbitration. Such arbitration shall be carried out under the rules of the American Arbitration Association, and shall be final and binding on the parties.

Alternatively, a more complex provision will specify a means for resolving disputes first by mediation, and failing that, arbitration. More complicated provisions also contain some *basic* guidelines for these procedures:

> In the event any dispute or controversy arising out of or relating to this Agreement, the parties agree to exercise their best efforts to resolve the dispute. Throughout the dispute resolution process, the parties shall continue to perform all their other obligations under this agreement.

> 1. MEDIATION. In the event that the parties cannot resolve the dispute, they shall first submit the dispute to Mediation. The party invoking mediation shall give to the other party written notice of its decision to do so. The parties shall attempt to resolve the dispute within a reason-

able time. If the dispute is not resolved within __ months, the dispute shall be submitted to binding arbitration in accordance with the Arbitration provision herein.

2. ARBITRATION. Any disputes arising out of or relating to this Agreement which are not resolved through mediation shall be resolved by binding arbitration in accordance with the then current Commercial Arbitration Rules of the American Arbitration Association. The award rendered by the arbitrator shall be final and binding on the parties, and judgment may be entered to this effect in any court having jurisdiction.

The arbitrator(s) shall not have the authority or right to modify, amend, add to, or subtract from any provision of this agreement. The arbitrator shall have the power to issue mandatory orders and restraining orders in connection with the arbitration, but shall not have the power to award punitive damages.

3. CONFIDENTIALITY. All documents and evidence submitted by the parties, as well as the dispute itself, proceedings, and outcome shall be kept strictly confidential by both parties in perpetuity.

In general, if the party you are negotiating with insists on specifying precise rules for an arbitration proceeding, it is recommended you do further research on this issue or check with an attorney. (Analyzing such legal rules is beyond the scope of this book.)

Notices between the Parties

During the term of the license, the licensor and/or licensee may need to notify the other party, as required by various provisions in the license. For instance, notification of a party may be required if a party decides to terminate or inform the other of a material breach.

Especially if you are dealing with a large company—with many branches, divisions, or affiliates—a *notice provision* becomes important. Such a provision defines the proper delivery method, address, and contact person to receive notices from the other party and will ensure that notices are *official*.

One example of such a notice provision is as follows:

Notices required under this Agreement shall be in writing and shall be sent by registered or certified mail, return receipt requested. Such notices shall be addressed to the parties at the addresses set forth below, or at such other address as may be specified by either party:

LICENSOR:

[Indicate Licensor's Contact Person & Address]

LICENSEE:

[Indicate Licensee's Contact Person & Address]

Of course, you may vary the specifics of this type of provision (i.e., registered or regular mail, number of contact people or addresses, and so on) depending on your business requirements.

Severability and Waiver

Severability

Severability and waiver are found in most license agreements. Though they are really two separate provisions, they are frequently dealt within the same license paragraph or section.

A *severability* provision basically states that each term or provision in the agreement is separate from the others and that if one or more of these terms or provisions is later found to be invalid (by a court of law), the others will still be valid. For example, if a license agreement becomes the subject of a lawsuit and the court finds that a warranty provision is invalid and/or unenforceable, this will not affect the rest of the license agreement. That invalid or unenforceable provision is, in effect, *severed* from the rest of the license agreement.

Waiver

Waiver is a bit harder to explain. To *waive* means to give up or to choose not to pursue a legal remedy against another party for a breach of the agreement. A *waiver provision* states that if one party breaches the agreement and the other party chooses not to enforce its rights by suing the breaching party, the former will still retain the right to sue in the future. In other words, the non-breaching party has not waived its rights by refusing to take immediate action.

The following language addresses *both* severability and waiver:

> If any provision, term, or clause in this Agreement is found to be invalid or unenforceable by any court of law, such invalidity or unenforceability shall not affect the validity of all other provisions, terms, or clauses in the Agreement. The failure of either party to enforce any of the provisions of this Agreement shall in no way be construed as a waiver of such provisions, nor affect any rights to enforce any provision of the Agreement in the future.

Entire Agreement

The *entire agreement* provision (also known as an *integration* or *merger* provision or clause) states that the signed agreement—including any exhibits, schedules and/or attachments—is the *entire* understanding between the parties. This means that the parties have not entered into any other agreements, contracts, or understandings (on the subject matter) apart from the agreement at issue.

This provision basically says that what the parties expected the final license to look like does not matter. Even if the parties have previously agreed upon certain points, this too does not matter. The only thing that counts is the *final, stated terms of the license agreement, as signed by the parties.*

This type of provision can be stated as the following:

> This Agreement constitutes the entire understanding between the parties, and supersedes all prior agreements, understandings, proposals, and/or discussions, whether written or oral, between the parties on this subject matter.

It is important to have an entire agreement provision in your license agreement in order to help avoid misunderstandings. Parties typically make statements, claims, and other promises to each other during negotiation of the license (and sometimes beforehand). Some of these may later change or turn out differently in the context of the entire license. Sometimes, based on these earlier statements, a party will form an inaccurate or incomplete understanding of one or more of the license's terms or issues. An entire agreement provision ensures that only the final agreement will control.

Modifications

Once any agreement is signed by every party, it may always be revised, amended, or modified if *all parties* agree to do so. In a license agreement, this means that both licensor and licensee must agree to the change. A *modifications* or *amendments* provision states this principle explicitly and further requires that any changes be written and signed by the parties.

An example of this type of provision is as follows:

> This Agreement may not be modified or revised, in whole or in part, except by a writing signed by both parties.

Sometimes, a party will also want to emphasize that once signed, a license agreement may not be canceled, rescinded, or terminated, except in accordance with the provisions of the license.

Relationship between the Parties

If the parties are entering solely into a license agreement, they may want to explicitly state that their agreement is a *license* and nothing else. In other words, the licensing arrangement will not constitute a joint venture between the parties, an employment relationship, or any kind of business partnership. This will help prevent misunderstanding as to the exact business relationship between licensor and licensee.

The following statement aptly summarizes this principle:

> The relationship between Licensor and Licensee is that of independent contractors, and nothing herein shall be construed as creating an employment, partnership, or a joint venture between them. Neither Party shall have the right to bind the other Party to any obligation or liability whatsoever.

Of course, parties who *do* decide to enter into a joint venture, partnership, or employment agreement may also license intellectual property between them. If the intention is to enter such a business relationship, as well as to license intellectual property, then the above provision would not be *applicable* to the agreement.

Headings

A *headings* provision simply states that the headings of the paragraphs or sections of the license agreement are for convenience only, and should not be used to interpret the actual provisions (in the event the license agreement is the subject of a lawsuit). The placement of a provision within the license agreement, as well as how such provision is named, should not have an effect on the provisions' legal meaning, or on the rights and obligations of the parties.

This can be stated as follows:

> The paragraph headings used in this Agreement are for convenience only and shall not be used in any way to interpret, construe, or govern this Agreement.

Counterparts

A *counterparts* provision states that the license agreement may be signed separately by each party and still be a properly executed license agreement. In other words, the manner of execution of the final agreement should not have any effect on the final agreement between the parties.

The following summarizes this provision:

> This Agreement may be executed in two or more counterparts, and all counterparts thus executed shall constitute one binding agreement.

NOTE: *The* counterparts *provision, as well as the heading provision discussed earlier, are not critical to the straightforward, relatively simple license agreement. However, more complicated licenses with many interrelated terms and conditions may benefit from these extra protections.*

9 MONITORING YOUR LICENSE

This chapter gives an overall birds eye view of the provisions covered in all the previous chapters. A quick checklist of the main questions you should ask yourself—whether you are licensor or licensee—before you sign your license agreement is provided. Lastly the chapter discusses how to keep track of the obligations to which you have committed yourself.

Before You Sign

Keeping track of all the provisions that go into a license agreement can certainly be a daunting task. The following is an overall scheme for all the provisions that typically go into a license agreement, as discussed in Chapter 4.

Main License Terms

The *main license terms* are the general business issues that provide the overall structure to your license, including:

- ✪ introduction and definition of parties;

- ✪ license grant;

✪ term;

✪ termination conditions;

✪ payment provisions; and,

✪ service provisions (if any).

Legal Protections

Legal protections protect the parties, as well as the intellectual property being licensed, both financially and legally speaking, and include:

✪ representations and warranties;

✪ indemnification;

✪ limitation of liability;

✪ insurance;

✪ protection of the intellectual property;

✪ third party infringement;

✪ confidentiality;

✪ force majeure;

✪ bankruptcy; and,

✪ injunction.

Standard or Miscellaneous Terms

Standard or miscellaneous terms are additional terms that are fairly consistent across many licenses, but deal with many important issues as well and include:

✪ assignment;

✪ corporate successors;

✪ choice of law / jurisdiction;

✪ alternative dispute resolution;

✪ notices between the parties;

✪ severability waiver;

✪ entire agreement;

✪ modifications;

✪ relationship between the parties;

✪ headings; and,

✪ counterparts.

At this point, you are probably asking yourself the following questions. Must all of these terms and provisions be included in every license agreement? The answer—like many answers to legal questions—lies in the circumstances of the situation. Depending on the kind of license you are entering, its complexity, the value and potential market of the intellectual property, the financial strength of your (and the other party's) business, as well as other factors, you may need most if not all, of the legal protections that will be examined in this and following chapters.

For example, if you own a potentially valuable intellectual property and intend to commercialize it by licensing a company to manufacture and sell your invention, you will probably need most of the provisions. However, there will also be many instances when you can make do with a simpler license agreement. However, you may need to consult with an intellectual property attorney if the material presented here and and later in the book does not fully address your particular circumstances.

If, however, you are drafting the license agreement yourself, the following is an overall checklist to help you keep track of most of the important questions, issues, and points to consider before you sign your license agreement.

Checklist   ✪   Have you properly defined the parties to the license?

As discussed in Chapter 4, you must carefully consider the business entity that is the licensor and licensee. Keep in mind that if the licensee is a company, there may be affiliates, subsidiaries, foreign branches, and so on. In addition, if you are the licensor, you should keep in mind who will be using your intellectual property.

✪   Does your license grant section accurately capture the license transaction?

This is the heart of your license. The license grant section consists of answers to the following questions. What intellectual property is being granted? What can the licensee do? Is the license exclusive or nonexclusive? In addition, this section may contain other information pertaining to ownership of the intellectual property. (Details of the license grant section are covered in Chapter 5.)

✪   Does the licensee have the right to sublicense?

This is an especially important issue of the *license grant*. To avoid any ambiguity in the license, this should be defined one way or the other. In some licenses, especially *make and sell licenses*, it may be beneficial for the licensee to have the right to sublicense. Other times, the licensor will clearly want to forbid it. (Sublicensing rights are discussed more fully in Chapter 5.)

✪   Have you set the right price for the license, and covered all payment provisions?

Have you adequately researched the *standard of the industry* in negotiating and agreeing on the price for the license—either *royalties* or *fixed payments*? Are there other related payment terms that need to be provided? (See Chapter 6 for more information about license payment and financial provisions.)

✪   Is the term of the license appropriate?

In other words, does the amount of time the license will be in effect reflect the type of license, the industry, and the requirements of both parties? (See Chapters 4 and 6 for a discussion of license term.)

✪ Have you considered how you can terminate the license if you need to?

Being able to terminate the license at any point during its term is an important business advantage. Consider which provisions of the license should *survive* termination or expiration of the license agreement. (Refer to Chapters 4 and 5 for the issue of termination.)

✪ Do you have all provisions in place relating to your specific intellectual property—patent, copyright, trademark, or trade secret?

While we have not covered specific provisions related to software, patents, trademarks, technology, and copyrighted works extensively, in most of these licenses, you may need to insert several additional provisions connected to your type of right.

✪ Have you put in sufficient *legal protections* in your license?

By *legal protections* we mean legal terms that protect the parties, their materials, and the intellectual property. Provisions such as representations and warranties, indemnification, and limitation of liability should be carefully considered. Additional protections such as an insurance provision, third party infringements, confidentiality, etc. should also be weighed. (For review of these types of legal provisions, see Chapter 7.)

✪ Do you have information or material that needs confidentiality?

If you are exchanging technical, financial, or other information with the other party, you most likely will need some confidentiality protection. This also holds true for the licensing of software. If you are licensing a trade secret, a confidentiality provision becomes especially important, since you may lose your rights to the trade secret without adequate confidentiality. (Confidentiality is discussed in Chapter 7.)

✪ Have you considered all the standard or miscellaneous legal terms?

Have you taken into account the *miscellaneous* or *standard* provisions such as assignment, choice of law and jurisdiction, alternative dispute resolution, and all the other terms covered in Chapter 8? If you are reviewing the other party's license agreement, remember that these provisions may be found anywhere in the agreement, so be on the alert for them.

Performing and Monitoring Your License

Once your license agreement is signed, you can breathe a sigh of relief. You have gotten through what is often a complicated and time-consuming process. But do not relax too long. You have now entered into a *new phase* of your licensing transaction. Your license agreement lists important obligations and responsibilities that you are now *legally* required to fulfill. In addition, you must actively review the *other party's* performance under the license agreement to make sure it is fulfilling all of its obligations. Sometimes this is relatively simple. For example, if the license is a basic *use-only* with fixed payments, then all the licensee really needs to do is make sure all payments are made and not misuse the intellectual property. However, if you are dealing with a *make and sell* license, especially those with royalties, your legal obligations can get more complicated.

The following quick reference for some of the obligations that you may be faced with in performing your license agreement is provided. If you are the *licensor*, depending on your type of license, you may have the obligation to:

- ❂ provide adequate levels of *support*, *maintenance*, and/or *service* to the licensee (See Chapter 10);

- ❂ adequately monitor the quality of the goods or services licensee is providing under your trademark and/or merchandising rights (See Chapter 12);

- ❂ provide all required information and materials under the license, including *confidential information*;

- ❂ take active steps to *monitor and maintain* your intellectual property (file registrations, pay requisite fees, file renewals, etc.); and,

- ❂ investigate potential infringement of your intellectual property, when you receive notice that this is occurring, where such infringement can be by licensee or by third parties.

In addition, you need to ensure that all *payments* have been made by the licensee or are being made on a *timely basis*. This includes carefully reviewing royalty statements and ensuring that payment are consistent and that the royalty rates and quantities of goods sold are correct.

If you are the *licensee*, again depending on your type of license, you may be obligated to do the following:

✪ make all *payments*—either royalties or fixed payments—required under the license, on a *timely basis*;

✪ for *make and sell licenses*, possibly submit *samples* of your products for quality control and approval purposes;

✪ *cooperate* with licensor in maintaining the licensed *intellectual property*, including providing documents and other materials; and,

✪ notify licensor of any *third party infringement* learned of during the term of the license.

If you perceive that the other party is not performing its obligations under the license or is breaching the license agreement in any significant way, you should carefully consider your options. Many disputes arise from misunderstandings and can be amicably resolved by the parties. For example, honest disputes about how much money is owed under the license or how the intellectual property may be used can often be corrected through discussions. Others—for instance, public disclosure of important confidential information or licensee's *willful misuse* of licensor's intellectual property—may require a different approach. An immediate consultation with an attorney for these more serious types of breaches is recommended.

While all situations and potential problems cannot be covered, here are some general rules about dealing with a licensing dispute.

✪ Review what your license agreement states regarding the specific breach (or material breaches in general), the opportunity to *cure* such breach, and your right to terminate the license.

✪ Raise the problem with the other party—oftentimes, simply notifying a party of a potential breach is sufficient to get them to correct the problem.

✪ Do not threaten litigation at this point or rush to terminate the license agreement too quickly.

Modifying or Terminating Your License

Finally, there are two important points regarding any modification or termination of your license agreement. Most often, a license will be performed without any modification or revision and will expire naturally. However, there may be circumstances that require either an early termination or modification of the license agreement. If this happens, keep in mind the following two points.

As noted in Chapter 8, an agreement may be modified or terminated if both parties agree to do so. Basically this involves either writing a brand new license agreement or drafting an *amendment* or *addendum* to the existing agreement. An amendment or addendum must identify itself as that and must make reference to the original agreement by name, date, and all parties. Actual modifications should be noted by section or paragraph number and it must be signed by all parties.

If you are *unilaterally* terminating the license pursuant to a *termination right* under the license agreement, you should give *written notice* to the other party. Keep a record that the party has received this notice. If *both parties* agree to terminate early, they should have this in signed, written form as well.

10 | SOFTWARE LICENSES

This chapter covers software licenses, however before starting, two *very important points* regarding the material and sample licenses need to be addressed. First, the discussion in this chapter assumes the licensor *owns* the software it is licensing and that the transaction is a basic license. Thus, this chapter does not cover reselling, distribution agreements, software development, or agreements where the licensee is allowed to modify the software.

Second, the sample software licenses provided in this chapter are all *nonexclusive, use-only licenses* that are most common in the industry. Though it is possible to license software on an *exclusive* basis or license in order to produce a product, you will need additional provisions dealing with exclusive grants for this type of license.

Types of Software Licenses

Software (otherwise known as a *programs* or *computer programs*) is instructions written in a computer language that instruct a computer to perform certain functions. There is a great diversity of software products and transactions and subsequently, many kinds of software licenses. The following lists some of these types and when they are typically used.

✪ *Use-Only Software License.* A software owner licenses a software program or product to a company for the company's internal use only.

✪ *Shrink-Wrap Software License.* A software owner mass-markets a standard software product (word processor, financial product, etc.) to consumers for their personal use only.

✪ *Click-Wrap Software License.* A software owner distributes a program through a website, either for payment or as shareware (for free) that users download and use.

✪ *Make and Sell Software License.* The licensed software is used by a company to generate some type of product or output, which it then sells to third parties. The licensor receives royalties for each product sold.

✪ *Software Escrow Agreement.* This is not really a license, but an agreement between the software licensor and licensee to deposit the software source code or software program with a third party (the *escrow agent*). The source code would be released to the licensee upon the occurrence of certain events.

Use Only Software License

A software license is a perfect example of a *use-only license*. A *software licensor*—sometimes referred to as the *vendor*—has a software program, application, or product that it wants to license to a company or sometimes an individual. The software is either developed for a specific industry or customized for a specific company. The licensee receives the right to use the software program or application for its own business needs. In addition, the software licensor promises to provide maintenance or fix *bugs* (software errors) in the licensed software. Common restrictions on the *licensee* include prohibition from copying, selling, or otherwise distributing the software outside its organization. See form 1 in Appendix F for an example of this type of license agreement.

Shrink-Wrap License

Let us say you have developed or acquired a software program or application that you want to sell to consumers. This could be a software program sold in a store or one that is downloaded through a website. A *shrink-wrap* or *click-wrap* license are the types of agreements that would apply to this situation. Shrink-wraps are discussed in this subsection, and click-wraps in the section below.

The *shrink-wrap license* agreement is typically a one-page written license that comes with software products that you would ordinarily buy in a retail store. For example, if you buy a word processor, financial program, or interactive game, you will find a short, but dense, written document enclosed that states terms of use for the product. See form 2 in Appendix F for an example of a shrink-wrap license agreement.

NOTE: *In the past, some courts have questioned the legal enforceability of these types of agreements. However, current law tends to favor them, and most software vendors use these types of agreements in order to maximize their legal protections.*

Click-Wrap License

With the growth of the Internet, there are now *electronic* versions of these types of licenses, known as *click wrap licenses*. For instance, when you download a software program or application from a website or sign up for a service or information online, you may see a box pop up with license terms and conditions for the downloaded product or application. After reading the terms, you then press one of two buttons: "*I Agree*" or "*I Disagree.*" Therefore, you signify acceptance of the terms of the license agreement in a direct way

In most respects, a click-wrap is very similar to its shrink-wrap cousin. There are, however, some differences relating to the fact that a shrink-wrap covers physical media such as floppy disks or CDs, as well as the fact that the reader of a click-wrap signifies consent by a click of a computer mouse. Form 3 in Appendix F provides an example of a click-wrap.

Unique license terms. As far as licenses go, shrink-wraps and click-wraps are unique. Since they accompany products that are mass-marketed, they do not identify an individual or company as the *licensee* and are not signed. The payment for the license is typically made up front when a consumer purchases the software. The term for these licenses is typically *perpetual.* For the user or the licensee, these types of licenses are take it or leave it situations. In other words, business negotiation of a shrink-wrap or click-wrap license is very rare.

Other terms found in these licenses reflect their target audience and types of uses. These type of licenses for mass-marketed software usually provide for use of the software on one computer. They typically allow the user to make one (or a handful) of copies for back-up purposes. And they state other restrictions on licensee's use of the licensed software, such as no reproduction, no distribution, no sublicense, etc.. In addition, the typical shrink-wrap and click-wrap licenses will contain the legal protections for the *licensor* found in most licenses.

Make and Sell
Software License

Though most software is use-only, software can also be licensed so that the licensee can produce and sell a product or service—typically, either data, or some kind of digital output.

If your software license is intended as a *make and sell*, review the other *make and sell* licenses in the chapters that follow, as well as the resources in Appendix B.

Software
Escrow
Agreement

A *software escrow agreement* is an agreement that is *sometimes* entered into *along with* a software license; however, it does not replace a license agreement. Escrow is common with software licenses where the software licensor promises to provide significant maintenance, error-correction, and service on the software. In an escrow arrangement, the *source code* (the computer program instructions) of the software is deposited in secrecy with a third party, the *escrow agent*. In the event the licensor does not provide the required maintenance on the software, the source code is released to the licensee.

Software-Specific Provisions

To begin with, many of the provisions in a software license will be identical to those in other licenses. For example, software licenses will contain a license grant, term, termination, payment, representations and warranties, indemnification, limitation of liability, as well as other business and legal provisions.

However, software has unique characteristics that necessitates the presence of certain software-specific provisions in your license. In addition, companies and individuals within the software industry, both on the licensor and licensee side, have developed certain expectations regarding how software is licensed. This *standard of the industry* must also be taken into consideration when drafting or negotiating software licenses.

NOTE: *Some types of software are eligible for* patent *rather than* copyright *protection. It is beyond the scope of this book to fully explore the details of patent versus software protection for software; however, for more information about this topic, refer to the resources and materials in* Appendix A.

Structure of the Software License

The way that the software license is structured will be one of the most important issues of your license. *Structured* means where the software is installed; how it is accessed; who will be allowed to use the software; as well as, how the license will be paid. There is no one, ideal way to structure a software license, but there are standardized types of software transactions common in the software industry.

✪ *User-Specific License*—This type of software license allows a given number of users to use the software at any one time. Payment for such a license will typically be based on number of users. If the licensee wants to add more users, it would likely have to pay the licensor an additional fee per user.

✪ *Machine-Specific License*—In a machine-specific license, the licensee is allowed to install the license on one computer or on a few specified computers.

NOTE: *With the advent of networked systems in most companies, machine-specific licenses have become problematic. This is because a company-wide network connects all computers, allowing users to share programs.*

✪ *Site-Specific License*—This gives the licensee the right to use the software in on any number of computers in a defined facility. Use of the software in additional facilities requires an additional fee.

✪ *Enterprise License*—This is a company-wide license, giving the licensee the freedom to install the software on any computer throughout the company in any facility without limit to the number of machines. This gives the licensee the most freedom in using the software.

It is up to the parties to decide how to structure their licensing transaction. Ultimately, the nature of the software, the size and complexity of the parties, the parties' technical requirements, as well as their relative bargaining power, will determine how the license is structured. For example, a large investment bank will require a different type of license than a small, start-up company with a few employees. (For more information about specific industry requirements and practices for software, see Appendix B.)

Common Restrictions on Licensee

Most license agreements, regardless of the intellectual property licensed, restrict the licensee's actions in some manner. Very few licensees get open, unlimited rights to use intellectual property. However, in the case of software, restrictions for licensed software are often written out in fairly standard ways.

Ordinarily, a *licensee* will get only those rights that are explicitly stated in the license agreement. Nevertheless, many *software licensors* prefer to spell out what the licensee can and cannot do. This will ensure that there will be no misunderstanding with respect to this most crucial element of the license. Most of the licensee restrictions are based on the general right of a copyright owner to control the reproduction, modification, and distribution of its copyrighted work.

NOTE: *Very often, a software licensor will also explicitly state that it retains ownership of the licensed software, even though ownership is not transferred in a license. A software licensor is especially vigilant regarding ownership when the licensee receives rights to make and sell a software product based on the licensed software.*

A typical software license will state that the licensee may *not* do the following.

- ✪ *Make additional copies of the software, with the exception of one copy for back-up or archival purposes.* This is a standard restriction forbidding the reproduction or copying of the licensed software.

- ✪ *Distribute the software, or any portion thereof, to any third party, by any manner whatsoever.* This is another standard restriction that ensures that the licensed software will stay with the licensee only. As worded, the restriction is quite broad.

- ✪ *Reverse engineer, decompile, or otherwise decode the software.* This restricts the licensee from trying to figure out the underlying algorithms, source code, or other trade secrets of the licensed software.

- ✪ *Post or distribute the software online or store the software in a data warehouse.* This restriction is an expansion of the distribution prohibition from above, taking into account more technical ways of distributing or sharing software.

✪ *Revise or modify the software or create derivative programs or works based on the software.* This is in line with any copyright owner's overall right to modify its existing work, and make derivative works.

Limited Warranties for the Software

Another common feature among software licenses is the licensor's *disclaiming* of at least some warranties pertaining to the licensed software. As you may recall from the earlier discussion of representations and warranties in Chapter 7, licensors often provide a warranty as to the *validity* and *noninfringement* of their intellectual property.

This is the case in software licenses as well. However, with software, there are additional issues. One very important issue is whether the licensed property will actually *work*—will perform its intended functions. Another issue involves errors in most software systems, regardless of how much development the software undergoes. Yet another potential problem with software is its dependence on the operating environment of the computers it is installed on, as well as the presence of other programs.

For these reasons, software licensors are generally *very careful* with the warranties they will provide in a software license. Many licensors will give a general warranty that the software will function and/or perform according to the technical representations and specifications made to the licensee. In other words, if the software licensor had previously claimed in brochures and/or technical specification sheets that its program will perform X, Y, and Z functions, it should warranty that the software will indeed perform these functions. *All other warranties should either be disclaimed or be very carefully adapted to the nature of the software and licensee's needs.*

One example of a fairly standard *disclaiming warranty* provision found in some software licenses is as follows:

ALL LICENSED SOFTWARE PROVIDED TO LICENSEE HEREUNDER IS PROVIDED "AS IS." LICENSOR MAKES NO WARRANTY, EITHER EXPRESS OR IMPLIED, WITH RESPECT TO THE LICENSED SOFTWARE, ITS QUALITY, MERCHANTABILITY, OR FITNESS FOR A PARTICULAR PURPOSE.

NOTE: *As previously stated, any type of disclaiming statement should be written in capital letters, preferably in boldface, in order to be conspicuous to the reader.*

Software Maintenance and Service Provisions

Software installation, error-correction, and general service and maintenance provisions are also very common when licensing software. Especially for more complex software licenses where the software application is complex or is vital to licensee's organization or business.

With the licensee's normal use of the software, especially over a significant period of time, it will likely encounter bugs, glitches, and other errors. These may often have an effect on the licensee's ability to effectively use the software. Hence, it is important that the licensor promise to correct these as soon as possible.

A standard maintenance provision could be a fairly simple one. Here are two examples:

> Telephone Support. Licensor will provide telephone consultation at Licensor's service location, to assist Licensee in identifying, verifying and resolving problems in the use and operation of Software. Telephone assistance services shall be limited to the Designated Users indicated in Exhibit A, which may be amended from time to time by Licensee upon written notice to Licensor.

> Problem Resolution. Licensor will respond to written problem reports concerning Software submitted by Licensee to Licensor. Upon written notification of a failure of Software to perform correctly, which failure can be reproduced at Licensor facility or via remote access to Licensee's facility, Licensor will use reasonable efforts to correct the failure and to provide Licensee with correcting product, a work-around or other solution to the problem.

However, when licensing more complicated software programs, the parties may desire more precise defining of responsibilities in the event of certain types of errors. One way of doing this is in the form of a chart that spells-out how soon the licensor must acknowledge or provide a plan for correction for specific types of errors (after notification by the licensee), as well as the actual deadline for repair of the error.

The following table shows one possibility for response times for various errors and problems with software.

Severity	Description	Response
Critical	Significant error that renders software unusable; may be major loss of data; no work-around exists.	Initial Response: 2 hours. Must be fixed by next day.
Serious	Error that disables major system functions and/or causes disruption in performance or corruption of data; difficult work-arounds are required.	Initial Response: 6 hours. Must be fixed in 3 business days.
Defect	Error that causes some loss of functionality and/or performance; ability to use program is impaired.	Initial Response: 1 day. Must be fixed in 5 business days.
Slight	Error which has no significant impact; work-around is readily available.	Initial Response: 1 week. Can be fixed in next release.

This is just *one* example of how potential problems and their possible solutions can be addressed. The definitions and the categorization in the above chart is arbitrary (though it is based on some real life license agreements). You will need to define the technical terms, response times, and solutions according to the technical needs of your situation.

Updates and Future Versions

Software is also unique in that updates and new versions of products are often churned out at a fairly rapid pace. It often happens that a new version of a software product will even become available within the term of a license agreement. Given this accelerated standard for software development, the licensee may want to receive the licensor's improvements and updates to the software, either for the original price of the software or for an additional fee. Likewise, the licensor may want to provide updates or revisions as an added incentive to the licensee to enter into a license.

If rights to updates, revisions, or future versions are granted, this needs to be explicitly stated in the license agreement. However, even if updates, revisions, or new versions will not be provided, it is a good idea to state this fact explicitly in the license agreement, so that there will not be any misunderstandings.

NOTE: *If your software product or application is one of several versions, you may want to identify the specific version when defining the* Licensed Property *or* Licensed Software *in your license. That way, it will be clear that what is being provided is that version only.*

Source Code Escrow

Before examining source code escrow, you must understand a distinction relevant to software technology. This is the distinction between *source code* and *object code*. Software is typically licensed as object code. These are the machine-level *instructions* understood by a computer. However, software can also exist as *source code*—a series of instructions written in a programming language (such as BASIC, JAVA, C ++ , and so on) that can be understood by a human user.

In most cases, when software is licensed, the licensee will typically receive its software in object code form, either on a physical media such as a CD or floppy disks, downloaded, or transferred online. Aside from an escrow provision, the delivery of source code becomes important when the licensee is given permission to make modifications or improvements to the software.

A source code escrow agreement is not a license, but an additional agreement that is signed along with a software license. Specifically, it is an agreement to deposit the source code to the licensed software with a third party, the *escrow agent*, who will hold it under strict confidentiality, and release it in the event certain *triggering events* take place. Typical triggering events include: licensor's failure to provide maintenance or error-correction services (as required by the license), breach of other obligations of the software license, licensor's bankruptcy, or licensor's cessation of its licensing business. Like the software *license* itself, the provisions of a software escrow agreement are also negotiated. Hence, triggering events may be drafted to fit the requirements of the parties.

Make sure that all important terms and concepts in your *escrow* agreement are consistent with the definitions in your *software license* agreement. Your escrow agent will be able to supply you with an escrow agreement and answer all questions regarding the escrow process.

Documentation and Technical Information

Finally, much licensed software comes with manuals, documentation, technical drawings and specifications, as well as other written information. As these materials are usually copyrighted as text, they should also be included in and protected by the license.

II | LICENSING TECHNOLOGY: PATENTS AND TRADE SECRETS

In this chapter, we turn to the licensing of technology and other technical information. This involves use of two more types of licenses: the patent and trade secret license. In these types of licenses, the licensor gives the licensee the right to use the licensor's technology to manufacture and sell a product and possibly confidential data to aid in implementing this. Like software licenses, patent and trade secret licenses can vary greatly and need to be written with the specific needs of the licensor and licensee in mind.

As with the chapter on software, the patent information in this chapter deals with a basic licensing scenario. Namely, the patent holder licenses its patent in a royalty-based, *make and sell license*. The licensor is not selling any products to the licensee as part of the patent license. Likewise, the licensee will be manufacturing and selling a licensed product based on the patent, but not making its own patentable improvements to such products.

NOTE: *As a general rule when licensing patents, you should be aware that certain types of actions on the part of the patent holder could be considered* illegal patent misuse *and result in a voidable contract or unenforceable patent. For example, if your patents expire before the end of the license term or if you condition your patent license on purchase of other products, this may be found illegal. Refer to the legal resources in the appendices or consult with a patent attorney for further information.*

Licensing Patents

Technology means any machine, device, material, chemical or biological combination, and/or process that produces a functional and useful result to its user. Technology can vary in complexity from the simple, to the very complicated. A new type of computer is a type of technology, but so is a new or improved garden tool.

New and original technology may be protected by either a *patent* or *trade secret*. Thus, the type of license agreement that applies to your situation will depend on the intellectual property right protecting your technology. If more than one right is involved, this too should be reflected in your license agreement. The parties should also consider whether there is any adjunct technology, know-how, and/or other information that needs to be licensed along with the main technology.

It is impossible to protect a particular invention by both an issued patent and trade secret. If you recall our discussion in Chapter 1, a trade secret is confidential information used in business that gives its owner a competitive advantage over rivals. However, when you patent an invention, the invention will be publicly disclosed in the issued patent. Thus, the issuance of a patent for an invention destroys the confidentiality of a trade secret on the same invention.

Using a Patent Attorney

Further, if you are unsure about whether a technology may be covered by another party's patent as well as your own, you will most likely need the advice of a qualified patent attorney. A patent attorney will review your planned product in light of all relevant patents in your field and make a reasonable legal assessment as to whether you may be infringing. Oftentimes, the attorney will draft an *opinion letter* that analyzes existing patents, your planned activity, and concludes with a judgment as to possible infringement. This is especially important in crowded fields or industries, where many patents cover very similar devices or processes. (For more information on locating the best legal counsel for your needs, see Appendix C.)

Technology License Provisions

Since technology can be protected by either patent or trade secret rights, in drafting (or reviewing) a technology license agreement, you need to be aware of both types of intellectual property.

A patent, as you learned in Chapter 1, is a twenty-year intellectual property protection covering new and original inventions. A patent gives its owner the right to exclude everyone else from using, making, and/or selling the patented device. So when a patent owner licenses its patent, it is permitting the licensee to use these rights in a way that would otherwise have been an infringement.

Therefore, two very critical definitions in your patent license will be:

✪ the licensed property (or, in patent licenses, may also be called the licensed patents); and,

✪ the licensed product—the manufactured product that is based on the intellectual property.

The Licensed Property
A licensor may license any number of its patents. However, regardless of quantity, all patents to be licensed must be listed and described in the agreement. This is preferably done in an attached exhibit or schedule. (See form 4 in Appendix F for an example.) Sometimes it may be helpful, for reference purposes to attach a copy of the actual patents being licensed to the license agreement.

NOTE: *A patent application may also be licensed. If you have submitted a patent application on your invention, but your patent has not yet issued, you can license your invention as a patent pending. The fact that the licensed property is a patent pending must be written in the definition. Keep in mind that if the patent issues, the terms of the license may have to change.*

If a patent owner possesses several patents, he or she may have to decide which patents to license. This is but one example of an intellectual property owner's choice whether to license, as opposed to using or not commercializing its intellectual property. A patent owner must carefully research the strategic choice of licensing some, as opposed to all, of its patents.

If you have a design patent on a manufactured article, this too can be licensed, either separately or in addition to utility patents. A design patent protects the ornamental features of an article of manufacture. Remember that if you are licensing a combination of utility and design patents, the design patents must be indicated as such and described along with all the licensed patents.

NOTE: *Unlike utility patents with a term of twenty years, design patents last for a term of only fourteen years. This earlier expiration of design patents must be taken into consideration if one is licensing a combination of utility and design patents. As we previously pointed out, the term of a patent license cannot exceed the duration of the patents being licensed.*

The Licensed Products

In a technology license, the licensor gives the licensee the right to use patent or trade secret rights in order to manufacture and sell licensed products. (See Chapter 5 for a discussion of licensed products.) The parties have wide latitude in defining and describing the licensed products. These may be a direct reproduction of all the elements in the licensor's patent or trade secret. Alternatively, the licensed product can be based on the licensor's patent, but with the addition of extra features or components.

Example: An inventor owns a patent for a new type of wrench with a uniquely adjustable socket. The inventor wants the invention manufactured and commercialized. He licenses it to ToolCo., a tool manufacturer, to manufacture and sell on the market. The wrench (licensed product) as manufactured by ToolCo., can be based on the inventor's patent, but contain other elements to make the product more marketable.

The license agreement must describe the licensed products. This is preferably done in an attached exhibit or schedule, but with a reference in the body of the license as well. For example, the following would be stated in a definitions section in the beginning of the license:

"Licensed Product" shall mean the products based on the Licensed Patents, and which are described in Exhibit A, attached hereto and incorporated herein.

In the Exhibit A, you would then describe the licensed product in greater detail. (See the patent licenses in Appendix F, for examples of this type of drafting.)

It is important to remember that regardless of how a licensed product is defined, you should make sure it is actually within the scope of the patent at issue. As you may recall from Chapter 1, a patent's scope is determined by the wording of its claims, as well as equivalents of these claims. If the licensed product falls outside this scope, then it is not covered by the patent in question and a license is not needed.

Know-How and Other Technical Information

Any important information, technical or otherwise, related to the licensed technology will sometimes be part of the license. Such information, often referred to as *Know-How*, is typically a trade secret of the licensor. This is technical information that, though not the main technology, will ultimately aid the licensee in implementing or manufacturing the licensed product. Know-how may also be required for the proper understanding and/or use of the main technology. A licensor will often license know-how to increase the economic value of the main technology and along with it, the license royalties.

Example: *In order to manufacture your wrench from the example above, your licensee might want your assistance, especially as to the best manufacturing techniques. Your technical assistance or know-how can and should be made a part of your patent license agreement.*

Any know-how or other technical information must also be described in the license agreement as part of the licensed property. As with patents, this information may be described in a schedule or exhibit attached to the license agreement and may be either defined separately or together with the main technology. In addition, you should have a confidentiality provision in the license, that protects this information from disclosure to anyone other than the licensee.

Technology Protected by Trade Secret

Finally, if you have a technology that is confidential and meets the legal definition of a trade secret, you may license this as well to a user who wants to use the technology. Trade secret licenses are similar in most essential respects to a patent license. In defining licensed property, the trade secret should be described and all technical information supplied under strict confidentiality conditions. Likewise, licensed product is described in the license or an attachment just as in a patent license.

One point that must be reiterated is that in a trade secret license, confidentiality provisions are very critical. Such confidentiality protection legally prevents the licensee from disclosing the trade secret to anyone outside the license. If a trade secret's confidentiality is not properly protected, the trade secret owner can lose all rights to it.

Sublicensing   If you are granting the licensee the right to sublicense the rights granted in your license, you may require additional provisions ensuring that:

- ✪ the licensee grant rights in a *written* license agreement; and,

- ✪ that all protections of the patent or other intellectual property must be included in the sublicensing agreement.

Patent Marking and Notice   According to patent law, any product incorporating a patent must, if commercially feasible, be marked with the patent number. The sample patent license makes reference to this requirement with respect to the licensed product.

Technology Cross-License

The *technology cross-license* is a special license agreement where two parties each license technology from the other. In other words, each party is both licensor and licensee.

Example: Company X needs to use certain patented technology as a component in its own product. Company Y that owns the patented technology Company X needs, itself desires to use technology owned by Company X. A cross-license provides the solution to this dilemma.

Though at first glance this scenario may seem unlikely, cross-licenses are actually quite common within certain industries. This is especially true in crowded fields or industries where there are numerous patents covering a given technology.

Example: EverCell has a patent on a new and improved battery that is used to power video cameras. One day it finds out that consumers are purchasing a battery similar to EverCell's battery, but with the newly added feature of a handle that allows the battery to be more easily inserted and taken out of the camera. This newly improved battery with handle is covered by a patent owned by another company, EasyHandle Co. The sale of the improved battery with a new handle infringes EverCell's patent because the claims in EverCell's patent are broad enough to cover EasyHandle's model.

However, EasyHandle has a patent on its version of the battery with the improved handle. Now, EverCell can sue EasyHandle for selling the new improved battery. But EverCell cannot sell the battery-plus-handle itself because that sale falls within the scope of the patent owned by EasyHandle. The best resolution here is for both parties to license each other's patents in a patent cross-license.

12 Copyright and Trademark Licenses

This chapter turns its attention to licensing copyrights and trademarks in an artistic, business, or merchandising context. These are two separate types of licenses, but are often interrelated. Trademarks tell consumers what the business source of a certain good is. A license of a trademark means the trademark owner is giving someone else permission to place its mark on goods. This entails some critical provisions in the license agreement.

Copyrighted Works

Licensing artistic works protected by copyright is a very complex area, involving a wide variety of license agreements. This is the area of *entertainment law*, a field often broken down into many subfields (many overlapping), including: publishing law, music law, permissions, art law, entertainment merchandising, performance licensing, as well as motion pictures licensing. (Though most of these topics are beyond the scope of the book, a general overview of what is involved in a copyright license is addressed.)

Copyright protects a wide variety of artistic works. Common copyrighted artistic works include the following:

✪ Written Works:

- books—both fiction and nonfiction

- magazine and journal articles

- short text, such as poems

- text posted on the web (online text)

✪ visual works:

- photographs

- designs

- cartoons

- fine art

- website pictures and graphics

✪ musical works:

- songs (with lyrics)

- instrumental musical works

- advertising jingles

- music samples

- sound recordings

✪ motion pictures and audiovisual works:

- film and movies

- video clips

Entertainment and artistic licenses vary tremendously, depending on the rights involved, their use, whether there is a performance, reproduction, or distribution of the work, as well as the type of user. In addition, each industry (music, painting, publishing, motion pictures, etc.) has a set of unique requirements, standards, and institutions. For instance, a music license to a record company to record a song is very different from a publishing agreement for a book or from a photography license. Even within an industry, licenses can differ greatly. Hence, a license to a music publisher to publish a song on sheet music is different from a license to record it on a CD. However, that being said, there are some commonalities for certain types of artistic licenses.

If you want to commercialize an artistic work or want to use someone else's copyrighted work, first review Chapters 13 and 14. If you are the potential user of someone else's artistic and copyrighted work, you do not always need a full-scale license. Depending on your type of use, you may only need permission from the copyright owner rather than a license agreement. Certain types of uses are permitted under the copyright *Fair Use Doctrine* that allows the use of the copyrighted work without any type of permission or license from the copyright owner.

Trademark Licenses

As you may recall from Chapter 1, a trademark is a word, logo, or other symbol that functions to indicate to consumers the business source of goods or services. There are other types of marks such as *service marks* and *trade names* that are included under our discussion of trademark.

Types of Trademark Licenses

The more common types of trademark licensing are the following.

- *Standard Trademark License*—a party licenses a trademark to another licensee to sell products under the trademark.

- *Business Franchising*—an established company like McDonald's licenses its name and other business information to a franchise.

- *Merchandising*—these are the placement of a trademark or a copyrighted picture or design on merchandise.

Popular, easy-to-recognize trademarks are extremely valuable to their business owners. For this reason, trademark licensors are generally active in enforcing their rights and making sure there is no infringement of their trademark. And also for this reason, you must be careful in following all the rules for trademark licensing, whether you are licensor or licensee

Trademark-Specific Provisions

When licensing a patent, copyright, or trade secret, many provisions are recommended for an effective and relatively problem-free license, but are not required by law. Trademark licenses, however, are unique. There are several key provisions that must be included with any trademark license. If the trademark owner does not include these, it could lose all rights to its trademark. They include:

- ✪ quality control of the licensed products;

- ✪ future *good will*;

- ✪ strict definition of *licensed product*; and,

- ✪ other trademark protections.

Quality Control of Licensed Products

Quality control or *quality standards* are a very important set of provisions that must be present in all licenses involving trademark rights. When a trademark owner licenses its trademark, it must allow itself to retain control over the quality of the products (that is, the licensed products) that will be marketed under the trademark. Furthermore, it is not enough to simply write such terms into the license. The trademark owner must actively exercise its right to control the quality of the products. It must inspect product samples and licensee facilities and generally take an active role in ensuring that the quality of the licensed product meets with licensor's overall standards.

The following is a sample quality control provision in a trademark license agreement. Though details may vary, this provision should put forth a general rule that licensee's products must conform to licensor's standards, provide for licensor's inspection and testing of product samples, and allow for licensor's inspection of licensee's production facilities.

QUALITY CONTROL PROVISION

Conformity to Quality Standards. Licensee shall apply the Licensed Trademark only to Products which have been manufactured by Licensee in accordance with Licensor's Quality Standards in materials, workmanship, design advertising, etc.

Product Samples. Licensee agrees to furnish to Licensor samples of the manufactured Products bearing the Licensed Trademark, as Licensor may request from time to time. Licensor shall inspect Products and test conformity of the Products with Licensor's Quality Standards.

Right to Inspect. Licensor shall have the right at any time during regular business hours to inspect all Products manufactured by Licensee at Licensee's facilities, in order to determine compliance of such Products with Licensor's Quality Standards. If at any time such Products shall, in Licensor's sole opinion, fail to conform with Licensor's Quality Standards, Licensor shall notify Licensee of such nonconformance. Licensee shall then cease all manufacture and sale of the nonconforming Products until further notice by Licensor.

The details of the quality control provisions will vary depending on the complexity of the license, the commercial value of the trademarks, as well as the business requirements of the parties. The licensor should also have a confidentiality provision that obligates licensee to protect the confidentiality of licensor's quality standards provided in the license.

Future Good Will

Simply put, *good will* is the tendency, formed over time, of consumers to associate a trademark with the positive qualities of the product such trademark represents. Good will is what essentially makes trademarks valuable.

If a trademark is licensed, it means a party other than the trademark owner will be selling products to consumers under the trademark. If such sales are very successful and if the license persists over a significant period of time, the trademark's good will may increase (sometimes greatly) under the licensee's sale of the products. This may be dangerous for the licensor, since the licensee may potentially claim that this additional good will is due to its own sales and marketing efforts. Therefore, a trademark license should have a provision stating that any newly acquired good will, value, or rights in the trademark will be for the benefit of the licensor only.

The following is one example of this type of provision:

> Any and all rights that may be acquired by the use of the Licensed Trademark by Licensee, including without limitation any good will in the Licensed Trademark acquired by Licensee, shall inure to the sole benefit of Licensor.

Strict Definition of Licensed Product

As with technology, and some data and software licenses, a trademark license will have a *licensed property* and a licensed product defined in the agreement. The licensed property, also called the *licensed trademark*, will identify the trademark, state whether it is federally or state registered, and provide a registration number if registered. The licensed products will be the products as manufactured and/or sold by the licensee, each of which bears the licensed trademark.

It is important in a trademark license to strictly define the licensed product as opposed to giving a general definition. Because trademarks are so connected to the qualities of their goods or services, the trademark licensor must ensure that only definite classes of products are associated with the mark.

Further Protection of Trademark

In addition to these provisions, trademark licenses often contain further protections of the licensed trademark. This often consists of prohibiting the licensee from using or registering similar trademarks to the licensed one. The following is one example of this type of provision:

> Licensee further agrees not to register any name or mark resembling or confusingly similar to the Licensed Trademark, in the U.S. or in any foreign country.

Merchandising Licenses

Though merchandising may involve copyrights as well as trademarks, or both, the essential provisions of a merchandising license will be similar to the quality control provisions found in trademark licenses.

Merchandising is the licensing of a copyright and/or trademark on physical goods. Among the goods and products are:

- ✪ clothing;

- ✪ posters, postcards, and stationery;

- ✪ dolls and action figures;

- ✪ toys and games;

- ✪ sports equipment; and,

- ✪ luggage and bags.

If you are the licensor entering into a merchandising relationship, you are giving permission to someone to place your trademark on the goods being produced. Some examples of merchandising relationships include the following.

- ✪ *Character/Entertainment.* This is a very popular type of licensing, involving television and movie characters, including cartoon characters for kids. Dominant companies in this industry include: Disney, Warner Brothers, Nickelodeon, and other movie studios and broadcast companies.

- ✪ *Brand Name Licensing.* Any company, school, or institution that has a popular name or trademarked logo may license this on a variety of merchandise.

- ✪ *Sports Licensing.* Sports brand names, logos, and characters can be licensed for placement on a variety of merchandise.

Many of the specific provisions necessary in merchandising licenses parallel those required for trademark licenses. The licensed product in merchandising license is the actual good upon which the copyrighted design, trademark, logo, etc. is placed.

Merchandising licenses are a unique and often complex area, combining elements of copyright and trademark licenses. As with trademark licensing, the practice of merchandising requires strict quality control. For example, the licensor will want to adopt certain quality standards for the licensed products produced by the licensee. Licensor must actively inspect sample products that the licensee manufactures and approve or disapprove of these samples based on the quality standards. (See Appendix B for more information about merchandising licenses.)

13 | PERMISSIONS

In this chapter, we turn to the subject of legal *permission*. Permission, in the legal sense, is similar to a license in that both involve getting authorization from an intellectual property owner for use of a copyrighted work or a trademark. However, permission is obtained for either one-time, simpler, or more limited uses of intellectual property. Typically, permission is sought for the reproduction, display, distribution, and sometimes transformation, of only a portion of a copyrighted work such as a book, or the use of a photograph, or mention of a trademark in a limited context. Permission agreements also do not typically entail royalty clauses, although a one-time fee to obtain permission is common.

Therefore, obtaining permission is typically much easier than writing and negotiating a license agreement. And while locating the proper intellectual property owner to get permission may sometimes be a painstaking endeavor, the actual *permission form* itself is relatively fast and uncomplicated. Obtaining permission to use that favorite photograph or poem in your own work can be a great way to increase the value of your new work and provide a means to get the word out about one's work.

Permission vs. License

Anytime you want to use a copyrighted work or a trademark in a way that would ordinarily be prohibited by intellectual property law, you will need *permission* from the copyright or trademark owner. If you want to reproduce, distribute, or display the copyrighted work or trademark, especially publicly, you most likely will need to obtain permission from the intellectual property owner.

Getting permission is similar in theory to entering into a *license*. However, permission is usually much faster and easier than signing a full-length license agreement. Most often, a permissions agreement is a one-page or even a half-page form. Obtaining permission may or may not cost you anything.

You could obtain permission for use of any artistic (copyrighted) work such as a book, article, song, video, picture, and so on, as well as for a trademark. The use could be for business, artistic, educational, or advertising purposes. And the type of use can itself vary. The following are *just some* of the situations where permission *may* be necessary, depending other factors.

- ✪ An author is writing a book and wants to use excerpts from another author's book or magazine article.

- ✪ A website for movie trivia wants to show a photo of various Hollywood stars.

- ✪ A dancer wants to use a popular song for a dance number she is performing on stage for the public.

- ✪ A company wants to distribute photocopies of a published business article to the company employees.

- ✪ A website that gives financial advice wants to post an article from the *New York Times* on the site.

Permissions are not for *patents* or for *trade secrets*. This is because the nature of these rights are such that full-length license agreements are typically needed, as opposed to a short permission form. In fact, even for *trademarks*, most uses will also require license agreements.

Works Covered by Copyright

Your first task in any permission inquiry will be to determine whether or not you need to seek permission for the work that you want to use. Knowing when you need permission is an important. If you can determine that you do not need permission to use a work, you will not need to go through the steps for obtaining permission.

The permission discussed is limited to U.S. law only. There is no such thing, for example, as an international copyright or trademark. Protection against unauthorized use in a particular country will depend on the national laws of the particular country you are examining. Thus even if you determine that you do not need to seek permission to use a particular work in the U.S., this does not mean that you also do not need permission to use the work abroad and vice versa.

To determine whether you need permission to use a work that might be the subject of copyright protection, you need to consider two factors:

1. *Is the artistic work in the public domain?*

2. *Even if the work is copyrighted, is your use "fair use"?*

Artistic Work and Public Domain

Assume that you want to use some work that could be protected by copyright such as an artistic work, a photograph, written article or excerpt, a song, painting, or some other work. You have identified the work you want. You must then determine if the work is covered by copyright or is the work in the *public domain*. A work can enter the public domain a number of ways.

✪ The copyright on the work has expired.

✪ The work could have been copyrighted, but requirements necessary to attach copyright were not completed.

✪ The work was created by a U.S. government official or employee as part of his or her official duties. This is a helpful exception to copyright protected. You do not need to seek permission to copy works prepared by U.S. government officials. (This means that we are safe here to go into the website at the Copyright Office and reproduce any one of their forms for you, here in this book.)

Subject to copyright. Permission is sought only for works that are still subject to copyright protection. This means that if the term of a copyright on a work has expired (i.e., the work is in the public domain), you are free to use that work without seeking permission from the owner of the copyright. Determining whether the copyright on a given work has expired is a task which is more difficult then it might initially sound, particularly when you are dealing with works created after 1978.

There are a set of rather complex rules with respect to how long a copyright term lasts depending on the whether the work was created *before* or *after* January 1, 1978. In addition, if you are dealing with works that were created prior to January 1, 1978, you will need to consider additional rules as to whether the work was ever published and also whether renewals of the copyright were ever sought in order to keep the copyright in force. Works created after January 1, 1978 are not subject to these additional rules because a copyright exists the moment the work is fixed in some tangible medium, and procedures like publication and renewals are not necessary.

To understand these difficult rules, examine the following chart that outlines the copyright rules with respect to the *magical* date of January 1, 1978. In the first row, you will see the rules for a work created in 1978 or later. You can see that the rules are relatively simple. The copyright term for works created after January 1, 1978 starts from the moment the work is created. But after this first row, you deal with works that are either created or published before the January 1, 1978 date.

You need to concern yourself not only with whether or not the work was published, but also with whether or not the copyright holder extended the life of the initial copyright term by properly seeking a renewal of any copyright registration. You may also notice, with respect to some of these older works, that registration of the copyright or publication with copyright notice is a necessary prerequisite even for a copyright to attach to the work in the first place.

Date of Work	Beginning of Copyright	Initial Term	Renewal Needed?
Created in 1978 or later	As soon as work is fixed in some tangible medium	Life of author (or last surviving author) + 70 years. If work is anonymous, pseudonymous, or work for hire, 95 years from publication or 120 years from creation, whichever is longer	No renewal necessary
Created, but not published, before 1978	January 1, 1978	Life of the author + 70 years or December 31, 2002, whichever is greater	No renewal necessary
Created before 1978, published between then and December 31, 1977	January 1, 1978	Life of the author +70 years or December 31, 2002, whichever is greater	No renewal necessary
Published between January 1, 1964 and December 31, 1977	As soon as work is published with copyright notice	Initial term of 28 years, another term of 67 years automatically starts at the end of the initial term (95 years total)	Automatic renewal by operation of law
Published between 1923 and 1963	As soon as work is published with copyright notice	Initial term of 28 years, another term of 67 years if copyright renewed (95 years total possible)	Renewal registration needed for additional 67 years
Published before 1923	These works are in the public domain		

Locate publication date. One of the easiest places to look for the date of publication, registration, or creation is on the work that you want to use. Most written works will have a copyright notice stating the date of publication, author, and publisher. If the work is a sound recording, examine the disk or cassette in which the recording is fixed or the cover in which the recording is sold.

For further investigation, you can search the records at the United States Copyright Office to see whether or not the work has been registered. Registrations made after January 1, 1978 can now be searched on the internet by going to the Copyright Office web site at **www.copyright.gov** and selecting *search copyright records.*

For works registered prior to that date, you will need to look at the Copyright Card Catalog at the Copyright Office in Washington D.C. You should also be able to find the catalog at various libraries.

For an even more detailed investigation, you can pay the Copyright Office to make this search for you. The fee was $75 per hour at the time this book was published. Check the Copyright Office website at:

www.copyright.gov

Copyrighted Work and Fair Use

Even if the artistic work you want to use is protected by copyright, you may still be able to use it without permission if your use falls under the *Fair Use Doctrine.* Courts have concluded that if your use is a *fair use*, then you do not need to obtain permission from the copyright owner.

The Copyright Act contains a list of purposes for which reproduction of a particular work may be considered *fair.* This includes criticism, comment, news reporting, teaching, scholarship, and research. The Act also sets out four factors to be used in determining whether or not a particular use is fair. Specifically, the following factors are considered:

Commercial vs. Noncommercial. Noncommercial uses are more likely to be considered fair use than commercial ones. Generally, two types of noncommercial uses nearly always found to be fair use are:

✪ *commentary and research.* For example, using excerpts from a copyrighted novel in a college essay or a newspaper review will likely be fair use and

✪ *parody.*

NOTE: *If the use is found to be commercial, the burden of proof as to market effect will be on the alleged infringer. On the other hand, if the use is found to be non-commercial, the burden of proof as to market proof will be on the copyright holder.*

Nature or type of work. This factor has to do with the amount of creativity of the work which is being copied. For example, something which is a highly creative work such as a poem will cut against a finding of fair use, whereas something which is not very creative such as a telephone book listing will weigh in favor of a finding of fair use.

Amount used. In general, the larger the volume (or the greater the importance) of what is copied, the less likely that the copying will be considered fair use. The larger the amount of material copied from an artist is considered a greater affront to the interests of the copyright owner.

Effect on the market. In 1985, the Supreme Court said that this fourth factor is the most important of all the factors that one looks at to determine whether or not there is fair use. Although more recent cases may suggest that the Supreme Court has abandoned its view that this is the most important factor, it remains a factor of considerable significance.

Where the use is intended for commercial gain, some meaningful likelihood of future harm is presumed. One test used for determining market harm is whether or not the use, should it become widespread, would adversely affect the potential market for the copyright work.

This was a key factor in recent decisions that held that copy shops do not have the right to copy selected works for professors and accumulate those selected works into course packs without seeking permission from each and every one of the copyright holders of the individual works. In arriving at its decision, the court noted that if copy shops across the country were to be allowed to make such copies without obtaining permission and paying the necessary fees, the potential value of the copyright works of scholarship published by the publishing houses would be diminished significantly.

The inquiry for market harm considers not only harm to the market of the original copyright work, but also harm to the market for derivative works. *Derivative works* are things like translations, abridgments, or any other type of work which recasts, transforms or adapts the original work. The *right to prepare derivative works* is an exclusive right which belongs to the copyright holder. This can be a somewhat difficult concept to understand and is probably why many people are under the false notion that if you simply transform a work into some other medium that this does not constitute infringement. This is simply not true.

Example: Tom, a renowned photographer, was hired by his good friend to take a photograph of his friend holding several puppies. Tom spent considerable time doing what he does best by adjusting the light and the position of his friends and puppies. After giving his friend 200 prints, Tom started to market prints of the photograph to galleries and the like with quite a bit of success.

Unknown to Tom, Harry, a rather famous sculptor in his own right, discovered the a print of the photograph and liked it so much that he decided he would attempt a 3-dimensional sculpture using the 2-dimensional photo as his guide.

The sculpture was such a success that Harry hired several associates to create even more sculptures. Harry was able to sell a few of these sculptures for a very handsome price.

Unfortunately for Harry, Tom later discovered one of Harry's sculptures depicted on the cover of an art magazine. A court found Harry liable for copyright infringement because the ordinary lay observer would recognize the sculptures produced by Harry haven been copied from Tom's copyrighted photo.

Works Covered by Trademark

Words, names, symbols, and logos are prime categories for protection as trademarks. If you go ahead and use a trademark without obtaining permission from the trademark owner, you could find yourself in a trademark infringement lawsuit down the road.

The U.S. is unique in comparison to the rest of the word in that it does not require that trademarks be registered with any governmental agency in order to constitute a trademark, although there are various advantages to registering your trademark in the U.S. Instead, U.S. trademark law allows for the acquisition of trademark rights through use of the trademark alone.

However, your job of determining whether a word, name, symbol, or logo that you want to use is the subject another person's trademark becomes more difficult. You need to be concerned not only with trademarks that are registered as such with the United States Patent and Trademark Office (USPTO), but also with trademarks that are not registered and have acquired trademark status through their use by the owner of the mark.

Despite all of this, the USPTO is still a very good place to start for determining whether or not the work you want to use is a trademark. You can, in fact, do a trademark search yourself by visiting the website of the USPTO at **www.uspto.gov** and then clicking on the "trademarks" icon at the home page.

If you determine that the work you want to use is not registered as a U.S. trademark, you should also inquire whether anyone is using the work as a trademark, nonetheless. You could make such an inquiry, for example, by searching for the mark on the Internet and looking to see whether any person is using the work as a designation of his or her services or origin of products. If you find that someone is using the mark as such, reconsider your use of the mark.

14 | OBTAINING PERMISSIONS

Assume that you have found out that using a specific artistic work or trademark *does* require permission. You may be considering at this point whether it is worth using the artistic work at all. Remember that you can always change your mind about whether to use the work at any time while you are obtaining permission. Sometimes, you may find that permission for using an artistic work is too difficult to secure or will simply cost too much. These are part of the business decisions you need to consider when you deal with intellectual property.

If, however, you have decided to proceed with obtaining permission, you need to follow specific steps. These will be examined in greater detail in the sections that follow. The three basic steps are:

1. find out who owns the copyrighted work or trademark;

2. find out any procedures that the copyright or trademark owner has for obtaining permission; and,

3. request permission to use the copyrighted work or trademark using a written *permission form* or agreement.

When locating the owner of a copyrighted work, keep in mind that the owner may not be (and most often is not) the *author* according to copyright law. The distinction between *copyright owner* and the author is the following:

✪ *Author*—this is the person who actually created the work that you want to use.

✪ *Owner*—the persons or company who has legal title to the copyright. This person is very often not the actual author of the work, since copyrights are often transferred by the author to a company (such as a publisher or magazine).

The remainder of this chapter, focuses on the process of obtaining permission for different types of copyrighted works. The following artistic works are covered:

✪ written works;

✪ photographs, graphic arts and artwork;

✪ musical works;

✪ film and video; and,

✪ performances and speeches.

Sometimes the work you want to use will not fit neatly into just one category. This is particularly true in the case of *multi-media* type works and online works. A *multi-media work* is a work, often instructional, which combines authorship in two or more media. The authorship may include text, artwork, sculpture, photography, sounds or music, and other types of media.

For works transmitted online, for example, the copyrighted authorship may consist of text, artwork, and music. You will need to be concerned with the copyright to each category.

Written Works

There are many types of written works, also known as *literary works*. These include: books (both fiction and nonfiction), magazine articles, pamphlets, and online text. Often, what you seek to use is not the entire written work, but rather small portions or excerpts from the written work. If the work from which you want to use these excepts is not yet in the public domain (as outlined at the beginning of the previous chapter), you will need to obtain permission from the copyright holder.

The following three categories are some of the most frequently used written works for which permission is sought:

- ✪ books;

- ✪ works used for educators and librarians; and,

- ✪ magazines and other periodicals.

Books   Your first step in obtaining permission to use an excerpt from a book will be to find out who owns the copyrighted work that you want to use. Your best place to start to find out the owner of the copyright is with the book itself.

A copyright notice is the familiar © symbol followed by the year of first publication and the name of the copyright author. You will also see additional years, if the book has been republished.

The name and address of the publisher should also appear very close to the copyright notice. The address of the publisher to whom you should send your request for permission will also typically be included near the copyright notice or publisher's name. If the written work does not include a means of contact for the publisher, most publishers maintain a website. Simply use one of the many various search engines like **www.google.com** to search for the website using the name of the publisher.

If the book does not contain the name of the publisher or the work simply has not been published, then you will need to approach the author of the work. There are a variety of ways that you can find the author of the work.

The most obvious and easiest way to locate the author of the work is to again look right on the work itself. Even if a book has not been published, most authors will include a copyright notice with their name. Sometimes you may also be able to find additional contact information right on the work itself such as the email, address or telephone number of the author. If you can not find this contact information, you will need to consult other references such as search engines and the like. One very useful resource is the *Author's Registry* that you can find online at:

www.authorsregistry.org

The *Author's Registry* maintains an extensive directory of authors with contact addresses, phone numbers, fax numbers, and email addresses. You do not actually complete the search yourself in this case, but rather email your request to the contact person listed at the Author's Registry. The registry will then get back to you with their search results with 24 hours. Searches for up to two author names is provided free of charge by the registry.

If you can not identify the name of the author on the work itself, then you may still not be out of luck. If the work has been published, the first place to check is with the *Library of Congress*. It can be found online at **www.lcWeb.loc.gov**. As of March 1, 1989, all works that are published in the United States are required by law to be deposited with the Library of Congress.

The Library of Congress will not provide contact information for the author. So you will need to take the name you have found and consult other references to locate this contact information such as the Author's Registry.

Publisher's procedures. Your next step to obtaining permission to use an excerpt from a book or magazine should be to determine whether the copyright owner already has any procedures in place for obtaining permission.

Most publishers will have permission departments whose task it is to evaluate and decide whether to grant permission. To save time, you are advised to consult the website of the Publisher to see whether or not they have an established permission process.

Written permission form. Your last step for obtaining permission to use the written work will be to complete a written permission form. Many of publishers will request that you use their own standard form. If, however, the publisher does not provide a form (or you are dealing with an individual artist), a general permission form is included at the end of this chapter. This sample request form also has an explanation of the major provisions of a permission request. Even if you use a form provided by the publisher, review the explanation of the sample form so that you will understand the form the publisher provides.

NOTE: *It will typically take several weeks before a Permissions Department has responded to your request. So you should send out your permission request well ahead of the date that need it. If your permission is denied, planning ahead will also allow you time to find a substitute for the work that you want to include in your own work.*

Works Used by Educators and Librarians

As you may recall from the previous chapter, whether or not a use is for commercial or non-commercial purposes weighs in on whether or not such a use could be considered a fair use. One of the largest noncommercial entities are educational institutions and libraries. As you might expect, the issue as to whether or not fair use protects such institutions from copying works has been a considerable topic of controversy.

One of the past, most hotly debated issues in this setting is whether or not instructors could take selected works and accumulate those selected work into one compilation (often referred to as an *anthology*) without having to obtain permission from each individual copyright holder of the works from which the selected readings were obtained.

This is still a common practice today. Professors and other academic instructors will commonly have copy shops order the selected readings and then copy the readings into what is referred to as a *course pack*. This process saves the student from having to read each one of the complete works in total. It also saves the students the considerable expense of having to buy multiple books just to read certain passages.

For a while, there was some uncertainty as to whether the copy shops who were putting these course packs together for the professors needed to obtain and pay for permission from the publishing houses that held the copyrights on the works. Several cases put an end to this uncertainty, however, and held that permission must absolutely be sought from the copyright holders of the works from which the selected readings are obtained.

If you want to obtain permission from the copyright holder of a selected reading from a copyrighted work for use in a course pack or the like, there are copyright clearance centers that will obtain the permission that you need for each work and then charge you a reasonable fee for the permission. The most well known clearance center is the Copyright Clearance Center (CCC). The website for the CCC can be found at **www.copyright.com**.

The Copyright Clearance Center (CCC) is a not-for-profit organization that provides owners of copyright materials, who have registered their works, royalties in exchange for the right to grant permission for the use of such works. The CCC is an excellent way that owners of copyrights can increase their revenue stream and provide the permission seeker with an easy way to go about obtaining permission from copyright holders represented by the CCC. In addition to the increase in revenues that you can gain when copy shops want to use your work as part of a course pack, you can gain potential revenue from corporations and law firms who want to photocopy materials for in-house use.

In addition to course packs, another common situation that arises in the educational setting is where teachers and the like make copies themselves of some selected portion of a literary work and then distribute these copies to their students in the classroom. This situation is different from the course pack situation because the teacher is not making any compilation or anthology, but is rather simply distributing portions of a selected work to students during the course. In this instance, there is considerable more leeway. Although not enacted into law, there are some guidelines that have been found to be quite persuasive in court to help you with this situation. These guidelines are known as the *Agreement on Guidelines for Classroom Copying in Not-For-Profit Educational Institutions with Respect to Books and Periodicals*. In short, these guidelines allow multiple copies for classroom use provided that the following conditions are met:

✪   copying meets the test of *brevity* (1,000 words or less);

✪   copying meets the test of *spontaneity*, under which the decision to use the work and the moment of its use for maximum teaching effectiveness is so close in time that it would be unreasonable to expect a timely reply to a request for permission;

✪   no more than nine instances of multiple copying take place during the term and only a limited number of copies are made from the works of any one author or from any collective work;

✪   each copy contains a notice of copyright;

✪   copying does not substitute for the purchase of books, publishers' reprints, or periodicals; and,

✪   the student is not charged any more than the actual cost of copying.

(For more information about these educational guidelines, consult *Circular 21* at the Copyright Office website. This circular also contains a lot of information about what is permissible in the library setting. If you work in the library setting and want to learn more about what is permissible from a copyright standpoint, consult that circular.)

Magazine and
other Periodical
Works

The steps for obtaining permission to magazine and other periodical articles are very similar to obtaining permission for the other types of written works. However, there are a few features that may be different.

Many articles that are written for newspapers, magazines, and the like are written by staff employees. In such instances, the newspaper or magazine periodical will own the copyright to the article as a *work-for-hire*. You will need to contact the magazine or newspaper directly to obtain permission to use the work.

In addition to regular staff, most periodicals also use *freelancers* to write articles. In such instances, the rules as to who you should seek permission from become more complex. You will need to determine from the periodical the type of rights in the copyright the freelancer is under with respect to the work that you want to use. Sometimes freelancers will only grant one-time rights to print the article, but retain the any *reprint rights* in the article. In such instances, you will need to approach the freelancer directly in order to obtain permission to use the article.

Freelance writers for newspaper columns also commonly submit their articles through *syndicates* that you can contact with respect to your desired use. A listing of the major syndicates in the U.S. can also be found at the website of the National Cartoonists Society at:

www.reuben.org/syndicate.asp

Photographs, Graphic Art, and Artwork

The Copyright Office sometimes refers to this category as *works of the visual arts* and *pictorial, graphic, or sculptural works*. Included in this category are the following:

- ✪ advertisements, commercial prints, labels;

- ✪ works of fine art;

- ✪ prints and art reproductions;

- ✪ maps and globes;

- ✪ photographs;

- ✪ posters; and,

- ✪ architectural and other technical drawings.

In the electronic age, many people like to scan or download photographs and then alter them using some computer package. In the alternative, you may want to recreate the copyright photo in some other medium. As discussed in the previous chapter with respect to recreating a photo into a sculpture, such activities constitute copyright infringement. This is true even if it takes you months to recreate the work.

Example: You look at a digital photo and use one of the various software packages out there to recreate the photograph. You spend one week, full time meticulously tracing the photo with your software package using different stunning colored inks and lines and come up with a recreation that looks remarkably similar to the photo, but is much more bright and stunning. Your recreation of the photo is copyright infringement if the photo is subject to copyright.

Another important thing to remember when using photographs, pictures, or artwork of any individual person or persons, you must also take into account rights of *publicity* and *privacy rights* of such persons. This is in addition to obtaining rights to the copyrighted photograph or other artwork. This means that you must either:

- ✪ get a warranty from the copyright owner that publicity and/or privacy rights have been obtained or

- ✪ secure these rights yourself.

If you need to secure publicity and/or privacy rights by yourself, the safest approach in such a circumstances is to obtain a *release* from the subject of the photograph. (The subject of publicity, privacy, and defamation is generally beyond the scope of this book.)

Some common types of visual works that this section will explain include:

- ✪ photographs;

- ✪ paintings and other works of fine art;

- ✪ on-line stock image banks/royalty-free art; and,

- ✪ cartoons and comic strips.

Photographs Just as with writings like books, the copyright to photographs may have been assigned to the publisher. In such a case, you will need to approach the publisher to obtain permission. Copyrights to photographs, however, are often held by the photographer or a photographic agency. If the photographer has not assigned the copyright, you will need to approach the individual photographer or agency.

You should approach locating the copyright holder much as you would approach locating the holder of a copyright for written works like books and periodicals. There are a number of references out there which can help you to locate the contact information for photographers. For example, the American Society of Media Photographers offers a way to search for photographers by last name. Their website is located at **www.asmp.org**.

Photographers who are looking to find ways to increase their revenue stream through the licensing of their photographs find that agencies in the business of representing such artists' photographs to the public are a practical and efficient way to license their works.

Paintings and Other Works of Fine Art

Someone who owns a painting or some other work of art does not necessarily own the copyright to the art. Just as in the case where a publisher does not own a copyright, where there is a lack of an assignment or a work-for-hire, a museum or other person who has not taken an assignment in a piece of artwork, does not own the copyright in that artwork. This is true even though the museum has bought and owns the painting itself.

A typical situation in the case of artwork is when what you want to use is a photograph of the artwork. In such a case, you need to be concerned not only with copyright to the original artwork (i.e., painting) itself, but also with the owner of the copyright to the photograph. Thus, in such a situation, you may actually need to obtain two sets of permissions—one from the owner of the original painting and another from the owner of the representation of that painting. Even if the original art work is in the public domain, you may still need to obtain permission from the owner of the copyright of the photograph.

Online Stock Image Banks/ Royalty-Free Art

There are a wide range of companies who maintain banks/databases online where you can find the perfect photograph, logo, artwork or other graphical representation. For photographs, one useful site is the Media Image Resource Alliance (MIRA). This site allows you to enter search terms to locate photographs of your liking. The website for MIRA is found at: **www.mira.com**. Once you have decided on the photograph that you want, you can purchase it and have it delivered by various means such as email, CD-ROM or FTP-delivery. The cost is between $15 to $25 per photograph. Your use of the photograph is subject to certain restrictions. For example, you are required to maintain a copyright notice near the photograph and most alterations are not allowed.

If you do a search on the Internet for *royalty-free* photographs or art, you can also locate hundreds of companies who will provide you with access to a bank containing thousands of photographs and graphical art such as logos and the like. To obtain access to the bank, you are sometimes required to pay a fee. However, many of these databases are entirely free. Such sites are often used by website designers and the like who need to find a logo or picture for use on their website. You can find some samples of these banks in Appendix D at the back of this book under *Graphics/Art*.

Another way to obtain access to royalty-free banks having thousands of photographs and other pictorial representations is through companies that sell CD-ROMS that contain such banks. Prices vary depending on the company and the number of pictures that you will have access to. On average you should expect to pay about $50 for a CD-ROM containing hundreds of thousands of such photographs and art.

Obtaining permission to use the photographs/art that come from royalty-free banks that you can find on the Internet and through purchase at your computer store involves reviewing the agreement which comes with your purchase. These agreements are frequently referred to as *shrink-wrap* agreements. If you are obtaining the art off the web, then such a shrink-wrap agreement will typically come just before you click on the *I Agree* button that signifies you accept the terms and conditions of the license agreement. If you are purchasing the art on CD-ROM, then the agreement will often come with your CD-ROM or it will be part of the installation process that requires you to agree to the terms and conditions of the license agreement before installation can continue.

Make sure that your intended use is in fact authorized under the terms of the agreement. These agreement are, in effect, your permission form. The downside of this is that you have to use the material according to the terms of the provider. If how you intend to use the copyrighted work extends beyond the *scope* allowed by the shrink-wrap agreement, then you will need to obtain permission for your intended use that extends beyond what you have been granted under the terms of the agreement.

Cartoons and Comic Strips

Cartoons and comic strips may be protected as copyrights with respect to the drawing, picture, or written description of the cartoon or comic strip character. The character may also be protected by a trademark.

Most of the big entertainment characters are licensed by syndicates. You should be able to find the name of the syndicate right next to the copyright or trademark notice near the character. A listing of the major syndicates in the U.S. can also be found at the website of the National Cartoonists Society at **www.reuben.org/syndicate.asp**.

Musical Works

Included within the definition of *musical works* is musical compositions and sound recordings. A *musical composition* refers to the underlying words to a song, as well as the music to that song. A *sound recording* refers to the fixation of a series of musical, spoken, or other sounds, but not including the sounds accompanying a motion picture or other audiovisual work.

The original copyright owner of the music composition has the right to make the first sound recording. Others are permitted to make subsequent sound recordings provided that they compensate the original owner of the composition under a set of compulsory licensing provisions that are beyond the scope of this book.

Sound recordings fixed before February 15, 1972 are not protected by federal copyright law. However, the selection and ordering of pre-existing sound recordings into a compilation work may be protected.

Example: If DJ's Record Company chooses the greatest hits of big bands recorded in the 1950s and orders them onto a disk, that compilation may be registered as a compilation, even though the individual recordings themselves are not protected by copyright because they were fixed before February 15, 1972.

Here are just a few additional examples of where you might get into problems with copyrights in musical works.

✪ You purchase a new CD and make an MP3 copy of it. The license agreement that came with your CD permits you to do this. You then place your MP3 copy onto the Internet to share with the public. You are now infringing upon the copyright holder's *right to distribute*.

✪ You download a copy of a copyrighted song using a file sharing network that is not authorized to copy or distribute the song. You have violated the *right to reproduce*. You burn copies of the song onto a writable CD that you then distribute to your friends. You have violated not only the *right to reproduce*, but also the *right to distribute*.

✪ You are fascinated by the one sound on a website and want to use that sound as a special effect when people hover their browser over your website button. You will need authorization from the copyright holder of that sound to use it on your own website. Copying it without some type of permission will violate the *right of reproduction*. In addition, when you place the sound on your website for others to hear, you will then be violating the *right to distribution*.

Sound Recordings

In respect to sound recordings, you need to be concerned with two separate copyrights as a permission seeker. The first copyright is the one to the actual underlying words and music (*musical composition*) to the recording. The second copyright is for the recording itself.

Example: Tom wants to pay a small fee to members of a local band to record several of his favorite U2 songs. Since Tom is not copying a recording disk to do this, he does not need permission from the record company who made the sound recording to the songs. But Tom still needs permission from the copyright holder to the underlying words and music (typically the music publisher) to legally record these songs.

Just as with printed works, authors who create the underlying music and songs that have been recorded have typically transferred or assigned their copyright to *music publishers*. In such instances, your best starting place is to contact the music publisher in order to obtain permission to use such works. The means that you can use to locate such publishers is similar to that for written works.

Your best starting place to locate the copyright owner of a sound recording is with the record company or producer or that recording.

Do you need permission if you want to play a song in public? One of the rights that copyright protection affords is the *right to perform publicly*. All other people must enter into a licensing arrangement to perform the music.

When you buy a CD or record, you have the right to listen to that CD or record. You do not purchase the right to play that CD or record in public. Examples where you might come into problems with the right to publicly perform includes such activities as the following:

✪ As a disc jockey for your local nightclub, you play one of your favorite tapes for the dance floor;

✪ You broadcast your favorite song using your website;

✪ As a DJ for your college radio station, you play one of your favorites records; or,

✪ As a small business owner, you play your favorites cassettes to keep your customers happy.

It would be literally impossible for individuals to monitor all of the establishments where music is publicly performed. In such instances, there are various organizations that can give blanket licenses to play recorded songs in public. These organizations are similar in nature to copyright clearance centers discussed with respect to literary works. The major organizations are BMI, ASCAP and SESAC. The websites for these various organizations can be found in Appendix B.

Organizations such as BMI acquire *performing rights* from writers and publishers of music and in return, grant licenses to establishments who publicly perform the music. The licenses are to the entire artist repertoire acquired by the organization. The organizations then take representative samples from selected establishments to come up with a figure on how much to distribute to each of its members.

Organizations like BMI do not license *dramatic performing rights* (the right, for example, to publicly perform a play on the stage). Moreover, these organizations do not license *mechanical* or *synchronization* rights. To obtain a mechanical or synchronization license you should contact the *Harry Fox Agency* that acts as a clearinghouse for both mechanical and synchronization licenses.

✪ *Mechanical License:* A mechanical license is permission to manufacture and distribute a phonorecord (this includes CDs, audio tapes or cassettes) for a specific copyrighted composition. The royalty of a mechanical license is usually determined by how many recordings are sold.

✪ *Synchronization License:* A synchronization license is permission to use music in combination with visual images (films, computer programs, TV, etc.).

Obtaining permission to use sound recordings is complex. Unfortunately, it is not something that can adequately be covered in a single chapter. If what you want to do requires the use of sound recordings, you should also take a look at a specific book that deals with licensing of music, some of which are listed in Appendix D. Even after you obtain permission to use the sound recording, there may be other things that you have to consider.

Film and Video

As with music, obtaining permission to use film and video is really a subject itself and one that cannot be adequately covered in a single chapter. In addition, *permission* is typically sought by a full fledged *licensing agreement,* rather than a simple *permission request letter* because of the complexity involved. You are advised to consult books that deal exclusively on this topic. (See Appendix D.*)*

The copyright to films and videos will typically be owned by the production company for the film or video. The exception to this is national news programming that is typically owned by the major TV networks. Usually the name of the production company will be included at the start of the film or the video. If you cannot locate the name of the production company on the film, two very useful resources to check are Screensite's at **www.sa.ua.du/screensite** and the Internet Movie Database at **us.imdb.com/search**.

Performances and Speeches

You will recall that for a copyright to exist, there must be some artistic expression in a *tangible medium.* Thus, truly extemporaneous speeches that have not been previously prepared are not protected by copyright. But if the speech has been previously prepared, you will need to deal with obtaining permission from the copyright owner.

In the case of speeches, you should keep in mind that the person who actually made the speech may not be the actual author of the speech (probably few presidents actually write their own speeches). Moreover, if the speech was recorded when it was made, you will also need to obtain permission from the copyright owner of the sound or videotape recording if you want to use that recording. If the speech was recorded by a news agency, then you should contact that agency if you want to use the recorded speech.

Recording the sounds or otherwise fixing the sounds or images of a live musical performance or transmitting to the public the sounds or images of such a performance is also copyright infringement unless you have permission to do this.

Penalties for Copyright Infringement

If you fail to obtain permission for a copyright work and go ahead and use that work, you are technically a copyright infringer. The Copyright Act allows for recovery of actual damages suffered as the result of your infringement and profits. *Actual damages* relate to the damage that you cause to the market value of the copyright. Because there may be cases where your infringement does not really cause much harm to the market value of the copyright, the Act also allows the copyright holder to collect what are called *statutory damages* instead. These statutory damages are between $500 and $20,000 for each work infringed. (17 U.S.C. Section 504(c)(1).) If the copyright holder elects statutory damages, the holder may even be able to claim enhanced statutory damages up to $100,000 if the court determines that your infringement is *willful*.

Willfulness means that you had knowledge that your conduct constituted copyright infringement. This does not mean that because you were not aware of the law that your infringement cannot be considered willful. As with other things, ignorance of the law is no defense. But, many aspects of copyright law are quite confusing, your infringement might, therefore, not be considered willful if you reasonably and in good faith did not believe that your actions constituted copyright infringement because you believed the copyright had expired or that your actions constituted fair use.

You will also find that if you seek permission now, rather than later, when your own work could have some commercial significance, you will find that obtaining your permission will be less expensive. People tend to charge more for things later on when they realize that what you have used has taken on some new commercial importance to you.

Unauthorized Use of Sound Recordings   In addition to all of the civil penalties discussed above that can attach for copyright infringement, the unauthorized reproduction, distribution, rental or digital transmission of copyright sound recordings is subject to criminal penalties under 17 U.S.C. Secs. 501, 506.

Trademarks

Copyright law does not extend to the following:

- ✪ names of products or services;

- ✪ names of businesses, organizations, or groups (including the name of a group of performers);

- ✪ names of pseudonyms or individuals (including pen name or stage name);

- ✪ titles of works; or,

- ✪ catchwords, catchphrases, mottos, slogans, or short advertising expressions.

However, all of these may be subject to trademark protection. One big difference that you need to keep in mind with trademarks as opposed to copyrights is the fact that a trademark can last indefinitely. As long as the owner of a trademark has not abandoned his/her use of the mark, you will need to obtain permission from the owner to use the mark.

Licensing of trademarks is typically not done through a simple permission because of the complexities involved. Trademark owners will usually insist upon a full-fledged trademark license to deal with these complexities. For example, the regular, non-exclusive grant of trademark permission to thousands of people who request such permission to use the trademark could result in the loss of that trademark to the owner. Owners of trademarks need to maintain good control over the use to which their trademarks are put. Full licensing agreements usually address this need.

Explanation of Terms
of the Permission Request

The permission forms used in Appendix G are basic forms that you should be able to adapt to your own particular situation. As already pointed out, many publishers will want to use their own forms. There will probably be no way to avoid this. But if you spend some time learning about the terms in a permission request, you will be in a better position to determine whether you want to go ahead with your request or perhaps whether you can negotiate terms that are more to your liking.

Just as you have gone through the other forms in this book with respect to licenses, remember that one of the major purpose of having a detailed agreement is that it can reduce your chances for a dispute later. Therefore, you need to be detailed orientated even when it comes to the permission process. If you think that you may need to use a work a certain way in the future, then put it in the agreement that such use will be covered by your request.

There is no need to create an elaborate permission request. Permission forms are meant to be simple and to provide a quick and inexpensive way to obtain permission to use the material that you want to use. But at the same time, it is worth your time to learn about the terms that commonly make up a permission request. Knowing something about the commonly used terms will assist you in adapting the form to your own situation. In addition, your knowledge will come in very useful when reading over the permission form a publisher requires that you use.

Mandatory Terms for Consideration

The terms of this section are vital to any well-drafted permission agreement and should be included if they fit your particular situation. These terms are referred to as *Mandatory Terms for Consideration to any Permission Request,* even though some of the terms will not apply to your unique situation.

Applicable fees. If a fee is being exchanged in return for the permission, then you will need a clause in the request that states the consideration. A clause you might use could be the following:

"In consideration of this permission, Licensee/Requester shall pay Licensor a fee of $_____ dollars which shall be due and payable within 30 days of execution of this agreement."

Description of owner's work. You need to adequately describe the work that you want to use. This includes the following information.

✪ **Details of Work Requested**. Try to include as much specifics about the work you want to use as possible. This includes information such as the following:

- **Full cite of the work:** Include the full title of the work that you want to use as well as the volume number if applicable. Include the authors name, and year of publication. If what you want to use comes from a magazine or periodical, then you can also include the ISSN number that is assigned to that magazine. If what you want to use comes from a book, then see if you can include the ISBN number assigned to that book.

- **Location of the material:** Provide the page numbers that includes the work that you want to use. If you are using a particular figure or chart, then refer to any referenced figure or chart number. (This is all particularly beneficial if you are the person who is granting permission since you do not want to inadvertently grant permission to use your entire work if the permission seeker is only paying for permission to use part of your work.) It is also a good idea to include a photocopy of the material that you want to use along with your request.

✪ **Details of New Work**. In addition to information about the work that you want to use, also include information about your own work in which you will make use of the copyright owner's work. This will include such information as:

- **Full cite of your work:** For example, if you will be using the work in a book that you intend to publish, you should state the title of your work, your publisher's name, the date of intended publication, and the number of copies expected to be published.

- **Other identifying information about your work:** if your own work will be published, you should include how much you expect to charge per copy. If you plan to offer a copy on the Internet, you should provide information such as the site on which the material will appear, as well as the starting and ending dates of publication that the material will be posted.

✪ **Scope of Rights that you Seek.** You need to define the rights that you seek. You need to make sure that the permission you receive is broad enough in scope to cover not only what you think you might want to do with the copyrighted work now, but also what you expect to do with the work in the future. If you later find that what you want to do is not including in the terms of use for your original permission agreement, you will need to send out a new permission letter requesting permission for your desired use. By that time, the copyright owner may have changed his or her mind about giving you permission, or may request an unreasonable fee to obtain the permission. If you go ahead without obtaining the required new permission, your actions will constitute infringement.

If you have an agreement with a publisher, then it is wise to consult your publisher right at the start for this information. Things to consider in the grant of rights section include some of the following.

- **Territory.** Permission to use the work only in the U.S. or to use the work in other countries, in which case you will want to specify the other countries or specify *world-wide*.

- **Languages:** If you want permission to publish the protected work abroad, you may also want to specify the languages that you expect to use the work. If you do not see yourself abroad, then you should probably not request foreign rights since the cost of your permission will probably be much greater.

- **Duration:** Permission grantors may want to grant permission for a specified amount of time such as a five or ten year period. Requesters will, of course, try to obtain permission for as long as they want to use the work. If a time limit is set, the requester will need to renegotiate permission for continued use of the work by completing a new permission agreement.

- **Your intended use of the work:** You should specify exactly how you intend to use the work. There are a wide range of possible uses, including such things as using the work in a book, magazine, website, in a presentation that you might be giving to colleagues, or to your students. If you are going to use the work in your own book, then you should also provide identifying information about your book including such things as the proposed title of your book; the estimated price that you will be charging for your book; the estimated circulation of your book; proposed date of publication of your book; and, the name and address of your publisher.

- **Exclusive vs. nonexclusive rights:** Permission requests by their very nature tend to be only for nonexclusive rights use of the work. It is a rare case where a right holder would want to grant permission to a requester on an exclusive basis. Permission grantors will want to insure that the rights granted are for nonexclusive rights only.

- **One time use or subsequent uses:** If you want to use a work in subsequent editions or publications of your work, then you should make sure that you specify this in your request. Permission grantors typically limit the use of their work to a *one-time* use only. Uses beyond this one-time use typically require another permission request.

- **Distribution process or media format:** If you plan to publish your work both electronically, in addition to print, you should make sure that you are granted electronic rights. A rights holder may want to restrict permission to use the work to print only because allowing electronic reproduction of the work may make it very easy for others to copy the work.

- **Other intended uses:** Make sure that you spell out what you want to do with the work if you are a permission seeker. Among some of the things you might want to specify in addition to electronic rights are the following:

  - posting material on the Web;

  - power point presentation; and,

  - overhead presentation.

There are, of course, many other intended uses for the material you may have. Be specific from both the perspective of the permission seeker as well as the permission grantor. Include the use. This will help you in avoiding any conflict later on as to what exactly the permission was granted to do. From a financial point of view too, a permission seeker will probably not want to insist upon a broad grant of rights if all he or she wants to do is to show the material at a conference. Such a request might appear absurd to the copyright holder, and be denied or require a hefty fee that would not make economic sense.

- **Alteration or manipulation of the work**: Include whether or not you intend to alter the work. For example, if you intend to manipulate a digitized image, you will need to obtain permission to alter the image. Some grantors of permission will typically not want to give permission for alteration of their work. It is a good idea to include a copy of what the alterations will look like. Grantors may want to insist on a copy of any alterations be approved as a condition to the permission.

Warranties and Representations

A permission grantor may want to include some type of disclaimer as to warranties about the material that is being provided. A sample disclaimer might be:

> Licensor makes no representations or warranties as the accuracy of any information contained in the Licensed Material, including any warranties of merchantability or fitness for a particular purpose. In no event shall Licensor have any liability to any part for special, incidental, tort, or consequential damages arising out of or in connection with the Licensed material.

From the requester's point of view, this is the section to put in any warranties where the grantor warrants that he or she owns the copyright to the material requested. Such warranties will most likely not be accepted by the grantor.

Indemnification

Permission grantors may want to include a clause in which the licensee agrees to hold the grantor harmless for any harm which might result from the use of the licensed material. This takes the permission closer to a full fledge license. A clause such as the following might be used:

> Licensee shall indemnify Licensor from any damages, lawsuits, claims, liabilities, costs, expenses, including attorney's fees, relating to the use of the licensed material.

Termination   A clause or two about when the grantor can terminate the permission might be in order as it would be in a full-fledged licensing agreement. For example, a grantor might want a clause such as:

> Licensor shall have the right to terminate this Agreement immediately upon written notice to Licensee if Licensee is in material breach of this Agreement.

Optional Terms to a Permission Request

Some terms to the permission agreement are truly optional, whether you stand in the shoes of the requester or the grantor. The following are a few of these optional provisions.

Credit Requirement   Although this clause does not appear in the sample provided, many permission agreements will require that you include a credit line for the work in your own work. If such a clause is included, it will often include terms as to where the credit line is placed, as well as the type of working that must be used.

A credit line, sometimes called an *acknowledgement,* will typically include the author, title, publisher, copyright notice of the creator of the work that you want to use as well as the words, *reprinted by permission* followed by the name of the copyright owner.

Example: You wish to use a chart in your own book which comes from a book entitled, "The New Season" which is published by Books Inc. The book has a copyright notice of 1984. The author of the book is Tom Nelson. You should include an *acknowledgment* section somewhere in your book (below the chart or in a separate acknowledgments section) as follows:

> From *The New Season* by Tom Nelson. Copyright ©1984 by Tom Nelson. Reprinted by permission of Books Inc.

Complimentary Copies   A grantor may request that the requester provide the grantor with one or more copies of the new work when it is published. Requesters should not object to this.

Cost of Permission

The cost of obtaining permission will depend on a range of factors including the following.

✪ *How well you negotiate.* Your negotiations skills will be an important factor to determining the cost of any permission.

✪ *Your status.* It will probably cost you less for permission if you are an individual or nonprofit institution, than if you are a company who is engaged in commercial enterprises.

✪ *Your intended scope of use.* The broader the scope or rights that you request in your permission request above, probably the costlier your permission request. If you are, for example, intending to use a photograph on page 360 of your new book as part of an illustration rather than on the front cover, the cost of obtaining permission is probably going to be less. If you are intending to use the work commercially as part of a company website, then the permission might costs more, than if you intend to use the work noncommercially as part of your own personal website.

✪ *The amount of the work that you want to use.* It goes without saying that permission to copy half of a book is probably going to cost you more than permission to copy a paragraph. Most right holders will want to limit you to the amount of material that you can use. Otherwise, your use might threaten their market for their work (people could, for example, simply go to your website to find the work).

✪ *How important the work is to you.* If the work that you want to use is very important to the creation of your own work, then you are probably going to be prepared to pay more to obtain permission for that work than if you have available substitutes for the work. As pointed out before, you always have the right to exclude the work that you want to use from your own work. Moreover, if the fees seem excessive, you can hire someone to create the work for you. (If you do this, however, be sure to complete a *work-for-hire* agreement or assignment.)

✪   *The work for which you are seeking permission.* The value of the work for which you seek permission may influence the cost of obtaining that permission. For example, it is going to cost a lot more to use a trademark coming from Disney, than a logo created by your Web design friend. Many freelance authors, in fact, will probably be more concerned that their work is distributed (so long as you give them proper credit) than making a big buck on their work.

Permission will probably cost you less if you obtain it right at the start, rather than if you wait until your work has itself gained some type of commercial value. It will certainly cost you less to obtain permission now, than if you become entangled in a copyright or trademark infringement action because you did not obtain the necessary permission.

As a final note to this chapter, you should seek permissions when you have determined that they are necessary, before you go ahead and use a work. Seeking permission is also a courtesy that should be afforded to the creators of original work.

GLOSSARY

A

acknowledgement. Sometimes known as a *credit line*, this is typically a sentence or two in which you identify the copyrighted work that you are using in your own work.

agreement. An exchange of promises between two or more parties to perform an action or actions in the future.

anthology. A term used in copyright law. You create *anthologies* when you arrange pre-existing works in a certain manner.

arbitration. A proceeding intended to resolve disputes between parties. Arbitration is like a litigation before a court of law, but is much faster and cheaper. Parties present evidence to a neutral party, the *arbitrator*, who is similar to a judge. The arbitrator's decision is binding on the parties, and may be enforced by a court if necessary.

assignment. A complete transfer of *ownership* in an intellectual property right or an agreement from one party to another, either for payment, or free of charge.

C

cease and desist letter. A letter sent by an owner of intellectual property to an individual or business suspected of infringing that owner's intellectual property, demanding that they cease the infringing activities. An offer to take a license under from the intellectual property owner may also be presented.

compilation. A term used in copyright law. A work formed by the collecting and assembling of preexisting materials that are selected, coordinated, or arranged in such a way that the resulting work as a whole constitutes an original work of authorship. *See also Anthology.*

computer program (software). A set of statements or instructions to be used directly or indirectly in a computer in order to bring about a certain result.

contract. *See agreement.*

copyright. A creator's right to his or her artistic expression, arising when the work is permanently created, and typically lasting the lifetime of its creator plus 70 years. The copyright owner has the exclusive right to: reproduce, distribute, display, perform, make derivative works, and publicly transmit the work.

D

derivative work. Translations, abridgments, or any other type of work that recasts, transforms or adapts an original copyrighted work.

design patent. A type of patent protection protecting the aesthetic or ornamental features of an article of manufacture. Design patents last for 14 years, and may in some cases overlap with copyright protection. *See also Patent.*

dramatic works. An artistic (and copyrightable) work that is intended to be performed, such as plays or radio and television scripts.

I

infringement. An unauthorized copying or use of a product, invention, mark, or artistic work protected by an intellectual property right. A type of *stealing* of intellectual property.

intellectual property (IP). A general term referring to property rights in inventions, artistic expression, and certain types of information. The main IP rights are patent, copyright, trademark, and trade secrets. All IP has an owner (or owners) who may be an individual or a company, and who have the right to use, license, or assign the rights.

L

letter of intent. A short agreement between parties, stating their intention to enter into a final, binding agreement sometime in the future. Letters of intent are generally not binding, and are used to summarize the final agreement's overall terms as well as show the parties' intent to enter into it.

license. Allowing someone to use intellectual property. A license is an authorization given by an owner of intellectual property to another party, so that the latter can use the intellectual property, usually for a limited time. Licenses are typically granted in exchange for payment.

license agreement. A written agreement providing the details of a license transaction. License agreements set forth all the terms and conditions of the license, including the rights granted, what the party receiving the IP may do, payment, as well as others.

licensee. A term used in licensing to refer to the party who is using intellectual property owned by the other party.

licensor. A term used in licensing to refer to the party who owns the intellectual property, and is allowing the other party use it.

likelihood of confusion. The standard in trademark law, by which it is judged whether a new mark or symbol *infringes* an existing trademark. If it can be shown that consumers will tend to be confused between the two marks, there is said to be *likelihood of confusion* and hence the new mark will infringe the existing trademark.

M

most favored nations. A provision in a license agreement in which the licensor guarantees the licensee the best business terms from all other licensees.

multimedia. A copyrightable work, often instructional, which combines authorship in two or more media. The authorship may include text, artwork, sculpture, photography, sounds or music and other types of media.

music composition. A copyrightable work of music, including any accompanying words. The author of a music composition is generally the composer, and the lyricist.

P

patent. An inventor's right to his or her new and unique invention, which can be a machine, manufacture, chemical composition, or process. A patent must be applied for through the U.S. Patent & Trademark Office, and the invention must at a minimum be novel, useful, and nonobvious. Patent protection typically lasts for 20 years.

permission. An authorization by an owner of intellectual property to someone so the latter can use the IP. Permission is similar to a license, but is much faster and simpler, typically requiring a very short form rather than a full-length license.

phonorecords. A term used in copyright law to refer to material objects in which sounds, other than those accompanying a motion picture or other audiovisual work, are fixed. Soundtracks are *not* considered phonorecords by the Copyright Office.

publication. Under copyright law, publication is defined as the distribution of copies or phonorecords of a work to the public by sale or other transfer of ownership, or by rental, lease, or lending.

R

release. A short agreement where an individual gives permission to someone else to use an image or picture of themselves, or other personal information. A release can also mean an agreement where one person promises not to sue another party, for an activity or in a certain context.

S

sound recordings. Copyrightable works that result from the fixation of a series of musical, spoken, or other sounds, but not including the sounds accompanying a motion picture or other audiovisual work. The author of a sound recording is the performers whose performance is fixed, or the sound producer who processes the sounds and fixes them in the final recording, or both.

substantial similarity. The legal standard in copyright law, by which it is judged whether a new artistic work infringes an existing copyrighted work.

T

trademark. A word, slogan, or symbol which identifies a good and indicates its business source to consumers. Trademarks arise from first use of a mark in commerce, within a given geographical territory. Trademarks vary in their distinctiveness and strength, which affects their ability to be federally registered.

trade name. The name of a company. Trade names function similarly to trademarks but have different rules for registration.

trade secret. Any confidential information used by a business that gives it a competitive advantage over others. A trade secret lasts indefinitely as long as the business maintains the information's confidentiality. Unlike other intellectual property rights, there is no application or registration process for trade secrets.

U

utility patent. Another name for a regular patent, as opposed to a design patent. *See also Patent and Design Patent.*

APPENDIX A
GENERAL RESOURCES

The easiest way to get quick information on any topic, issue, or law in intellectual property or other areas of law is through the many websites (and organizations) listed.

However, if you need more in-depth analysis and discussion of *patents, copyrights, trademarks,* or *trade secrets,* refer to the various books and publications. We also indicate which books are professional legal guides (used by the lawyers) and which are more accessible to the general public.

COPYRIGHTS

Copyright Statutes: Title 17
www4.law.cornell.edu/uscode/17
Actual U.S. copyright law

Online Copyright Resources
www.library.yale.edu/~okerson
 /copyproj.html#nonucopy
Extensive list of links to copyright sites and
resources.

Overview of Copyright Law
www.law.cornell.edu/topics/copyright.html
Brief introduction to copyright law

U.S. Copyright Office
www.loc.gov/copyright
Official government office for copyright; the
place to start for any copyright information
or research; contains regulations, forms.

Books

**Copyrighting America: America's
Copyright Guide & Workbook**
 by William J. S. Murphy
 (PATACCO, 2000)

**How to Register Your Own Copyright:
With Forms, 3rd Edition**
 by Mark Warda
 (Sphinx Publishing, 2000)

Nimmer on Copyright
 Melville B. Nimmer
 (Matthew Bender & Co., Inc., 2001)
 The definitive professional legal treatise on
 copyright law; can be found in some general
 libraries with law section.

Associations

**American Intellectual Property Law
Association**
www.aipla.org
One of the top legal associations for intellectual property attorneys.

International Offices

European Patent Office
www.european-patent-office.org

Japanese Patent Office
www.jpo.go.jp

United Kingdom Patent Office
www.patent.gov.uk

World Intellectual Property Organization
www.wipo.int

www.bountyquest.com
Offers rewards to people who can dig up
prior art that may invalidate a patent.

www.bustpatents.com
Site devoted to helping you find prior art to
invalidate software patents.

www.cipa.org.uk
Site you can use to locate patent agents in
the UK.

**http://dir.yahoo.com
/Business_and_Economy/Companies/Law
/Intellectual_Property/Trademarks/Services**
Yahoo is a great site to go for intellectual
property information and listings of websites
that cover this area of law

www.heckle.org
Information for the individual inventor.

www.ipo.org
Intellectual Property Owners Association

www.lexis-nexis.com
A commercial database for prior art.

www.micropatent.com
Allows you to search for patents.

www.patents.ibm.com
Another website where you can search for patents.

www.patentminer.com
Another commercial database for patents.

PATENTS

U.S. Patent & Trademark Office: Patents
www.uspto.gov/main/patents.htm
The official government office for patents and trademarks; the place to start for everything patent.

Books

Chisum on Patents
by Donald S. Chisum
(Matthew Bender & Co., Inc.)
(multivolume)
The most complete and comprehensive professional legal treatise on patent law; available mostly in law libraries (and some business libraries).

Protect Your Patent
by James L. Rogers
(Sphinx Publishing, 2003)
All about using and protecting your patent.

The Complete Patent Book: Everything You Need to Know to Obtain Your Patent
by James L. Rogers
(Sphinx Publishing, 2003)
All about patent law for the general public.

TRADEMARKS

International

International Guide to Trademarks.
http://ttdomino.Thomson-thomson.com/www/internat-vis.nsf

Searches

Thomson & Thomson – Trademark Searching Company
www.thomson-thomson.com

Trademark Center
www.tmcenter.com
Company that does trademark searches and has information about trademarks.

Trademark Express
www.tmexpress.com
Another trademark company that does searches and offers other services.

U.S. Patent & Trademark Office:
Trademark Information & Searching
www.uspto.gov/main/trademarks.htm
Search federally registered trademarks for
free online using TESS (Trademark
Electronic Search System); note that the
search is for registered trademarks only.

TRADE SECRETS

Trade Secret Law
www.execpc.com/~mhallign

GENERAL LEGAL WEBSITES

FindLaw.com
www.findlaw.com
Huge site full of business and legal resources
You can also find many court cases as well as
sample contracts and licenses.
Links to many other organizations and
resources.

GigaLaw.com – "Legal Information for
Internet Professionals"
www.gigalaw.com

KuesterLaw: Technology Law Resources
www.kuesterlaw.com
General legal resources for technology and
intellectual property law.

Legal Information Institute
www.law.cornell.edu/topical.html
Resource for quick information of many
areas of law, organized by topic
Succinct summaries, with references to
statutory and case law.

Appendix B
Licensing

The information in this appendix is designed to assist the reader in finding additional resources specific to licensing their invention including finding potential licensees.

COPYRIGHT (ARTISTIC WORKS & ENTERTAINMENT)

American Library Association
www.ala.org

ASCAP: American Society of Composers, Authors & Publishers
http://ascap.com
Largest performing rights organization for the music industry.

American Society of Journalists & Authors
www.asja.org

BMI: Broadcast Music, Inc.
www.bmi.com/home1.asp
Music performing rights organization.

Copyright Clearance Center
http://copyright.com
Provides licensing systems and permissions for the reproduction and distribution of copyrighted content such as book excerpts and articles.

Film, Television & Multimedia Production
www.marklitwak.com
Website of entertainment attorney with articles and information on film and television contracts and licenses; also contains useful glossary of "industry" terms.

Literary Market Place
www.literarymarketplace.com/lmp/us /index_us.asp
Comprehensive listing of publishers (*the Literary Market Place*, by R.R. Bowker, is a book available at most local libraries.)

Motion Picture Licensing Corporation
www.mplc.com

National Music Publisher's Association
www.nmpa.org

Recording Industry Association of America
www.riaa.com
Largest association of record companies; contains information on the music industry and licensing.

SESAC
www.sesac.com
Music performing rights organization.

The Association of American Publishers
www.publishers.org/about/rpacurls.cfm
Lists names and addresses of publishers.

The Harry Fox Agency
www.harryfox.com
"Mechanical" rights agency for the music industry.

U.S. Copyright Office: Licensing Division
www.copyright.gov/carp
Administers certain types of licensing – e.g., retransmission of radio broadcasts, digital audio, etc.

Books

The Writer's Legal Guide: An Authors Guild Desk Reference, 3rd Edition
by Tad Crawford & Kay Murray (2002)
Excellent, readable guide to copyright law, contracts, and legal issues for writers.

Business and Legal Forms for Graphic Designers, 3rd Edition
by Tad Crawford, et al.
(Allworth Press, 1999)
Other titles by same author includes business and legal forms for: photographers, visual artists, fine artists, crafts, and so on.

The Musician's Business and Legal Guide, 3rd Edition
Edited by Mark E. Halloran, et al.
(Prentice Hall, 2001)

This Business of Music: The Definitive Guide to the Music Industry (This Business of Music, 8th Edition)
by M. William Krasilovsky, et al.
(Watson-Guptill Pub., 2000)

Dealmaking in the Film and Television Industry, 2nd Edition
by Mark Litwak

Contracts for the Film and Television Industry, 2nd Edition
by Mark Litwak

Licensing Art & Design
by Caryn R. Leland
(Allworth Press, 1995)

FINDING LICENSORS & LICENSEES

2XFR: Intellectual Property Licensing & Marketplace
www.2xfr.com/how_to_use.asp
Online "business accelerator" which connects prospective licensors with licensees.

Industry Trade Journals
www.patentcafe.com/resource_industry
  /tradejournals.html
Website lists the top 50 trade journals in patent-related industries.

International Licensing Industry Merchandisers' Association (LIMA)
www.licensing.org
Resources, services, and licensing industry information for entertainment, trademark, fashion, sports, and art licensing. Huge site with plenty of information on merchandising.

Jacob Javits Center Trade Show: International Licensing (New York City)
www.javitscenter.com/content/events
/webcast/main.htm
Also check events, trade shows, and conventions on licensing in convention centers in major cities.

Licensing World Website
www.licensingworld.com
Resources, tools, and information to locate licensors or licensees.

New York New Media Association (New York City)
www.nynma.org
Huge organization connecting technology and business professionals in the New York City area, especially in internet & new media; also contains resources on raising venture capital.

Small Business Administration (SBA)
www.asbdc-us.org
Resources to help the patent owner locate manufacturers and potential licensees.

U.S. Patent & Trademark Office: Official Gazette
www.uspto.gov – Click on "Index" icon and "O" for "Official Gazette"
Weekly periodical listing new patents; will publish notice of a patent's availability for sale or license (cost: $25).
Official Gazette

GENERAL LICENSING

Books

Franchising & Licensing: Two Ways to Build Your Business, 2nd Edition
by Andrew J. Sherman
(AMACOM, 1999)

How to License Technology
(John Wiley & Sons, Inc., 1996)

How to License Your Million Dollar Idea
by Harvey Reese
(The Inventor's Bookstore)

Licensing: A Strategy for Profits
by Edward P. White
(KEW Licensing Press, 1990)

Licensing Intellectual Property: Legal, Business and Market Dynamics
(John Wiley & Sons, Inc., 1996)

The Licensing Business Handbook, 4th Edition
by Karen Raugust
(EPM Communications Inc., 2001)

The Licensing Business Handbook, 4th Edition
by Karen Raugust
(EPM Communications, Inc., 2002

PATENTS (SOFTWARE & TECHNOLOGY)

DSI Technologies Escrow Services
www.dsiescrow.com
Well-known software escrow agent.

National Technology Transfer Center
www.nttc.edu
Has a wealth of information on commercialization of inventions.

New York Software Industry Association
www.nysia.org

Patent Café: Intellectual Property Management
www.patentcafe.com

Software Information Industry Association
www.siia.net

Will It Sell?
www.willitsell.com
Useful in determining whether your invention will be marketable before you invest time and money getting a patent.

Yet2.com
www.yet2.com
A market place site where you can locate patent rights for sale or licensing.

Books

The Complete Idiot's Guide to Cashing In on Your Inventions
by Richard C. Levy
(Alpha Books, 2002)

Cyberlaw: Your Rights in Cyberspace
by Gerald R. Ferrera, et al.
(Southwestern College Pub., 2001)

CyberRegs: A Business Guide to Web Property, Privacy, and Patents
by Bill Zoellick
(Addison Wesley Professional, 2001)

GigaLaw Guide to Internet Law
by Doug Isenberg
(Random House Trade Paperbacks, 2002)

Technology Licensing: Corporate Strategies for Maximizing Value
edited by Russell L. Parr & Patrick H. Sullivan
(John Wiley & Sons, 1996)

The Technology Transfer System: Inventions - Marketing - Licensing - Patenting - Setting - Practice - Management - Policy
by Albert E. Muir
(EPM Communications, Inc., 2002)

TRADEMARK LICENSING & MERCHANDISING

International Licensing Industry Merchandisers' Association (LIMA)
www.licensing.org
Resources, services, and licensing industry information for entertainment, trademark, fashion, sports, and art licensing.

Movie Merchandising
www.marklitwak.com/movmerc.html
Excellent sample merchandising agreement, checklist, and basic information on film-related merchandising on entertainment attorney's website.

Merchandising & Licensing
www.grr.com/aboutlicense.html
Summary of merchandising

APPENDIX C
FINDING AN ATTORNEY

The information in this appendix will assist you in finding an attorney, as well as resources for alternative dispute resolution.

ALTERNATIVE DISPUTE RESOLUTION
(ARBITRATION & MEDIATION)

American Arbitration Association

www.adr.org/index2.1.jsp

The place to start for arbitration, mediation, and general alternative dispute resolution; find alternative dispute professionals; website also contains rules and procedures related to ADR.

Arbitration & Mediation Resources

www.thecre.com/fedlaw/legal89.htm

Links to arbitration and mediation websites, regulations, and resources.

Martindale Hubbell Legal Directory

www.martindale.com

Comprehensive legal directory; contains locator for Dispute Resolution professionals, investigators, expert witnesses, consultants, and other legal professionals.

Books

Arbitration Advocacy
by John W. Cooley
(National Institute for Trial Advocacy, 1997)

Online Dispute Resolution: Resolving Conflicts in Cyberspace
by Ethan Katsh & Janet Rifkin
(Jossey-Bass, 2001)

FINDING AN ATTORNEY

American Bar Association
www.abanet.org
Nationwide association of attorneys; contains a wealth of resources and information.

American Intellectual Property Law Association
www.aipla.org
One of the top legal associations for intellectual property attorneys.

AttorneyFind
www.attorneyfind.com
Resource to find attorneys in various legal specialties.

Bar Association of the City of New York
www.abcny.org
Citywide attorney association; similar association in major cities.

KuesterLaw: Technology Law Resources
www.kuesterlaw.com
Contains links to numerous technology and intellectual property law firms and lawyers across the nation, from small to large.

Martindale Hubbell Legal Directory
www.martindale.com
Comprehensive legal directory and search tool for finding any attorney practicing in the United States; you can do a search by attorney name, law firm, or practice area within a city or state; also contains locator for investigators, expert witnesses, consultants, and other legal professionals.

New York State Bar Association
www.nysba.org
Statewide attorney association; contains resources, links, and information; similar association in every state.

Volunteer Lawyers for the Arts
www.vlany.org
As the name implies, you can get free legal assistance with creative works & entertainment matters; website contains a directory of similar organizations in different cities.

APPENDIX D
PERMISSIONS

The information in this appendix will assist the reader seeking to obtain permission to use the work of another. It contains additional materials to help the reader learn about permissions in general, as well as specific locations of contacts to obtain permissions.

FILM

Motion Picture Licensing Corporation
www.mplc.com

Books

Clearance & Copyright: Everything the Independent Filmmaker Needs to Know
by Michael C. Donaldson
(Silman-James Press)

GENERAL

U.S. Copyright Office
www.loc.gov/copyright
www.copyright.gov
The U.S. Copyright Office is a great starting place to determine the copyright status of a creative work; for information on how to search the records at the Copyright Office, request the following:

(i) Circular 22 -- "How to Investigate the Copyright Status of a Work"

(ii) Circular 23 -- "The Copyright Card Catalog and the Online Files of the Copyright Office."

GRAPHIC ARTS/ VISUAL WORKS

American Society of Media Photographers
www.asmp.org

Artists Rights Society
www.arsny.com

Graphic Artists Guild
www.gag.org

International Federation of Reproduction Rights Organizations
www.ifrro.org

Miscellaneous Graphic Arts Websites:
www.acidfonts.com
www.artres.com
http://cartoonbank.com
www.clipart.com
http://clip-art.com
http://clipartdownload.com
www.doctorstock.com
www.flamingtext.com
www.fontsnthings.co
http://iconbazaar.com
www.lifeart.com
www.nystockphoto.com
www.novadevelopment.com
www.stockphoto.com
www.artres.com
www.lifeart.com
www.htmlgoodies.com

Picture Archive Council of America
www.pacaoffice.org

MUSIC

Music Library Association
www.musiclibraryassoc.org

National Music Publisher's Association
www.nmpa.org

Performing & Mechanical Rights Organizations

ASCAP: American Society of Composers, Authors & Publishers
http://ascap.com
Largest performing rights organization for the music industry.

BMI: Broadcast Music, Inc.
www.bmi.com/home1.asp
Performing rights organization.

SESAC
www.sesac.com
Performing rights organization.

WRITTEN WORKS

American Library Association

www.ala.org

Author's Registry

www.authorsregistry.org/autcondir.html

American Society of Journalists & Authors

www.asja.org

Copyright Clearance Center

http://copyright.com/
A great resource for getting permission; provides licensing systems and permissions for the reproduction and distribution of copyrighted content such as book excerpts and articles.

Literary Market Place

www.literarymarketplace.com/lmp/us
  /index_us.asp
Comprehensive listing of publishers; the Literary Market Place, by R.R. Bowker, is a book available at most local libraries.

National Writers Union

www.nwu.org

The Association of American Publishers

www.publishers.org/about/rpacurls.cfm
Lists names and addresses of publishers.

APPENDIX E
BUSINESS RESOURCES

The information below provides the reader with additional business resources that could be critical to preparing and negotiating their license agreement.

CONTRACTS & NEGOTIATION

FindLaw: Contracts Law & Resources
www.findlaw.com/01topics
/07contracts

LawDepot.com Contract Center
www.lawdepot.com/contracts/usa
Online source for all types of personal and business contracts.

Legal Information Institute: Contracts
www.law.cornell.edu/topics
/contracts.html

Books

Beyond Winning: Negotiating to Create Value in Deals and Disputes
by Robert H. Mnookin
(Harvard Univ Pr, 2000)

Contracts in a Nutshell (Nutshell Series), 4th Edition
by Claude D. Rohwer, Gordon D. Schaber
(West Information Pub. Group, 1997)

Essentials of Negotiation, 2nd Edition
by Roy J. Lewicki, et al.
(McGraw-Hill/Irwin, 2000)

Getting to Yes: Negotiating Agreements Without Giving In
by R. Fish & W. Ury
(Penguin)

Guidelines For Advertiser/Agency Contracts
by Lawrence J. Flink
(Association of National Advertisers, 2001)

Negotiating Terms of Employment
by Carolyn Buppert
(Law Office of Carolyn Buppert, 2002)

ROYALTIES, IP VALUATION & BUSINESS STRATEGY

Intellectual Property Law Primer
http://sciencelawyer.com/faq-1.htm
Attorney website with overview and strategy for intellectual property.

Patent Café: Intellectual Property Management
www.patentcafe.com
Excellent information and resources for management and valuation of patents and technological-related intellectual property.

Books

e-Patent Strategies for Software, e-Commerce, the Internet, Telecom Services, Financial Services, and Business Methods (with Case Studies and Forecasts)
by Stephen C. Glazier
(LBI Law & Business Institute, 2000)

Early-Stage Technologies: Valuation and Pricing
by Richard Razgaitis
(John Wiley & Sons 1999)

Essentials of Intellectual Property
by Alexander I Poltorak & Paul J. Lerner
(John Wiley & Sons,2002)
Very readable guide to the business and financial aspects of intellectual property; also contains an excellent summary of the various intellectual property rights.

Hidden Value: Profiting From the Intellectual Property Economy
edited by Bruce Berman

IP Strategy: Complete Intellectual Property Planning, Access and Protection
by Howard C. Anawalt & Elizabeth E. Powers

Licensing Royalty Rates, 2003
by Charles W. Battersby, et al.
(Aspen Publishers, Inc., 2003).

Patent Strategies for Business
by Stephen C. Glazier
(Euromoney Publications, 1995)

Patent Strategies for Researchers and Research Managers
by Jackson H. Knight
(John Wiley & Sons, 1996)

Protecting Your Company's Intellectual Property: A Practical Guide to Trademarks, Copyrights, Patents & Trade Secrets
by Deborah E. Bouchoux
(AMACOM 2001)

Rembrandts in the Attic: Unlocking the Hidden Value of Patents
by Kevin G. Rivette & David Kline
(Harvard Business School Press)

APPENDIX F
SAMPLE LICENSE
AGREEMENTS

These licenses and agreements are fairly standard, and are balanced between the interests of licensor and licensee. None include any service, maintenance, or technical support provisions of any kind. Form 1, however, is more protective of the Licensor. If you are the Licensee (and have sufficient bargaining power), you may want to revise the warranties, limitation of liability, confidentiality, and other provision to be more in your favor.

These full-length agreements are a starting point for your own license agreement only. Many of the terms and conditions provided in the sample licenses will in fact apply to your license. Others, however, may not be applicable. You will need to structure your own license grant, payment terms, service and maintenance provisions, representations and warranties, indemnification, limitation of liabilities, as well as other business and legal considerations according to the specific needs of your licensing transaction.

If the parties are exchanging confidential material, a mutual confidentiality provision will also be necessary.

Table of Forms

This patent license is a make and sell license based on royalties. As such, the parties will need to define net sales, royalty rates, and other financial information. If there is no know-how being licensed, all such references in the license agreement should be removed.

The content here is copyright only (artistic copyright, not data or technical information). Trademarks require separate provisions—see form 6, below. The rights and responsibilities of the parties in 1(B) & (C) should be precisely defined by the parties and described in the agreement.

In the following license, the trademarks being licensed are federally registered trademarks. Licensor needs to supply its own product quality standards for manufacture of the licensed products; provisions regarding inspection, delivery of product samples, trademark notices, and so on, need to be specified. This license is nonexclusive, royalty-based make and sell license; payment terms need to be finalized (i.e., net sales deductions).

SOFTWARE LICENSE AGREEMENT

This Software License Agreement ("**Agreement**") is made and entered into this ___day of _____, 200_ ("**Effective Date**") by and between _____, a _____ corporation with a principal place of business at _____ ("**Licensor**"), and _____, a _____ corporation with a principal place of business at _____ ("**Licensee**").

WITNESSETH:

WHEREAS, Licensor has developed certain computer software defined herein, and is willing to grant a license in such software to Licensee on the terms and conditions contained herein; and

WHEREAS, Licensee desires to use such computer software for its own internal business purposes, on the terms and conditions contained herein.

NOW, THEREFORE, in exchange for and in consideration of the mutual promises, premises, and covenants herein, and for other good and valuable consideration, the receipt and sufficiency of which are hereby acknowledged, Licensor and Licensee hereby agree as follows:

1. DEFINITIONS.

A. "**Licensed Software**" shall mean the computer software programs and/or routines known as [*describe software program*].

B. "**Documentation**" shall mean all manuals, materials, and information provided by Licensor to Licensee together with the Licensed Software.

2. LICENSE GRANT.

A. **License Grant.** Subject to the terms and conditions of this Agreement, Licensor hereby grants to Licensee a nonexclusive, nontransferable license to use the Licensed Software on a single computer processor with an unlimited number of concurrent users, solely for its own internal business purposes. This license grant does *not* include the right to sublicense the Licensed Software or any part thereof.

B. **Proprietary Rights.** Notwithstanding the above license grant or anything else to the contrary, all rights, including without limitation trade secret and copyright rights, in and to the Licensed Software and the Documentation shall remain the sole and exclusive property of Licensor.

C. **Restrictions on Licensee**. The license grant above is for licensee's own internal business purposes. Licensee may *not*:

(1) make additional copies of the Software or the Documentation, with the exception of one (1) copy for back-up or archival purposes;

(2) revise or modify the Software, or create derivative programs or works based on the Software;

(3) distribute the Software or the Documentation, or any portion thereof, to any third party, by any manner whatsoever;

(4) reverse engineer, decompile, or otherwise decode the Software;

(5) post or distribute the Software online, or store the Software in a data warehouse.

D. **Future Updates**. The license granted above does **not** provide for, and Licensor is under no obligations to provide, any updates of the Licensed Software.

3. TERM.

The term of this Agreement shall be one (1) year. This Agreement shall automatically renew for successive one year terms, unless either Party shall notify the other in writing, not less than thirty (30) days prior to expiration of the then current term, of such Party's intent **not** to renew this Agreement.

4. TERMINATION.

A. **Termination Conditions**. Subject to Subsection B below, either party shall have the right to terminate this Agreement upon the occurrence of any of the following events (hereinafter referred to as a "Default"):

(1) a party files a petition under any of the United States bankruptcy laws;

(2) voluntary proceedings under the United States bankruptcy laws are commenced by creditors against a party;

(3) licensee's distribution, exchange, or offer to distribute or exchange one or more copies, whether in source code or machine readable form, of the Licensed Software, whether by sale, license, lease or otherwise;

(4) licensee breaches of any of the restrictions set forth in Section 1(C) above;

(5) one of the parties voluntarily dissolves or attempts to dissolve itself as a corporation; or

(6) a material breach of a term or condition of this Agreement.

B. Notification and Cure. If any of these events occurs, the non-defaulting party shall give the defaulting party written notice, and shall have the right to terminate this Agreement if the defaulting party does not cure such default within thirty (30) days from receipt of such notice. The parties' rights as set forth in this section shall not be deemed exhaustive of their rights in law and equity.

C. Return of Software. Upon termination of this Agreement under this section, or expiration of the Agreement at the end of its term, Licensee shall immediately return to Licensor all copies of the Licensed Software, including all archival and backup copies.

5. PAYMENT.

Licensee agrees to pay the Licensor a license fee in the amount of $_____ per year for the license granted herein. Payment shall be made within thirty (30) days of the Effective Date, or the date of renewal of the then current term.

6. REPRESENTATIONS AND WARRANTIES.

A. Corporate Warranties. Each party hereby represents and warrants that: (i) it has the right, power, and authority to enter into this Agreement; (ii) the Agreement has been duly executed by the Party's authorized representative; and (iii) this Agreement does not contravene or otherwise conflict with any other agreement entered into by that Party.

B. Licensor's Warranties. Licensor represents and warrants that it has all title, rights, and interest in and to the Licensed Software and that Licensee's use of the Licensed Software will not infringe any patent, copyright, trademark, or other intellectual property right of any third party.

C. Licensor warrants that the Licensed Software shall be produced in a good and workmanlike manner and be substantially free from physical defects. EXCEPT FOR THE PRECEDING, LICENSOR MAKES NO WARRANTY, EITHER EXPRESS OR IMPLIED WITH RESPECT TO THE LICENSED SOFTWARE, ITS QUALITY, MERCHANTABILITY, OR FITNESS FOR A PARTICULAR PURPOSE. ALL LICENSED SOFTWARE PROVIDED HEREUNDER IS "AS IS," AND LICENSOR DOES NOT WARRANT THAT IT WILL BE ERROR-FREE. LICENSOR SHALL NOT BE LIABLE FOR ANY DAMAGES CAUSED, IN WHOLE OR IN PART, BY THE USE OF THE LICENSED SOFTWARE.

7. INDEMNIFICATION.

Licensor will indemnify and hold harmless the Licensee from any and all third party claims, liabilities, damages, and/or costs, including without limitation reasonable attorneys' fees, arising from the breach of its warranties in Section 6(B) of this Agreement.

8. LIMITATION OF LIABILITY.

IN NO EVENT SHALL LICENSOR'S ENTIRE LIABILITY UNDER THIS AGREEMENT EXCEED THE FEES PAID BY LICENSEE HEREUNDER DURING THE PRECEDING TWELVE (12) MONTHS.

IN NO EVENT WHATSOEVER SHALL EITHER PARTY BE LIABLE TO THE OTHER OR TO THIRD PARTIES FOR ANY LOST REVENUES OR LOST PROFITS OR OTHER DIRECT OR INDIRECT, INCIDENTAL, SPECIAL, PUNITIVE OR CONSEQUENTIAL DAMAGES INCURRED BY ANY PERSON, EVEN IF ADVISED OF THE POSSIBILITY OF SUCH DAMAGES OR CLAIMS.

9. CONFIDENTIALITY

A. Licensee understands and agrees that the Licensed Software contains certain information that is confidential and proprietary. Licensee agrees to maintain all information in the strictest confidence and to use the Licensed Software solely in accordance with the terms of this Agreement. Licensee further agrees to keep any materials, documentation, and technical information disclosed by Licensor strictly confidential.

B. Licensee's obligations with respect to such confidential information shall survive the termination of this Agreement. Not withstanding anything to the contrary in Section A, Licensee shall not be prohibited from using or disclosing information which: (i) is already available to the public as of the date of this Agreement; (ii) becomes publicly available through no fault of Licensee (or the fault of its employees or agents); (iii) is already known to Licensee at the time of its receipt thereof, as shown by written records existing and is available to Licensee from a third party who is not under an obligation of non-disclosure with respect to such information.

10. MISCELLANEOUS TERMS.

A. Assignability. The license granted hereunder is personal to Licensee and shall not be assigned by any act of Licensee or by operation of law unless in connection with a transfer of substantially all of the assets of Licensee, or with the consent of Licensor.

B. Choice of Law/Jurisdiction. This Agreement shall be governed in accordance with the laws of the State of _____, without regard to its choice of law or conflicts of law provisions. The parties consent to the jurisdiction of such courts.

C. Successors. The provisions of the Agreement shall be binding upon and shall inure to the benefit of the parties hereto, their heirs, administrators, successors and assigns.

D. Waiver/Severability. No waiver by either party of any default shall be deemed as a waiver of prior or subsequent default of the same or other provisions of this Agreement. If any term, clause or provision hereof is held invalid or unenforceable by a court of competent jurisdiction, such invalidity shall not affect the validity or operation of any other term, clause or provision and such invalid term, clause or provision shall be deemed to be severed from the Agreement.

E. Notices Between the Parties. Any notice required to be given pursuant to this Agreement shall be in writing and delivered personally to the other designated party at the above-stated address or mailed by certified or registered mail, return receipt requested or delivered by a recognized national overnight courier service. Either party may change the address to which notice or payment is to be sent by written notice to the other in accordance with the provisions of this paragraph.

F. No Joint Venture. The relationship between Licensor and Licensee is that of independent contractors, and nothing herein shall be construed as creating an employment, partnership, or a joint venture between them. Neither Party shall have the right to bind the other Party to any obligation or liability whatsoever.

G. Entire Agreement/Modification. This Agreement constitutes the entire understanding between the parties, and supersedes all prior agreements between the parties on this subject matter. This agreement shall not be modified or amended except in a writing signed by both parties. This Agreement shall take precedence over any other documents which may be in conflict with this Agreement.

H. Survival. Sections 1, 2(B) & (C), 6, 7, 8, 9, and 10(B) shall survive the expiration or termination of this Agreement.

IN WITNESS WHEREOF, the parties have caused their authorized representatives to make and sign this Agreement.

_____   _____
LICENSOR   LICENSEE

_____ _____   _____ _____
Name   Date   Name   Date

_____   _____
Title   Title

SHRINK-WRAP SOFTWARE LICENSE

PLEASE READ THIS LICENSE CAREFULLY BEFORE USING THE SOFTWARE. YOUR USE OF THE SOFTWARE SIGNIFIES THAT YOU AGREE TO BE BOUND BY THE TERMS OF THIS LICENSE. IF YOU DO NOT AGREE TO THE TERMS OF THIS LICENSE, PROMPTLY RETURN THE SOFTWARE FOR A FULL REFUND.

1. <u>License to Software.</u> The software accompanying this license ("**Software**"), is licensed to you by [*insert name of your company*] ("**Vendor**"). You own the medium on which the Software is recorded, but Vendor and Vendor's Third Party Suppliers own the Software and all documentation. This License gives you the right **solely** to:

(1) use the Software on a single computer;

(2) make **one copy** of the Software for backup purposes or archival purposes only. You must reproduce on such copy the Vendor's copyright notice and any other proprietary legends that were on the original copy of the Software;

(3) transfer your rights to the Software given to you under this License, to another party, provided such other party agrees to all terms and conditions of this License.

2. <u>Restrictions</u>. The Software contains copyrighted material, trade secrets and other proprietary material owned by Vendor and Vendor's Third Party Suppliers. In order to protect them, and except as permitted by applicable legislation, you may ***not***:

(1) modify, sell, sublicense, or distribute the Software in any way, or create derivative works based upon the Software;

(2) decompile, reverse engineer, or otherwise decode the Software, in whole or in part, in any way;

(3) electronically transmit the Software from one computer to another or over a network; or,

(4) post or distribute the Software online, or store the Software in a data warehouse.

3. <u>Termination</u>. This term of the License will continue indefinitely, or until it is terminated by a party. You may terminate this License at any time by destroying the Software, documentation and any copies of the Software. This License will terminate immediately without notice from Vendor if you fail to comply with any provision of this License. Upon termination you must destroy the Software, related documentation, and any copy you made of the Software.

4. Export Law Assurance. You agree and certify that neither the Software nor any other product or technical data received from Vendor will be exported outside the United States except as permitted and authorized by the laws and regulations of the United States.

5. Government Restricted Rights. The Software and documentation are provided with "Restricted Rights." Use, duplication, or disclosure by the Government is subject to restrictions as set forth in FAR52.227-14 and DFAR252.227-7013, et seq. Use of the Software by the Government constitutes acknowledgment of Licensor's proprietary rights to it.

6. Limited Warranty. Vendor warrants the tangible media which contains the Software to be free from defects in materials and workmanship under normal use for a period of ninety (90) days, starting from the date purchase. **VENDOR'S ENTIRE LIABILITY FOR SUCH DEFECTS, AND YOUR EXCLUSIVE REMEDY, WILL BE REPLACEMENT OF THE DEFECTIVE MEDIA.**

ANY IMPLIED WARRANTIES ON THE TANGIBLE MEDIA, INCLUDING THE IMPLIED WARRANTIES OF MERCHANTABILITY AND FITNESS FOR A PARTICULAR PURPOSE, ARE LIMITED IN DURATION TO NINETY (90) DAYS FROM THE DATE OF DELIVERY. THIS WARRANTY GIVES YOU SPECIFIC LEGAL RIGHTS, AND YOU MAY ALSO HAVE OTHER RIGHTS WHICH VARY BY JURISDICTION.

7. Disclaimer of Warranty on Software. The Software and related documentation are provided "As Is" and without warranty of any kind. **VENDOR EXPRESSLY DISCLAIMS ALL WARRANTIES, EXPRESS AND IMPLIED, INCLUDING, BUT NOT LIMITED TO, THE IMPLIED WARRANTIES OF MERCHANTABILITY AND FITNESS FOR A PARTICULAR PURPOSE. VENDOR DOES NOT WARRANT THAT THE SOFTWARE WILL MEET YOUR REQUIREMENTS, OR THAT THE OPERATION OF THE SOFTWARE WILL BE UNINTERRUPTED OR ERROR-FREE, OR THAT THE SOFTWARE WILL BE FREE OF DEFECTS.**

SOME JURISDICTIONS DO NOT ALLOW THE EXCLUSION OF IMPLIED WARRANTIES, SO THE ABOVE EXCLUSION MAY NOT APPLY TO YOU.

8. IN NO EVENT SHALL VENDOR'S TOTAL LIABILITY TO YOU FOR ALL DAMAGES, LOSS, AND CAUSES OF ACTION, INCLUDING WITHOUT LIMITATION CONTRACT, TORT, NEGLIGENCE, EXCEED THE AMOUNT PAID BY YOU FOR THE SOFTWARE.

UNDER NO CIRCUMSTANCES SHALL VENDOR, OR ITS DIRECTORS, OFFICERS, EMPLOYEES OR AGENTS, BE LIABLE TO YOU FOR ANY INCIDENTAL, INDIRECT, SPECIAL, PUNITIVE, OR CONSEQUENTIAL DAMAGES, INCLUDING WITHOUT LIMITATION LOST PROFITS, ARISING OUT OF THE USE OF THE SOFTWARE OR

DOCUMENTATION, EVEN IF VENDOR HAS BEEN ADVISED OF THE POSSIBILITY OF SUCH DAMAGES.

SOME JURISDICTIONS DO NOT ALLOW THE LIMITATION OR EXCLUSION OF LIABILITY FOR INCIDENTAL OR CONSEQUENTIAL DAMAGES, SO THE ABOVE LIMITATION OR EXCLUSION MAY NOT APPLY TO YOU.

9. <u>Miscellaneous.</u> This License is governed by the law of [***insert State***], without regard to its choice of law or conflicts of law provisions. Any action arising under, relating to or connected with this License or the use of the Software will be filed only in an appropriate court located in [***insert State***], and the parties agree to submit to the personal jurisdiction of such courts. No modification of any provision of this License will be effective, except by a written document signed by both parties. No waiver by either party of any default shall be deemed as a waiver of prior or subsequent default of the same or other provisions of this Agreement. If any term is held invalid or unenforceable by a court, this shall not affect the validity or operation of any other term, and such invalid or unenforceable term shall be deemed to be severed from this License.

CLICK-WRAP SOFTWARE LICENSE

PLEASE READ BEFORE DOWNLOADING OR COPYING. BY SELECTING THE "I ACCEPT" BUTTON BELOW, OR BY DOWNLOADING OR COPYING THE SOFTWARE, YOU ARE AGREEING TO BE BOUND BY THE TERMS AND CONDITIONS OF THIS LICENSE. DO NOT SELECT "I ACCEPT," DOWNLOAD, OR COPY THIS SPECIFICATION UNTIL YOU HAVE CAREFULLY READ, UNDERSTOOD, AND AGREED TO ALL THE TERMS AND CONDITIONS LISTED BELOW.

IF YOU SELECT "I DO NOT ACCEPT," THE DOWNLOAD PROCESS WILL NOT PROCEED. IF YOU DO NOT WISH TO AGREE TO THESE TERMS AND CONDITIONS DO NOT DOWNLOAD OR COPY THE SPECIFICATION.

1. License to Software. The software accompanying this license ("**Software**"), is licensed to you by [*insert name of your company*] ("**Licensor**"). Licensor and Licensor's Third Party Suppliers own the Software and all documentation. This License gives you the right **solely** to:

(1) use the Software on a single computer;

(2) make **one copy** of the Software for backup purposes or archival purposes only. You must reproduce on such copy the Vendor's copyright notice and any other proprietary legends that were on the original copy of the Software;

(3) transfer your rights to the Software given to you under this License, to another party, provided such other party agrees to all terms and conditions of this License.

2. Restrictions. The Software contains copyrighted material, trade secrets and other proprietary material owned by Licensor and Licensor's Third Party Suppliers. In order to protect them, and except as permitted by applicable legislation, you may not:

(1) modify, sell, sublicense, or distribute the Software in any way, or create derivative works based upon the Software;

(2) decompile, reverse engineer, or otherwise decode the Software, in whole or in part, in any way;

(3) electronically transmit the Software from one computer to another or over a network; or,

(4) post or distribute the Software online, or store the Software in a data warehouse.

3. <u>Termination.</u> This term of the License will continue indefinitely, or until it is terminated by a party. You may terminate this License at any time by destroying the Software, documentation and any copies of the Software. This License will terminate immediately without notice from Licensor if you fail to comply with any provision of this License. Upon termination you must destroy the Software, related documentation, and any copy you made of the Software.

4. <u>Export Law Assurance.</u> You agree and certify that neither the Software nor any other product or technical data received from Licensor will be exported outside the United States except as permitted and authorized by the laws and regulations of the United States.

5. <u>Government Restricted Rights.</u> The Software and documentation are provided with "Restricted Rights." Use, duplication, or disclosure by the Government is subject to restrictions as set forth in FAR52.227-14 and DFAR252.227-7013, et seq. Use of the Software by the Government constitutes acknowledgment of Licensor's proprietary rights to it.

6. <u>Disclaimer of Warranty on Software.</u> The Software and related documentation and information are provided "As Is" and without warranty of any kind. **LICENSOR EXPRESSLY DISCLAIMS ALL WARRANTIES, EXPRESS AND IMPLIED, INCLUDING, BUT NOT LIMITED TO, THE IMPLIED WARRANTIES OF MERCHANTABILITY AND FITNESS FOR A PARTICULAR PURPOSE. LICENSOR DOES NOT WARRANT THAT THE SOFTWARE WILL MEET YOUR REQUIREMENTS, OR THAT THE OPERATION OF THE SOFTWARE WILL BE UNINTERRUPTED OR ERROR-FREE, OR THAT THE SOFTWARE WILL BE FREE OF DEFECTS.**

SOME JURISDICTIONS DO NOT ALLOW THE EXCLUSION OF IMPLIED WARRANTIES, SO THE ABOVE EXCLUSION MAY NOT APPLY TO YOU.

7. IN NO EVENT SHALL LICENSOR'S TOTAL LIABILITY TO YOU FOR ALL DAMAGES, LOSS, AND CAUSES OF ACTION, INCLUDING WITHOUT LIMITATION CONTRACT, TORT, NEGLIGENCE, EXCEED THE AMOUNT PAID BY YOU FOR THE SOFTWARE.

UNDER NO CIRCUMSTANCES SHALL LICENSOR, OR ITS DIRECTORS, OFFICERS, EMPLOYEES OR AGENTS, BE LIABLE TO YOU FOR ANY INCIDENTAL, INDIRECT, SPECIAL, PUNITIVE, OR CONSEQUENTIAL DAMAGES, INCLUDING WITHOUT LIMITATION LOST PROFITS, ARISING OUT OF THE USE OF THE SOFTWARE, ANY INFORMATION, OR DOCUMENTATION, EVEN IF LICENSOR HAS BEEN ADVISED OF THE POSSIBILITY OF SUCH DAMAGES.

SOME JURISDICTIONS DO NOT ALLOW THE LIMITATION OR EXCLUSION OF LIABILITY FOR INCIDENTAL OR CONSEQUENTIAL DAMAGES, SO THE ABOVE LIMITATION OR EXCLUSION MAY NOT APPLY TO YOU.

8. Miscellaneous. This License is governed by the law of [*insert State*], without regard to its choice of law or conflicts of law provisions. Any action arising under, relating to or connected with this License or the use of the Software will be filed only in an appropriate court located in [*insert State*], and the parties agree to submit to the personal jurisdiction of such courts. No modification of any provision of this License will be effective, except by a written document signed by both parties. No waiver by either party of any default shall be deemed as a waiver of prior or subsequent default of the same or other provisions of this Agreement. If any term is held invalid or unenforceable by a court, this shall not affect the validity or operation of any other term, and such invalid or unenforceable term shall be deemed to be severed from this License.

PATENT LICENSE AGREEMENT

This Patent License Agreement (**Agreement**) is made and entered into this ___day of _____, 200_ (**Effective Date**) by and between _____, a _____ corporation with a principal place of business at _____ ("**Licensor**"), and _____, a _____ corporation with a principal place of business at _____ ("**Licensee**").

WITNESSETH:

WHEREAS, Licensor is the owner of certain patents, as further defined in Section 1 herein, relating to [*identify general field*] technology;

WHEREAS, Licensor desires to have the patents developed and commercialized and is willing to grant a license for this purpose; and,

WHEREAS, Licensee desires to obtain a license to use the Licensed Patents in order to manufacture and sell the Licensed Products, as further defined in Section 1 herein, in accordance with the terms and conditions set forth below.

NOW, THEREFORE, in consideration of the premises and the mutual covenants contained herein, the parties hereto agree as follows:

1. DEFINITIONS

A. "**Licensed Know-How**" is the information described in Schedule A, as may be amended.

B. "**Licensed Patents**" are all the patents listed in Schedule A, attached hereto and incorporated herein, as well as any patents resulting from the reissue or reexamination of such patents.

C. "**Licensed Product**" shall mean any product which incorporates any of the Licensed Patents, and as further identified and described in Schedule A.

D. "**Net Sales**" shall mean Licensee's billings for the Licensed Products less the sum of the following: [**list "net sales" deductions**].

E. "**Territory**" shall mean [**describe territory of the license grant**].

2. LICENSE GRANT

A. License Grant. Subject to the terms and conditions of this Agreement, Licensor hereby grants to Licensee a limited, nontransferable, nonexclusive right to manufacture and sell the Licensed Products solely in the Territory. Licensor further grants to Licensee the right to use the Licensed Know-How solely in connection with the manufacture of the Licensed Products. Licensee shall not have any rights of sublicense with respect to any of the rights granted herein.

B. Ownership and Proprietary Rights. Licensor shall at all times retain sole ownership in the Licensed Patents and the Licensed Know-How. Nothing in this Agreement or Licensee's use of the Licensed Patents or Licensed Know-How shall be deemed to grant Licensee any right, title, or interest in the Licensed Patents or Licensed Know-How, in whole or in part.

3. TERM

The Term of this Agreement shall begin on the Effective Date and continue for a period of _____ years, or the expiration of any of the Licensed Patents, unless this Agreement is terminated sooner, as provided herein.

4. PAYMENT

A. Royalty Provision. During the term of this Agreement, Licensee shall pay Licensor royalties of _____ % for each Licensed Product sold by Licensee, on a Net Sales basis. Royalties shall be calculated on a quarterly calendar basis, and each royalty payment shall be due within thirty (30) days after the end of the preceding quarter, for example on the 1st day of January, April, July, and October. Royalties shall commence on [***insert beginning date for royalties***] and continue until the expiration or earlier termination of this Agreement.

B. Royalty Statements and Reports. On a quarterly basis throughout the term of this Agreement, Licensee shall deliver to Licensor an accurate royalty statement, setting forth the number of Licensed Products sold and description, gross invoice, amount billed customers, net sales discounts, and royalty paid. Licensee shall provide such royalty statements to Licensor regardless whether any sales were actually made during the quarter.

C. Records and Accounting. Licensee shall keep full and accurate accounting information on the sales of the Licensed Products and the royalty amounts paid payable to Licensor, as provided hereunder.

During the term of this Agreement, and for a period of __ years thereafter, Licensor shall have the right to inspect Licensee's books, records, and all other materials and information relating or pertaining to this license and Licensee's payment of the royalties hereunder. Licensor shall conduct such inspections only during business hours and not more than once in any calendar year, and provide two (2) days notice to Licensee before such inspection. In the event that such inspection reveals a discrepancy of more than 5% between what Licensor was owed versus Licensee's actual payments, Licensee shall immediately pay the difference and shall further reimburse Licensor for all reasonable costs of such inspection.

Licensor shall keep all information obtained from such disclosures strictly confidential and shall not disclose any confidential or proprietary business information belonging to Licensee, unless agreed to by Licensee in writing or required by law. Notwithstanding the preceding, such confidential or proprietary information may be used in any legal proceeding based on Licensee's failure to pay the royalties due hereunder.

D. Late Payments. The royalty payments set forth in this Agreement shall, if overdue, bear interest until payment at a per *month* rate of ___%. The payment of such interest shall not prevent Licensor from exercising any other rights it may have in law and equity with respect to Licensee's late payments.

5. MARKETING OF LICENSED PRODUCTS

Licensee shall use all commercially reasonable efforts to actively and diligently market the Licensed Products, as provided herein, throughout the term of this Agreement.

6. TERMINATION

A. Licensor's Right to Terminate. Licensee shall, upon prior written notice, have the immediate right to terminate this Agreement if Licensee breaches the license grant provisions in Section 2(A) or the confidentiality obligations in Section 13. The Licensor's rights as set forth in this section shall not be deemed exhaustive of their rights in law and equity.

B. Mutual Termination Conditions. Subject to Subsection C below, either party shall have the right to terminate this Agreement upon the occurrence of any of the following events (hereinafter referred to as a "Default"):

(1) a party files a petition under any of the United States bankruptcy laws;

(2) voluntary proceedings under the United States bankruptcy laws are commenced by creditors against a party;

(3) one of the parties voluntarily dissolves or attempts to dissolve itself as a corporation; or,

(4) a material breach of a term or condition of this Agreement other than those set forth in subsection A, above.

C. Notification and Cure. If any of these events in Subsection B occurs, the non-defaulting party shall give the defaulting party written notice, and shall have the right to terminate this Agreement if the defaulting party does not cure such default within thirty (30) days from receipt of such notice. The parties' rights as set forth in this section shall not be deemed exhaustive of their rights in law and equity.

D. Post-Termination Rights and Obligations. Upon termination of this Agreement for any reason, Licensee shall immediately cease manufacturing and selling the Licensed Products, provided that: (i) Licensee shall immediately pay off all amounts due Licensor; and (ii) Licensee shall have the right to sell any of its remaining inventory of the Licensed Products for a period of _____ months thereafter. Licensee shall provide Licensor with a written accounting of such remaining inventory and shall continue to make all royalty payments (and provide royalty statements) as provided in Section 4, during such inventory sell-off period. Upon termination, each Party shall also immediately return to the other all materials and documents, including copies, belonging to the other Party.

7. REPRESENTATIONS AND WARRANTIES.

A. Corporate Warranties. Each party hereby represents and warrants that: (i) it has the right, power, and authority to enter into this Agreement; (ii) the Agreement has been duly executed by the Party's authorized representative; and (iii) this Agreement does not contravene or otherwise conflict with any other agreement entered into by that Party.

B. Licensor's Warranties. Licensor represents and warrants that it has all title, rights, and interest in and to the Licensed Patents and Licensed Know-How. Licensor further represents and warrants that to the best of its knowledge, Licensee's use of the Licensed Patents and/or Licensed Know-How will not infringe any intellectual property right of any third party.

8. INDEMNIFICATION.

A. Indemnification by Licensor. Licensor shall indemnify and hold License, its directors, officers, and employees, harmless against all claims, proceedings, demands, and liabilities of any kind whatsoever, including reasonable attorneys' fees, arising out of breach of its warranties in Section 7 hereunder.

B. Indemnification by Licensee. Licensee shall indemnify and hold Licensor, its directors, officers, and employees, harmless against all claims, proceedings, demands, and liabilities of any kind whatsoever, including reasonable attorneys' fees, arising out of: (i) breach of its warranties in Section 7 hereunder; (ii) death of or injury to any person or persons or out of any damage to property, result-ing from the production, manufacture, sale, of the Licensed Product; or (iii) breach of Section 2(A) or Section 13 hereunder.

9. LIMITATION OF LIABILITY.

NEITHER PARTY SHALL BE LIABLE TO THE OTHER FOR ANY LOST REV-ENUES OR LOST PROFITS OR OTHER INDIRECT, INCIDENTAL, SPECIAL, PUNITIVE OR CONSEQUENTIAL DAMAGES INCURRED BY ANY PERSON, EVEN IF ADVISED OF THE POSSIBILITY OF SUCH DAMAGES OR CLAIMS.

10. PATENT PROSECUTION AND MARKING.

A. Licensor's Prosecution of Licensed Patents. Licensor shall, in its sole discretion, apply for, seek prompt issuance of, maintain the Licensed Patents during the term of this Agreement.

B. Licensee's Marking Obligations. To the extent commercially feasible, Licensee shall mark all Licensed Products that are manufactured or sold under this Agreement with the number of each issued patent under the Licensed Patents that applies to such Licensed Product.

11. THIRD PARTY INFRINGEMENT

Licensee shall make all commercially reasonable efforts to inform Licensor if it learns of any third party infringement of the Licensed Patents by a third party, and shall provide Licensor with any avail-able evidence thereof.

12. INSURANCE

Licensee shall, for the Term of the Agreement, obtain and maintain at its own cost and expense a stan-dard Product Liability Insurance in the amount of $_____ naming Licensor as an additional insured. Such policy shall provide protection against any and all claims, demands and causes of action arising out of any defects or failure to perform, alleged or otherwise, of the Licensed Products. Licensee shall furnish Licensor a certificate of insurance from this policy within thirty (30) days after execution of this Agreement.

13. CONFIDENTIALITY

Licensee understands and acknowledges that the Licensed Know-How is a confidential trade secret belonging to Licensor. Licensee agrees to maintain all Know-How, Licensor information, and the terms and information contained in this Agreement in the strictest confidence. Licensee shall not disclose any such Know-How or information to any third party under any circumstances. This provision shall survive expiration or earlier termination of this Agreement.

14. MISCELLANEOUS TERMS

A. Assignability. The license granted hereunder is personal to Licensee and shall not be assigned by any act of Licensee or by operation of law unless in connection with a transfer of substantially all of the assets of Licensee or with the consent of Licensor.

B. Choice of Law/Jurisdiction. This Agreement shall be governed in accordance with the laws of the State of [*insert State*], without regard to its choice of law or conflicts of law provisions. The parties consent to the jurisdiction of such courts, agree to accept service of process by mail, and hereby waive any jurisdictional or venue defenses otherwise available to it.

C. Successors. The provisions of the Agreement shall be binding upon and shall inure to the benefit of the parties hereto, their heirs, administrators, successors and assigns.

D. Waiver/Severability. No waiver by either party of any default shall be deemed as a waiver of prior or subsequent default of the same or other provisions of this Agreement. If any term, clause or provision hereof is held invalid or unenforceable by a court of competent jurisdiction, such invalidity shall not affect the validity or operation of any other term, clause or provision and such invalid term, clause, or provision shall be deemed to be severed from the Agreement.

E. Notices Between the Parties. Any notice required to be given pursuant to this Agreement shall be in writing and delivered personally to the other designated party at the above-stated address or mailed by certified or registered mail, return receipt requested or delivered by a recognized national overnight courier service. Either party may change the address to which notice or payment is to be sent by written notice to the other in accordance with the provisions of this paragraph.

F. No Joint Venture. The relationship between Licensor and Licensee is that of independent contractors, and nothing herein shall be construed as creating an employment, a partnership, or a joint venture. Neither Party shall have the right to bind the other Party to any obligation or liability whatsoever.

G. Entire Agreement/Modification. This Agreement constitutes the entire understanding between the parties, and supersedes all prior agreements between the parties on this subject matter. This agreement shall not be modified or amended except in a writing signed by both parties. This Agreement shall take precedence over any other documents which may be in conflict with this Agreement.

H. Survival. Sections 1, 2(B), 4(C), 6(D), 7, 8, 9, 13 and applicable provisions in Section 14 shall survive the expiration or termination of this Agreement.

IN WITNESS WHEREOF, the parties have duly executed this Agreement the day and year set forth below.

LICENSOR   **LICENSEE**

_____   _____

Name   Date   Name   Date

_____   _____

Title   Title

SCHEDULE A

(1) Licensed Patents. The following *United States Patents* are to be licensed under this Agreement:

1. U.S. Patent No. _____—titled _____, issued on _____, _____.

2. U.S. Patent No. _____—titled _____, issued on _____, _____.

3. U.S. Patent No. _____—titled _____, issued on _____, _____.

(2) Licensed "Know-How". The following technical information is licensed:

(3) Licensed Product. The following products are to be manufactured and sold by Licensee under this Agreement:

1. [*Describe Product*]

WEB LICENSE AGREEMENT

This Content License Agreement ("**Agreement**"), effective as of this __ day of _____, 20__, by and between _____, a _____ corporation, with a principal place of business at _____ ("**Licensor**"), and _____, a _____ corporation with a principal place of business at _____ ("**Licensee**").

WITNESSETH:

WHEREAS, Licensee has a World Wide Web site on the Internet at **www._____.com** ("Website"), which is intended to [**describe general purpose of the website**];

WHEREAS, Licensor is the sole and exclusive owner of certain [generally describe content], described more fully in Schedule A, attached hereto and incorporated herein ("Content"); and

WHEREAS, Licensor desires to grant Licensee the right to reproduce and post the Content on the Website, subject to the terms and conditions of this agreement.

NOW, THEREFORE, in consideration of the premises and the mutual covenants of this Agreement, the parties hereto agree as follows:

1. LICENSE GRANT

A. License Grant. Subject to the terms and conditions of this Agreement, Licensor hereby grants to Licensee a nontransferable, nonexclusive, worldwide right solely to use, reproduce, distribute, and publicly display the Content on the Website. Licensee shall not have the right to sublicense this Content, in whole or in part.

B. Licensee Rights. Licensee may, at its sole discretion, use reasonable excerpts or portions of the Content on [***describe how Content will be used***]. Licensor will not materially alter the Content without Licensee's prior written consent. Licensee shall have sole control over the overall "look and feel" of the website. Licensee shall have sole responsibility for hosting and maintaining, at its own expense, the website.

C. Rights and Responsibilities of the Parties. Licensor and Licensee agree to the following:

(1) [***describe delivery of the Content***];

(2) [***describe provision of any update, revisions***];

(3) *[describe any Licensor attribution and copyright notices for Licensor's Content on the Website.*

2. TERM

The term of this Agreement shall be one (1) year. This Agreement shall automatically renew for successive one year terms, unless either Party notifies the other in writing, not less than thirty (30) days prior to expiration of the then current term, of such Party's intent not to renew this Agreement.

3. TERMINATION

A. Termination for Breach. This Agreement may be terminated by either Party for the material breach of the other party, provided that the non-breaching Party gives written notice to the breaching Party and a thirty (30) day opportunity to cure such breach.

B. Post-Termination Rights and Obligations. Upon the expiration or earlier termination of this Agreement, Licensee shall immediately cease using the Content as provided herein. In addition, all payments that are owed Licensor shall be immediately payable in full.

4. PAYMENT

Licensee agrees to pay the Licensor a license fee in the amount of $_____ per year for the license granted herein. Payment shall be made within thirty (30) days of the Effective Date, or the date of renewal of the then current term.

5. OWNERSHIP

A. Licensor's Property. Licensor shall retain all right, title and interest in and to the Content, subject to the license grant to Licensee hereunder.

B. Licensee's Property. Licensee will retain all right, title, and interest in and to the website worldwide including without limitation ownership of all copyrights, trademarks, look and feel, and other intellectual property rights therein, as well as all right, title, and interest in and to its trademarks, service marks and trade names worldwide, including any goodwill associated therewith.

6. WARRANTY AND INDEMNITY

A. Corporate Warranties. Each party hereby represents and warrants that: (i) it has the right, power, and authority to enter into this Agreement; (ii) the Agreement has been duly executed by the Party's authorized representative; and (iii) this Agreement does not contravene or otherwise conflict with any other agreement entered into by that Party.

B. Licensor's Warranties. Licensor represents and warrants that it has all title, rights, and interest in and to the Content and that Licensee's use of the Content will not infringe any intellectual property right of any third party.

7. INDEMNIFICATION

A. Indemnification by Licensor. Licensor will indemnify and hold harmless Licensee, its officers, directors, and employees from any and all third party claims, liability, damages, and/or costs (including, but not limited to, attorneys fees) arising from its breach of any of its warranties in Section 6 herein.

B. Indemnification by Licensee. Licensee will indemnify and hold harmless Licensor, its officers, directors, employees, from any and all third, party claims, liability, damages, and/or costs (including but not limited to, attorneys fees) arising from its breach of its warranties in Section 5 herein or breach of the license grant in Section 6 herein.

8. LIMITATION OF LIABILITY

NEITHER PARTY SHALL BE LIABLE TO THE OTHER FOR ANY LOST REVENUES OR LOST PROFITS OR OTHER INDIRECT, INCIDENTAL, SPECIAL, PUNITIVE OR CON-SEQUENTIAL DAMAGES INCURRED BY ANY PERSON, EVEN IF ADVISED OF THE POSSIBILITY OF SUCH DAMAGES OR CLAIMS.

9. MISCELLANEOUS TERMS

A. Assignability. The license granted hereunder is personal to Licensee and shall not be assigned by any act of Licensee or by operation of law unless in connection with a transfer of substantially all of the assets of Licensee, or with the consent of Licensor.

B. Choice of Law/Jurisdiction. This Agreement shall be governed in accordance with the laws of the State of *[insert State]*, without regard to its choice of law or conflicts of law provisions. The parties consent to the jurisdiction of all such courts.

C. Successors. The provisions of the Agreement shall be binding upon and shall inure to the benefit of the parties hereto, their heirs, administrators, successors and assigns.

D. Waiver/Severability. No waiver by either party of any default shall be deemed as a waiver of prior or subsequent default of the same or other provisions of this Agreement. If any term, clause or provision hereof is held invalid or unenforceable by a court of competent jurisdiction, such invalidity shall not affect the validity or operation of any other term, clause or provision and such invalid term, clause or provision shall be deemed to be severed from the Agreement.

E. Notices Between the Parties. Any notice required to be given pursuant to this Agreement shall be in writing and delivered personally to the other designated party at the above-stated address or mailed by certified or registered mail, return receipt requested or delivered by a recognized national overnight courier service. Either party may change the address to which notice or payment is to be sent by written notice to the other in accordance with the provisions of this paragraph.

F. No Joint Venture. The relationship between Licensor and Licensee is that of independent contractors, and nothing herein shall be construed as creating an employment, partnership, or a joint venture between them. Neither Party shall have the right to bind the other Party to any obligation or liability whatsoever.

G. Entire Agreement/Modification. This Agreement constitutes the entire understanding between the parties, and supersedes all prior agreements between the parties on this subject matter. This agreement shall not be modified or amended except in a writing signed by both parties. This Agreement shall take precedence over any other documents which may be in conflict with this Agreement.

H. Survival. Sections 3B, 5, 6, 7, 8, and applicable subsections of 9 shall survive the expiration or termination of this Agreement.

IN WITNESS WHEREOF, the parties hereto have caused this Agreement to be duly executed on the date below written.

_____	_____
LICENSOR	LICENSEE
_____	_____
Name Date	Name Date
_____	_____
Title	Title

EXHIBIT A

The following content is to be licensed under the terms and conditions of this Agreement:

1.

2.

3.

4.

5.

TRADEMARK LICENSE AGREEMENT

This Trademark License Agreement ("Agreement"), effective as of this __ day of _____, 20__, by and between _____, a _____ corporation, with a principal place of business at _____ ("Licensor"), and _____, a _____ corporation with a principal place of business at _____ ("Licensee").

WITNESSETH:

WHEREAS, Licensor is the owner of the federally registered trademarks identified in Schedule A, attached hereto and incorporated herein (the "Licensed Marks").

WHEREAS, Licensee desires to use the Licensed Marks on and in connection with certain products in accordance with Licensor's product quality standards, further described in Schedule B, attached hereto and incorporated herein ("Product Quality Standards"); and

WHEREAS, Licensor desires to license the Licensed Marks to Licensee under the terms and conditions of this Agreement.

NOW, THEREFORE, in consideration of the mutual covenants and promises contained herein, the receipt and sufficiency of which are hereby acknowledged, the parties hereto agree as follows.

1. LICENSE GRANT

A. License Grant. Subject to the terms and conditions of this Agreement, Licensor grants to Licensee a nonexclusive, nontransferable, license to use the Licensed Marks in connection with and on certain products further described in Schedule A ("Licensed Products"), solely within the territory of [*define territory*], and which conforms and is in compliance with Licensor's Product Quality Standards. This license shall not give Licensee the right to sublicense any of the Licensed Marks.

B. Use of the Licensed Marks. Licensee shall use the Licensed Marks in accordance with the terms and conditions of this Agreement and in compliance with all applicable laws and regulations regarding the use and designation of trademarks. Licensee shall comply with Licensor's terms and conditions, set forth in writing from time to time, with respect to the style, appearance, and manner of use of the Licensed Marks. Licensee shall apply the appropriate legends and notices, as set forth in Exhibit B, to the Licensed Marks.

2. QUALITY CONTROL

A. Conformity to Product Quality Standards. Licensee shall apply the Licensed Marks only to Products which have been manufactured by Licensee in accordance with Licensor's Product Quality Standards in materials, workmanship, design, advertising, and promotion. Licensee expressly agrees that it will not use the Licensed Marks with any products that do not meet such Product Quality Standards. Licensor shall have the right to revise the Product Quality Standards from time to time, at its sole discretion, provided it gives reasonable notice to Licensee of any revisions.

B. Product Samples. Licensee agrees to furnish to Licensor samples of the Licensed Products bearing the Licensed Marks, as Licensor may request from time to time. Licensor shall inspect Licensed Products in order to test the conformity of the Products with Licensor's Product Quality Standards. Licensor shall notify Licensee of compliance or noncompliance of the samples with such Product Quality Standards. In the event of noncompliance, Licensee shall immediately cease all manufacture and sale of the nonconforming Licensed Products until further notice from Licensor. Licensee shall bear all costs for the shipment and return of samples.

C. Right to Inspect Licensed Products. Licensor shall have the right, upon reasonable notice, at any time during regular business hours, to inspect all Licensed Products manufactured by Licensee at Licensee's facilities, in order to determine compliance of such Products with Licensor's Product Quality Standards. If at any time such Products shall, in Licensor's sole opinion, fail to conform with Licensor's Quality Standards, Licensor shall notify Licensee of such nonconformance. Licensee shall then cease all manufacture and sale of the nonconforming Products until the further notice by Licensor.

D. Confidentiality. The Product Quality Standards are proprietary to Licensor and Licensee shall maintain these in the strictest confidence, and shall not disclose such to any third party.

3. OWNERSHIP AND PROPRIETARY RIGHTS

Licensee acknowledges that all right, title and interest in and to the Licensed Marks is and shall remain with the Licensor, and that Licensee shall not oppose or do anything inconsistent with such ownership, and shall not use or register any trademark which resembles or is confusingly similar to the Licensed Marks. Licensee further agrees that it shall not challenge the validity of such ownership or make any claim to the Licensed Marks or against Licensor's title in same. Licensee agrees and acknowledges that any and all rights that may be acquired by use of any of the Licensed Marks shall inure solely for the benefit of and on behalf of Licensor. Licensee agrees to execute all papers reasonably requested by Licensor relating to the registration, maintenance, and/or renewal of the Licensed Marks. Licensee agrees that nothing in this Agreement shall give Licensee any right, title or interest in or to the Licensed Marks other than the limited rights granted herein.

4. TERM

The term of this Agreement shall be _____ years. This Agreement shall automatically renew for successive one year terms, unless either Party shall notify the other in writing, not less than thirty (30) days prior to expiration of the then current term, of such Party's intent not to renew this Agreement.

5. TERMINATION

A. Licensor's Right to Terminate. Licensor shall, upon prior written notice, have the right to immediately terminate this Agreement if Licensee breaches any of the provisions of Section 1 (License Grant), Section 2 (Quality Control) or Section 3 (Ownership and Proprietary Rights). The Licensor's rights as set forth in this section shall *not* be deemed exhaustive of their rights in law and equity.

B. Mutual Termination Conditions. Subject to Subsection C below, either party shall have the right to terminate this Agreement upon the occurrence of any of the following events (hereinafter referred to as a "Default"):

(1) a party files a petition under any of the United States bankruptcy laws;

(2) voluntary proceedings under the United States bankruptcy laws are commenced by creditors against a party;

(3) one of the parties voluntarily dissolves or attempts to dissolve itself as a corporation; or,

(4) a material breach of a term or condition of this Agreement other than those set forth in subsection A, above.

C. Notification and Cure. If any of these events in Section 5(B) occurs, the non-defaulting party shall give the defaulting party written notice, and shall have the right to terminate this Agreement if the defaulting party does not cure such default within thirty (30) days from receipt of such notice. The parties' rights as set forth in this section shall not be deemed exhaustive of their rights in law and equity.

D. Post-Termination Rights and Obligations. Upon the expiration or termination of this Agreement for any reason, Licensee shall immediately cease manufacturing and selling the Licensed Products, provided that Licensee shall have the right to sell any of its remaining inventory of the Licensed Products for a period of _____ months thereafter. Licensee shall provide Licensor with a written accounting of such remaining inventory and shall continue to make all royalty payments (and provide royalty statements) as provided in Section 6 herein, during such inventory sell-off period. Licensee shall destroy all printed materials bearing the Licensed Marks. All amounts due Licensor before expiration or termination of this Agreement shall also be immediately payable. Each Party shall also immediately return to the other all materials and documents, including copies, belonging to the other Party.

6. PAYMENT

A. Royalty Provision. During the term of this Agreement, Licensee shall pay Licensor royalties of _____ % on Net Sales of each Licensed Product sold by Licensee. Royalties shall be calculated on a quarterly calendar basis, and each royalty payment shall be due within thirty (30) days after the end of the preceding quarter, for example on the 1st day of January, April, July, and October. Royalties shall commence on *[insert beginning date for royalties]* and continue until the expiration or earlier termination of this Agreement.

B. Net Sales. "Net Sales" as used herein shall mean Licensee's gross sales, as indicated by customer invoices, minus *[indicate net sales deductions]*.

C. Royalty Statements and Reports. On a quarterly basis throughout the term of this Agreement, Licensee shall deliver to Licensor an accurate royalty statement, setting forth the number of Licensed Products sold and description, gross invoice, amount billed customers, net sales discounts, and royalty paid. Licensee shall provide such royalty statements to Licensor regardless whether any sales were actually made during the quarter.

D. Records and Accounting. Licensee shall keep full and accurate accounting information on the sales of the Licensed Products and the royalty amounts paid payable to Licensor, as provided hereunder.

During the term of this Agreement, and for a period of __ years thereafter, Licensor shall have the right to inspect Licensee's books, records, and all other materials and information relating or pertaining to this license and Licensee's payment of the royalties hereunder. Licensor shall conduct such inspections only during business hours, not more than once in any calendar year, and shall provide two (2) days notice to Licensee before any such inspection. In the event that such inspection reveals a discrepancy of more than 5% between what Licensor was owed versus Licensee's actual payments, Licensee shall immediately pay the difference and shall further reimburse Licensor for all reasonable costs of such inspection.

Licensor shall keep all information obtained from such disclosures strictly confidential and shall not disclose any confidential or proprietary business information belonging to Licensee, unless agreed to by Licensee in writing or required by law. Such confidentiality shall survive the termination of this Agreement. Notwithstanding the preceding, such confidential or proprietary information may be used in any legal proceeding based on Licensee's failure to pay the royalties due hereunder.

E. Late Payments. The royalty payments set forth in this Agreement shall, if overdue, bear interest until payment at a per *month* rate of ____%. The payment of such interest shall not prevent Licensor from exercising any other rights it may have in law and equity with respect to Licensee's late payments.

7. REPRESENTATIONS AND WARRANTIES

Each party hereby represents and warrants that: (i) it has the right, power, and authority to enter into this Agreement; (ii) the Agreement has been duly executed by the Party's authorized representative; and (iii) this Agreement does not contravene or otherwise conflict with any other agreement entered into by that Party.

8. INDEMNIFICATION

A. Indemnification by Licensor. Licensor shall indemnify and hold License, its directors, officers, and employees, harmless against all claims, proceedings, demands and liabilities of any kind whatsoever, including reasonable attorneys' fees, arising out of breach of any of its warranties in Section 7 hereunder.

B. Indemnification by Licensee. Licensee shall indemnify and hold Licensor, its directors, officers, and employees, harmless against all claims, proceedings, demands and liabilities of any kind whatsoever, including reasonable attorneys' fees, arising from a: (i) breach of any provision in Section 1 (License Grant), Section 2 (Quality Control) and Section 3 (Ownership & Proprietary Rights); (ii) death of or injury to any person or persons or out of any damage to property, resulting from the production, manufacture, sale, of the Licensed Products; or (iii) breach of Section any of its warranties in Section 7 hereunder.

9. LIMITATION OF LIABILITY

NEITHER PARTY SHALL BE LIABLE FOR ANY SPECIAL, INCIDENTAL, PUNITIVE, OR CONSEQUENTIAL DAMAGES, INCLUDING WITHOUT LIMITATION LOST PROFITS, EVEN IF IT HAS BEEN ADVISED OF THE POSSIBILITY OF SUCH DAMAGES.

10. THIRD PARTY INFRINGEMENTS

Licensee agrees to promptly notify Licensor of any unauthorized use of the Licensed Marks by others as such use comes to Licensee's attention. Licensor shall have the sole right and discretion to bring infringement or any other proceeding in law or equity to protect the Licensed Marks, but shall not be obligated to do so.

11. INSURANCE

Licensee shall, for the Term of the Agreement, obtain and maintain at its own cost and expense a standard Product Liability Insurance in the amount of $_____ naming Licensor as an additional insured. Such policy shall provide protection against any and all claims, demands and causes of action arising out of any defects or failure to perform, alleged or otherwise, of the Licensed Products. Licensee shall furnish Licensor a certificate of insurance from this policy within thirty (30) days after execution of this Agreement, as well as proof of premium payments as may be requested by Licensor from time to time.

12. MISCELLANEOUS TERMS

A. Assignability. The license granted hereunder is personal to Licensee and shall not be assigned by any act of Licensee or by operation of law unless in connection with a transfer of substantially all of the assets of Licensee or with the consent of Licensor.

B. Choice of Law/Jurisdiction. This Agreement shall be governed in accordance with the laws of the State of *[Insert State]*, without regard to its choice of law or conflicts of law provisions. The parties consent to the jurisdiction of such courts, agree to accept service of process by mail.

C. Successors. The provisions of the Agreement shall be binding upon and shall inure to the benefit of the parties hereto, their heirs, administrators, successors and assigns.

D. Waiver/Severability. No waiver by either party of any default shall be deemed as a waiver of prior or subsequent default of the same or other provisions of this Agreement. If any term, clause or provision hereof is held invalid or unenforceable by a court of competent jurisdiction, such invalidity shall not affect the validity or operation of any other term, clause or provision and such invalid term, clause or provision shall be deemed to be severed from the Agreement.

E. Notices Between the Parties. Notices required under this Agreement shall be in writing and shall be sent by registered or certified mail, return receipt requested. Such notices shall be addressed to the parties at the addresses set forth below, or at such other address as may be specified by either party:

LICENSOR:

[Indicate Licensor's Contact Person & Address]

LICENSEE:

[Indicate Licensee's Contact Person & Address]

F. No Joint Venture. The relationship between Licensor and Licensee is that of independent contractors, and nothing herein shall be construed as creating an employment, partnership, or a joint venture between them. Neither Party shall have the right to bind the other Party to any obligation or liability whatsoever.

G. Entire Agreement / Modification. This Agreement constitutes the entire understanding between the parties, and supersedes all prior agreements between the parties on this subject matter. This agreement shall not be modified or amended except in a writing signed by both parties. This Agreement shall take precedence over any other documents which may be in conflict with this Agreement.

H. Survival. Sections 2(D), 3, 5(D), 7, 8, 9, and applicable provisions of Section 12 shall serve the expiration or earlier termination of this Agreement.

IN WITNESS WHEREOF, the parties hereto have caused this Agreement to be duly executed on the date below written.

_____   _____
LICENSOR   LICENSEE

_____   _____
Name   Date   Name   Date

_____   _____
Title   Title

SCHEDULE A

1. Licensed Marks. The following trademarks are being licensed under this Agreement:
[*identify and describe trademarks, whether registered, and registration number*]

2. Licensed Products. The following Licensed Products form part of this Agreement:
[*describe products on which trademarks will be placed*]

<u>SCHEDULE B</u>

1. Product Quality Standards:

[*Detailed description of Licensor's Product Quality Standards for manufacture of the Licensed Products*]

2. Notices to be Placed on Licensed Products:

3. Additional Conditions for the style, appearance, and use of Licensed Marks:

APPENDIX G
SAMPLE PERMISSION
DOCUMENTS

This appendix provides forms you can use to request permission. Response times to a permission request will generally take several weeks to complete. Plan ahead accordingly. If you do not obtain a response after sending in your response, you can send out a second request. Just remember to label your request as a SECOND REQUEST in bold letters so as not to confuse the people to whom you have sent your request.

This is a general form that you can adapt for your request. The form is simplified in that it does not include many of the terms in respect to the scope of rights requested that can be included in a permission request. You should insert such terms only after you understand them from reading the Explanation of Terms. The use of these terms will of course depend on which point of view you take (i.e., the view of a permission grantor is going to be different than a permission seeker).

If you are the grantor of permission, you can use this form (or your own adapted one) to notify the requester that you have approved the permission request.

You can use a form similar to this one if you have been asked for permission but do not own the rights which the requester seeks.

SAMPLE PERMISSION REQUEST COVER LETTER

A sample permission request for appears below. If you are mailing or faxing your request form, you should also include a cover letter to the rights holder. A sample cover letter that you can use also appears below.

[Date]

[Company Name]

Attention: Permission Department

Re: Permission Request

Dear Sir or Madam:

I would like to obtain permission to use certain material that I believe is protected by copyright owned by you. Attached to this cover letter is a request form that sets out the applicable information for my request.

Kindly grant my request for the foregoing rights by signing and returning to me a signed copy of the request form. I would greatly appreciate it if you could return the letter to me no later than _____

If you do not own the rights for which I seek permission, or if additional copyright permissions are needed, kindly indicate who I can contact to obtain these rights.

Sincerely,

_____

SAMPLE PERMISSION REQUEST FORM

My name: _____

My address: _____

My Phone: _____

My Fax: _____

My email: _____

Details of Work Requested:

Title of work: _____

Author(s): _____

Volume/Edition: _____

Date of Publication: _____

Location of desired material:

_____

Details of New Work:

Author: _____

Publisher: _____

Proposed number of pages: _____

Expected Publication Date: _____

Proposed list price: _____

Quantity of first printing: _____

Scope of Rights Sought:

Territory:_____

Distribution Process (include whether electronic/print or both):

_____
_____-
_____

Other Terms:

_____
_____

AGREED AND ACCEPTED:

BY: _____
(Print Name and Title) (Licensor)

BY: _____
(Print Name and Title) (Licensee/Requester)

SAMPLE PERMISSION ACCEPTANCE LETTER

[Date]

[Company Name]

Re: Permission Request

Dear Sir or Madam:

We are pleased to grant permission to you as outlined under the terms of the attached *permission request form.* This permission is subject to your payment of a one time fee of $_____ dollars.

Should you elect not to use this material, please return a copy of the *permission request form* with the words *cancelled* on the face of the form.

Sincerely,

_____

PERMISSION REFERRAL LETTER

[Date]

[Company Name]

Re: _____ (title/author)

Dear Sir or Madam:

Thank you for your recent request to use material from the reference title. Unfortunately, we do not control the rights for the material that you wish to use for the following reasons:

_____ The material you have requested is subject to a copyright owned by another person. We were granted permission to use this material from _____. Thus, you may want to contact that person to determine the current copyright holder.

_____ The material you have requested is now in the public domain.

INDEX

SPHINX® PUBLISHING ORDER FORM

BILL TO:		SHIP TO:	
Phone #	**Terms**	**F.O.B.** Chicago, IL	**Ship Date**

Charge my: ☐ VISA ☐ MasterCard ☐ American Express

☐ **Money Order or Personal Check**

Credit Card Number

Expiration Date

Qty	ISBN	Title	Retail	Ext.	Qty	ISBN	Title	Retail	Ext.
		SPHINX PUBLISHING NATIONAL TITLES				1-57248-089-0	Neighbor v. Neighbor (2E)	$16.95	
	1-57248-238-9	The 529 College Savings Plan	$16.95			1-57248-169-2	The Power of Attorney Handbook (4E)	$19.95	
	1-57248-349-0	The Antique and Art Collector's Legal Guide	$24.95			1-57248-332-6	Profit from Intellectual Property	$28.95	
	1-57248-148-X	Cómo Hacer su Propio Testamento	$16.95			1-57248-329-6	Protect Your Patent	$24.95	
	1-57248-226-5	Cómo Restablecer su propio Crédito y Renegociar sus Deudas	$21.95			1-57248-344-X	Repair Your Own Credit and Deal with Debt (2E)	$18.95	
	1-57248-147-1	Cómo Solicitar su Propio Divorcio	$24.95			1-57248-350-4	El Seguro Social Preguntas y Respuestas	$14.95	
	1-57248-166-8	The Complete Book of Corporate Forms	$24.95			1-57248-217-6	Sexual Harassment: Your Guide to Legal Action	$18.95	
	1-57248-229-X	The Complete Legal Guide to Senior Care	$21.95			1-57248-219-2	The Small Business Owner's Guide to Bankruptcy	$21.95	
	1-57248-201-X	The Complete Patent Book	$26.95			1-57248-168-4	The Social Security Benefits Handbook (3E)	$18.95	
	1-57248-163-3	Crime Victim's Guide to Justice (2E)	$21.95			1-57248-216-8	Social Security Q&A	$12.95	
	1-57248-251-6	The Entrepreneur's Internet Handbook	$21.95			1-57248-221-1	Teen Rights	$22.95	
	1-57248-346-6	Essential Guide to Real Estate Contracts (2E)	$18.95			1-57248-236-2	Unmarried Parents' Rights (2E)	$19.95	
	1-57248-160-9	Essential Guide to Real Estate Leases	$18.95			1-57248-218-4	U.S. Immigration Step by Step	$21.95	
	1-57248-254-0	Family Limited Partnership	$26.95			1-57248-161-7	U.S.A. Immigration Guide (4E)	$24.95	
	1-57248-331-8	Gay & Lesbian Rights	$26.95			1-57248-192-7	The Visitation Handbook	$18.95	
	1-57248-139-0	Grandparents' Rights (3E)	$24.95			1-57248-225-7	Win Your Unemployment Compensation Claim (2E)	$21.95	
	1-57248-188-9	Guía de Inmigración a Estados Unidos (3E)	$24.95			1-57248-138-2	Winning Your Personal Injury Claim (2E)	$24.95	
	1-57248-187-0	Guía de Justicia para Víctimas del Crimen	$21.95			1-57248-333-4	Working with Your Homeowners Association	$19.95	
	1-57248-103-X	Help Your Lawyer Win Your Case (2E)	$14.95			1-57248-162-5	Your Right to Child Custody, Visitation and Support (2E)	$24.95	
	1-57248-164-1	How to buy a Condominium or Townhome (2E)	$19.95			1-57248-157-9	Your Rights When You Owe Too Much	$16.95	
	1-57248-328-8	How to Buy Your First Home	$18.95				**CALIFORNIA TITLES**		
	1-57248-191-9	How to File Your Own Bankruptcy (5E)	$21.95			1-57248-150-1	CA Power of Attorney Handbook (2E)	$18.95	
	1-57248-343-1	How to File Your Own Divorce (5E)	$26.95			1-57248-337-7	How to File for Divorce in CA (4E)	$26.95	
	1-57248-222-2	How to Form a Limited Liability Company (2E)	$24.95			1-57248-145-5	How to Probate and Settle an Estate in CA	$26.95	
	1-57248-231-1	How to Form a Nonprofit Corporation (2E)	$24.95			1-57248-146-3	How to Start a Business in CA	$18.95	
	1-57248-345-8	How to Form Your Own Corporation (4E)	$26.95			1-57248-194-3	How to Win in Small Claims Court in CA (2E)	$18.95	
	1-57248-224-9	How to Form Your Own Partnership (2E)	$24.95			1-57248-246-X	Make Your Own CA Will	$18.95	
	1-57248-232-X	How to Make Your Own Simple Will (3E)	$18.95			1-57248-196-X	The Landlord's Legal Guide in CA	$24.95	
	1-57248-200-1	How to Register Your Own Copyright (4E)	$24.95			1-57248-241-9	Tenants' Rights in CA	$21.95	
	1-57248-104-8	How to Register Your Own Trademark (3E)	$21.95				**FLORIDA TITLES**		
	1-57248-233-8	How to Write Your Own Living Will (3E)	$18.95			1-57071-363-4	Florida Power of Attorney Handbook (2E)	$16.95	
	1-57248-156-0	How to Write Your Own Premarital Agreement (3E)	$24.95			1-57248-176-5	How to File for Divorce in FL (7E)	$26.95	
	1-57248-230-3	Incorporate in Delaware from Any State	$24.95			1-57248-177-3	How to Form a Corporation in FL (5E)	$24.95	
	1-57248-158-7	Incorporate in Nevada from Any State	$24.95			1-57248-203-6	How to Form a Limited Liability Co. in FL (2E)	$24.95	
	1-57248-250-8	Inmigración a los EE.UU. Paso a Paso	$22.95			1-57071-401-0	How to Form a Partnership in FL	$22.95	
	1-57071-333-2	Jurors' Rights (2E)	$12.95			1-57248-113-7	How to Make a FL Will (6E)	$16.95	
	1-57248-223-0	Legal Research Made Easy (3E)	$21.95			1-57248-088-2	How to Modify Your FL Divorce Judgment (4E)	$24.95	
	1-57248-165-X	Living Trusts and Other Ways to Avoid Probate (3E)	$24.95			1-57248-144-7	How to Probate and Settle an Estate in FL (4E)	$26.95	
	1-57248-186-2	Manual de Beneficios para el Seguro Social	$18.95			1-57248-339-3	How to Start a Business in FL (7E)	$21.95	
	1-57248-220-6	Mastering the MBE	$16.95			1-57248-204-4	How to Win in Small Claims Court in FL (7E)	$18.95	
	1-57248-167-6	Most Valuable Bus. Legal Forms You'll Ever Need (3E)	$21.95			1-57248-202-8	Land Trusts in Florida (6E)	$29.95	
	1-57248-130-7	Most Valuable Personal Legal Forms You'll Ever Need	$24.95			1-57248-338-5	Landlords' Rights and Duties in FL (9E)	$22.95	
	1-57248-098-X	The Nanny and Domestic Help Legal Kit	$22.95						

Form Continued on Following Page   **SUBTOTAL**

To order, call Sourcebooks at 1-800-432-7444 or FAX (630) 961-2168 (Bookstores, libraries, wholesalers—please call for discount)

Prices are subject to change without notice.

Find more legal information at: www.SphinxLegal.com

SPHINX® PUBLISHING ORDER FORM

Qty	ISBN	Title	Retail	Ext.
		GEORGIA TITLES		
_____	1-57248-340-7	How to File for Divorce in GA (5E)	$21.95	_____
_____	1-57248-180-3	How to Make a GA Will (4E)	$21.95	_____
_____	1-57248-341-5	How to Start a Business in Georgia (3E)	$21.95	_____
		ILLINOIS TITLES		
_____	1-57248-244-3	Child Custody, Visitation, and Support in IL	$24.95	_____
_____	1-57248-206-0	How to File for Divorce in IL (3E)	$24.95	_____
_____	1-57248-170-6	How to Make an IL Will (3E)	$16.95	_____
_____	1-57248-247-8	How to Start a Business in IL (3E)	$21.95	_____
_____	1-57248-252-4	The Landlord's Legal Guide in IL	$24.95	_____
		MARYLAND, VIRGINIA AND THE DISTRICT OF COLUMBIA		
_____	1-57248-240-0	How to File for Divorce in MD, VA and DC	$28.95	_____
		MASSACHUSETTS TITLES		
_____	1-57248-128-5	How to File for Divorce in MA (3E)	$24.95	_____
_____	1-57248-115-3	How to Form a Corporation in MA	$24.95	_____
_____	1-57248-108-0	How to Make a MA Will (2E)	$16.95	_____
_____	1-57248-248-6	How to Start a Business in MA (3E)	$21.95	_____
_____	1-57248-209-5	The Landlord's Legal Guide in MA	$24.95	_____
		MICHIGAN TITLES		
_____	1-57248-215-X	How to File for Divorce in MI (3E)	$24.95	_____
_____	1-57248-182-X	How to Make a MI Will (3E)	$16.95	_____
_____	1-57248-183-8	How to Start a Business in MI (3E)	$18.95	_____
		MINNESOTA TITLES		
_____	1-57248-142-0	How to File for Divorce in MN	$21.95	_____
_____	1-57248-179-X	How to Form a Corporation in MN	$24.95	_____
_____	1-57248-178-1	How to Make a MN Will (2E)	$16.95	_____
		NEW JERSEY TITLES		
_____	1-57248-239-7	How to File for Divorce in NJ	$24.95	_____
		NEW YORK TITLES		
_____	1-57248-193-5	Child Custody, Visitation and Support in NY	$26.95	_____
_____	1-57248-351-2	File for Divorce in NY	$26.95	_____
_____	1-57248-249-4	How to Form a Corporation in NY (2E)	$24.95	_____
_____	1-57248-095-5	How to Make a NY Will (2E)	$16.95	_____
_____	1-57248-199-4	How to Start a Business in NY (2E)	$18.95	_____
_____	1-57248-198-6	How to Win in Small Claims Court in NY (2E)	$18.95	_____
_____	1-57248-197-8	Landlords' Legal Guide in NY	$24.95	_____
_____	1-57071-188-7	New York Power of Attorney Handbook	$19.95	_____
_____	1-57248-122-6	Tenants' Rights in NY	$21.95	_____

Qty	ISBN	Title	Retail	Ext.
		NORTH CAROLINA TITLES		
_____	1-57248-185-4	How to File for Divorce in NC (3E)	$22.95	_____
_____	1-57248-129-3	How to Make a NC Will (3E)	$16.95	_____
_____	1-57248-184-6	How to Start a Business in NC (3E)	$18.95	_____
_____	1-57248-091-2	Landlords' Rights & Duties in NC	$21.95	_____
		OHIO TITLES		
_____	1-57248-190-0	How to File for Divorce in OH (2E)	$24.95	_____
_____	1-57248-174-9	How to Form a Corporation in OH	$24.95	_____
_____	1-57248-173-0	How to Make an OH Will	$16.95	_____
		PENNSYLVANIA TITLES		
_____	1-57248-242-7	Child Custody, Visitation and Support in PA	$26.95	_____
_____	1-57248-211-7	How to File for Divorce in PA (3E)	$26.95	_____
_____	1-57248-094-7	How to Make a PA Will (2E)	$16.95	_____
_____	1-57248-112-9	How to Start a Business in PA (2E)	$18.95	_____
_____	1-57248-245-1	The Landlord's Legal Guide in PA	$24.95	_____
		TEXAS TITLES		
_____	1-57248-171-4	Child Custody, Visitation, and Support in TX	$22.95	_____
_____	1-57248-172-2	How to File for Divorce in TX (3E)	$24.95	_____
_____	1-57248-114-5	How to Form a Corporation in TX (2E)	$24.95	_____
_____	1-57248-255-9	How to Make a TX Will (3E)	$16.95	_____
_____	1-57248-214-1	How to Probate and Settle an Estate in TX (3E)	$26.95	_____
_____	1-57248-228-1	How to Start a Business in TX (3E)	$18.95	_____
_____	1-57248-111-0	How to Win in Small Claims Court in TX (2E)	$16.95	_____
_____	1-57248-110-2	Landlords' Rights and Duties in TX (2E)	$21.95	_____

SUBTOTAL THIS PAGE _____

SUBTOTAL PREVIOUS PAGE _____

Shipping — $5.00 for 1st book, $1.00 each additional _____

Illinois residents add 6.75% sales tax _____

Connecticut residents add 6.00% sales tax _____

TOTAL _____

To order, call Sourcebooks at 1-800-432-7444 or FAX (630) 961-2168 (Bookstores, libraries, wholesalers—please call for discount)
Prices are subject to change without notice.
Find more legal information at: www.SphinxLegal.com